Labor of the Heart

Labor of the Heart

A Parent's Guide to
the Decisions and
Emotions in Adoption

Kathleen L. Whitten, Ph.D.

M. Evans

Lanham • New York • Boulder • Toronto • Plymouth, UK

Published by M. Evans
An imprint of The Rowman & Littlefield Publishing Group, Inc.
4501 Forbes Boulevard, Suite 200, Lanham, Maryland 20706
www.rlpgtrade.com

Estover Road, Plymouth PL6 7PY, United Kingdom

Distributed by NATIONAL BOOK NETWORK

Library of Congress Cataloging-in-Publication Data
Whitten, Kathleen L.
    Labor of the heart : a parent's guide to the decisions and emotions in adoption /
Kathleen L. Whitten.
        p. cm.
    Includes bibliographical references and index.
    ISBN-13: 978-1-59077-133-4 (pbk. : alk. paper)
    ISBN-10: 1-59077-133-8 (pbk. : alk. paper)
    1. Adoption—Psychological aspects. 2. Adoptive parents—Psychology. I. Title.
HV875.W47 2008
362.73401'9—dc22

                                                                2007032298

∞" The paper used in this publication meets the minimum requirements of American National Standard for Information Sciences—Permanence of Paper for Printed Library Materials, ANSI/NISO Z39.48-1992.

Manufactured in the United States of America.

Dedicated with love

to

Stevenson A. W. Richardson and

Katherine A. Q. Richardson

875

BY EMILY DICKINSON

I stepped from Plank to Plank
A slow and cautious way
The Stars about my Head I felt
About my Feet the Sea.

I knew not but the next
Would be my final inch—
This gave me that precarious Gait
Some call Experience.

Contents

Acknowledgments

Special thanks to Erika Raskin for her excellent, detailed suggestions on the manuscript. Thanks also to Roussie Jacksina, Kathleen Valenti Knaus, Chi Lam, Virginia Moran, Steve Richardson, and Faye Satterly, and for review, critiques, and moral support.

I am grateful to The Deadline Club (a.k.a. Columbia Literary Exchange): Lynn Felder, Jo Ann McCracken, Anne Creed, Libby Bernardin, and Ruth Nicholson. You gave me a great start.

I appreciate all that I learned from my teachers: Robert E. Emery, Robert S. Marvin, Greg Orr, and Charlotte Patterson.

Thanks to my editors at Rowman & Littlefield, Dulcie Wilcox and Rick Rinehart, for launching this book, and to my agent, Jennifer DeChiara, for her enthusiastic support.

I am grateful to the many parents who entrusted their stories to me: Jenny White, Nancy Adams, Kendall Mosburg, Sen. Mary Landrieu (D–La.), Toni Ayers, Maureen Oswald, Jody Boulet, Susie Hoffman, Michele McCormick, Julie Govan, Heidi Senderovitz, and the anonymous ones. Most parents asked that their names be changed to protect their privacy and that of their families.

Thanks to Malayna Ford, for her excellent research assistance.

I am privileged to have worked with many adoption professionals, and social workers, who were also my teachers: Chris Walker, Dana Neidley, John Freeman, Anne J. Atkinson, Phyllis Colman, Constance Barry, Karen Horridge, and Theresa King.

Thanks to Mark Mendelsohn, director of the International Adoption Clinic at the University of Virginia, for his excellent clinical skills and warm heart.

I am grateful to the women who believed before I did: Nancy Maseng, Curry Edwards, Marie Shervais, Suzanne Williams, Rose Scheibler, Rhonda Olson, Deanie Tourville, and Kay Roman.

Thanks to Rev. David Stoddart, rector of Church of Our Savior in Charlottesville, Virginia, for inspiration and material for chapter 8.

To Ruby Lumpkin Whitten and Katherine A. Q. Richardson, who taught me how to be a mother, gratitude beyond words.

Preface

The emotions unique to bringing a child into the family through adoption aren't obvious at first, but they can create significant stress. Adoptive parents often experience the double trial of emotional responses to infertility and to the process of adoption itself—which one adoptive mother called "excruciating labor with no end in sight."

When we were preparing to adopt our daughter, I wanted a book to help me validate my feelings about infertility, and to spell out the emotional aspects of all the decisions we had to make. There wasn't one, so I decided to combine my personal experience with my professional experience as a developmental psychologist to create *Labor of the Heart*.

Would-be adoptive parents cycle through grief, anger, fear, anxiety, frustration, and guilt—and back again, and again. Psychologists who study these emotions know that they cloud decision-making, at exactly the same time that adoptive parents are making life-altering, irrevocable decisions: will we adopt at all, will we adopt an older child or an infant, can we parent a child with developmental delays? Adoptive parents often must decide within a couple of weeks whether to take a particular child home with no more information than a video and a one-page medical report. These decisions can cause extreme stress for even the healthiest, best informed, and most serene parents.

Here's the silver lining: The demands of the adoption process give parents-to-be many opportunities to practice empirically tested ways of coping. These methods include optimism, social support, and spiritual practice. Psychologists have found that each one has many benefits. If adoptive parents use these before their child comes home, they will be even better parents. Research in developmental psychology shows that parents' psychological health is the main factor in children's secure attachment. For the children, secure attachment means better behavior, higher grades in school, and closer relationships with peers.

I decided that it was time for adoptive parents to have easy access to the latest research in developmental and clinical psychology. New scientific research, including mine, contradicts many of the negative ideas about adopted children and adoptive families in widely used adoption guides. New adoption practices demand a book that includes parents' emotional histories and capabilities. *Labor of the Heart* gives readers access to current research from the United States and Europe translated into practical form for busy parents-to-be.

Labor of the Heart will be especially useful for first-time adoptive parents, because it discusses the transition to adoptive parenthood and the challenges of making decisions during the adoption process. It includes special techniques to help parents resolve their feelings about infertility and their emotions and uncertainties about adoption. The book explodes negative myths about adopted children with positive scientific findings. The chapter on commitment gives parents concrete guidance on one of the most important decisions they will ever make—whether to adopt a particular child. Waiting is widely recognized as a difficult part of adoption, so the relevant chapter shows parents how to use that time to begin giving their child a secure, loving home to come into. The chapter on the spiritual aspects of adoption continues a theme from chapter 1: how a spiritual or religious practice supports parenting.

The book includes exercises in a workbook format. These are based on reliable and valid psychological measures. Some might overlap with questions a social worker will ask during a home study, but they are meant as a tool for private reflection. They can also be used by readers and their spouses, partners, and extended family members to spark discussion about the issues involved in becoming an adoptive family.

Labor of the Heart does not include adoption logistics. This information can be found in other books and on the Web—the best source because the legal requirements and countries' policies on adoption change rapidly, especially in international adoption. You can use *Labor of the Heart* along with books on logistics to help you explore your feelings about the difficult emotions and life-changing decisions involved in adopting a child. *Labor of the Heart* is the only book to weave together the most recent empirical research on adopted children's adjustment, clinical observations, and personal stories.

This book is solidly grounded in peer-reviewed, published studies in professional journals from psychology, social work, public health, and medicine. Social workers and psychologists working with adoptive families can therefore recommend it with confidence to clients as part of their home study or as homework in psychotherapy.

I hope that reading this book will be like chatting over coffee with a good friend who has an adopted child and is a developmental psychologist. I include stories of my own family's adoption as well as stories from other people who've adopted. These stories will help you to identify and validate your feelings throughout the long process of adoption.

The Agony and the Art of Becoming
an Adoptive Parent

Here's how I thought it would be: I'm in a birthing center or hospital, with my husband, parents, and friends surrounding me. I'm holding our baby, perfect and healthy. Even though the baby's just been born, she's rosy and plump. Even though I've just given birth, I look gorgeous and feel well rested. After an overnight to make sure everyone's okay—and, of course, we are—we head home to happily ever after. My husband and I might talk a little about the miracle of birth, but we take it for granted, really, because that's how it's supposed to be.

That's how it *was* supposed to be, but the reality of our journey to parenthood was very different. Here's how it went:

On Thanksgiving morning in 1997, we got our wake-up call at 3:30 a.m. My husband Steve and I were already awake, anxious and jet-lagged. The van would leave our hotel in Saigon at 4 a.m. for the four-hour drive to Vinh Long, where our daughter waited for us. The three adoption agency staff and the driver loaded us into a van with an image of Quan Yin, the goddess of mercy, hanging from the rearview mirror. Cathy and Dave, the parents-to-be from Minneapolis, were as bleary-eyed as we were.

We bounced over potholes through dark Saigon streets. Someone mentioned a curfew. If there was one, we were breaking it. In the shadows, whole families slept on park benches and in the roundabout with the monument to one of the People's Heroes.

At 6 a.m., dawn pulled away the curtain of dark to show the countryside, totally green. Rice paddies with coconut palms on the borders stretched to the horizon. At home, our families would be eating pumpkin pie and watching college football on television. In the Mekong Delta, Highway 1 was crowded with motorcycles, bicycles, and pedestrians, with an occasional truck sharing the center lane with our van. Along the roadside, children walked to school carrying book bags. They wore white shirts, black pants, and—still—the red neckerchiefs of Communist youth. The girls had long, straight black hair, spilling down their white shirts. I thought, "Our daughter will look like them."

Each village had a market, a line of little shops as basic as three-walled woven pandanus or bamboo with thatched roofs and dirt floors, most neatly swept and stocked with soft drinks, cigarettes, bags of rice, and hanging clumps of dried octopus. Mechanics' shops had signs that read *Va Vo* or *Hon Da*. Open-air barbershops, complete with barber chairs, are known as *Hot Toc*. In this Communist country slowly opening to capitalism, everyone was in business.

We took a ferry across one branch of the Mekong, into the heart of the delta. Ours was the only van. Vendors crowded onto the ferry. Two women were cooking rice and noodles over portable stoves beside the van. A beggar opened the driver's window, shouted something in Vietnamese, and thrust in a can that already had a few *dong* in it.

At 8 a.m. we arrived in Vinh Long, our daughter's birthplace. We met our agency's Vietnam director at a restaurant—a shed with a wooden floor and screens, set on pilings in the Mekong River. We had a superb view of the river and of a tropical island in the middle. It was a Viet Cong stronghold during the "American War," they said.

After breakfast we drove to a two-story, yellow stucco building, with a tile roof and ceramic tile floors, the provincial capital building. Inside, the staff had lined up their shoes in the hall. We were ushered upstairs to the conference room. One wall was covered with red drapery with a large gold star in the center. Under the star stood a plaster bust of Ho Chi Minh, leader of the Communist movement that defeated the French, and then the Americans. Steve, Dave, Cathy, and I looked at the bust, then back at each other. Both Steve and Dave had been of draft age when "Uncle Ho" was the United States' Enemy No. 1. The strangeness and irony of the scene left us speechless.

The room was long and narrow, with windows on both sides, all open to the river. Small electric fans stirred humid air around us. Steve and Dave were starting to look damp in their long-sleeved shirts and ties. But we had been assured that long sleeves are a mark of respect, and that the ties would impress everyone since so few men in Vietnam wear them, or even have them.

A small woman, all in black, brought in a tray with Pepsis in bottles. She opened them and put a straw in each one, then placed them on the table in front of each chair. The bottles, too, were sweating. The straws bobbed like the junks on the river.

Everyone smiled at everyone else. The translator scurried from group to group. I was already sweating but my mouth was dry. Where was my baby? We all took seats, with the officials at the head of the table, the highest ranking man nearest the bust of Ho Chi Minh. An official spoke in Vietnamese, with pauses from time to time for the translator. During moments of quiet, we heard the Mekong lap the dock outside.

I kept thinking, "Where are the babies?"

Finally, they appeared, each in the arms of a Vietnamese nanny. The larger, more animated one must be ours, I thought. Cathy and Dave's daughter was a month younger, so I expected her to be smaller. But the little one was our daughter-to-be. She was all eyes, her large head on a newborn-sized body, with very thin arms. She gazed around at everyone, then dozed off. I was instantly anxious, because she looked so small and fragile—and because anxiety had been a constant companion. But I knew she was mine, and my happiness at finally seeing her mixed with my longing to hold her so much I cried.

More speeches. My husband spoke for the American parents, slowly and deeply, with appropriate pauses for the translator, as if he'd done this all his life. I cried some more. I listened only to little snatches of the other speeches. I just gazed at her, my baby, during the rest of the ceremony.

After we signed the official register—of what, I'm not sure—the nanny handed my baby gently to me. Her thin body felt hot and sticky in her ruffled white satin dress bought for this special occasion. Through my tears I saw the polyester rose stuck on the front of her dress. The center of the rose had silver glitter pasted onto it. Her legs and bottom were wrapped in a thin blue towel, printed with green roses. I felt ecstatic, and scared, surrounded by strangers from Vietnam and two people from Minnesota I'd known for twenty-four hours.

The reality of my first moments as a mother were as different from my fantasy as they could possibly have been. But I have come to believe that my experience was absolutely right, the way it was meant to be. The important pieces were exactly as I had hoped, only more intense than I had ever dreamed possible. We were—and often still are—overwhelmed by the miracle of *her*, and by our incredible good fortune to be her parents. When our plane lifted off from Than Son Nhut Airport a week after her adoption, we were certain that we were headed home to happily ever after. It had taken my husband and me three years to repaint our original picture of parenthood to include our daughter's Mekong River reality. In those years, we endured and were privileged to experience the agony and the art of becoming adoptive parents.

The Transition to Parenthood

The transition to parenthood is one of the most challenging that adults ever face. The arrival of the first child brings profound changes, whether that child is adopted or biological. Personal time nearly disappears. Scheduling becomes as complicated as air traffic control. Time with spouses or partners and friends is elbowed out by the baby's needs and parents' sleep deprivation. There is a constant rumble of suggestions from well-meaning people.

Before the child arrives, though, parents have an "expectancy" period. If you are considering adoption, you are already in this period—you are expecting to become a parent. Parents' attitudes and actions during the expectancy period predict attitudes toward their new parenthood (Levy-Shiff, Zoran, & Shulman, 1997). In practical terms, the research of Dr. Levy-Shiff and colleagues shows that we adoptive parents have a golden opportunity to embrace the child who will be given to us—before he or she is even placed in our arms. With some preliminary work we can make a smooth transition to parenthood. This work has three main parts:

1) Re-visioning parenthood to include adoption.
2) Making the long series of difficult, emotional decisions that
   adoption requires.

Is the glass . . .

Half empty?	Or half full?
We lack cultural models of adoptive parenthood.	We can create family models in our own image.
Nature doesn't hard-wire us to *decide* to be parents.	We can reaffirm our commitment to our children many times before they come home.
We have a jumble of stressful emotions about infertility and adoption.	We can practice emotional awareness and positive coping.

3) For anyone adopting after infertility, resolving emotions that can be very intense.

These steps don't march along in a neat line. We might have to work on all three at the same time. This presents a major challenge for adoptive parents: we may be faced with emotions related to infertility while trying to prepare an adoption dossier, and at the same time we may have to confront anti-adoption prejudice or racism from friends and family.

The difficult emotional context of adoptive parenting has a silver lining. It gives us opportunities to create unique images of parenthood, to reaffirm our commitment to our children over and over before they come home, and to develop awareness of our own emotions. If we use our "expectancy" opportunities well, we will be stronger parents throughout the next demanding years after our children arrive. The "Views of Adoptive Parenthood" above shows two ways of looking at the process of adoptive parenthood. We can choose to keep looking at, and believing, the "half empty" side or the "half full" side. Throughout this book, I'll encourage you to focus on the positive aspects in order to grow through your experience.

While we have countless examples of the transition to biological parent-hood and the ways people become biological parents in the United States, there are no general cultural models here or in Western Europe for adop-tive parenthood. A major family transition needs a cultural model—a real-life or fictional character whose experience we can relate to and check our reality against. Without models, we're making everything up as we go along. Biological parents may sometimes feel this way, too, but their method of bringing their children into the world is as old as mammal love. On the other hand, adoptive parents sometimes feel anxiety about how we fit into the model of "family"—we know we don't fit into the biological model. Current adoptive models are either vague or exotic. We might have seen news reports about celebrities adopting children from abroad. But most of us aren't Hollywood stars or pop singers, scheduling a home study between multimillion-dollar films or tours. The resulting unease and anxi-ety can reinforce our fears that our family is different from others, or that our child is too unlike the one we imagined, if we first tried for a preg-nancy. Most of us grew up in biological families, with few openly adoptive families close to home as models. The example of a happy adoptive family, though, can be a powerful influence on the decision to adopt.

Senator Mary Landrieu said, "Ever since I was a young child I had the idea I wanted to adopt. My aunt, who was also my godmother, had two adopted children. I thought it was wonderful, the happiness and joy it brought to my aunt and uncle. When I got married, I married an adoptee, a man adopted from an orphanage in Ireland. I thought, 'He certainly can't object to adopting.' It was a natural from there. We went through some tra-ditional fertility issues, then went through an agency and came to be adop-tive parents."

Julie, the American mother of a toddler from China, also had had an up-close view of adoption. She said, "Some friends of ours had adopted a little girl from Russia just before we got married. Her legs were so atro-phied from staying in her crib that she couldn't stand up. But after just three weeks she was stronger, and starting to speak English. It was really magical. They had a hard transition after she came home, but I could see something wonderful happening."

For Hanne, the Danish mother of two girls, adoption from Asia was always part of her family plan. "There was no logical reason—just that the picture we both had in our heads was of a child with Asian features. I think I was probably influenced by the fact that when I grew up, nearly all internationally adopted children I knew were from South Korea. And then, I must admit, I think Asian children and people are beautiful."

Although it is usually obvious that transracially adopted children are not birth children, many adults today didn't grow up recognizing adoptive families. Before 1980, adoptions were "closed." Adopted children in same-race families often were not told that they had been adopted. If they were not told that they were adopted, they certainly were not told anything about their birth parents, much less allowed to have regular visits with them, as many families do today. According to Dr. Harold Grotevant, a leading open adoption researcher at the University of Minnesota, social workers in the 1950s and 1960s wanted to shield children from the presumed stigma of "illegitimacy" or "bad blood." Social workers tried to place children with families who looked like them, to make it easier for them to pass as their parents' biological children. Most of us probably knew adopted children but didn't know that they were adopted because they didn't know it themselves. This secrecy reinforced the stigma of adoption—which, like premarital pregnancy, was not spoken about openly and was considered taboo.

"Adoption has changed radically in thirty years," says Theresa King, a veteran Philadelphia social worker who specialized in placing African-American children in same-race adoptive families. "But the main issues of adoption are the same as they always were, and it's a lifelong journey."

ANTI-ADOPTION PREJUDICE

Difficulties linked to adoption include prejudice against adopted children and their families. Such views gave impetus to the secrecy that has often been associated with adoption (Wegar, 2000, 2006). Biased attitudes about adopted children and their biological families have unfortunately been evident from the 1960s to the present. The first large U.S. study of adoption attitudes by the Evan B. Donaldson Adoption Institute found that most people believed adoption served a useful purpose in society, but 30 percent questioned adoptees' mental health. Anti-adoption bias can affect social workers' attitudes toward their clients, parents' attitudes toward their children, and the reception of adopted children in their schools and communities. I worked with another psychologist, Dr. Dawn Kriebel, on a survey of mental health professionals' attitudes about adoption. Sadly, we found that 28 percent of mental health professionals we surveyed said that adopted children were more likely than non-adopted ones to have problems in school, or with delinquent behavior or drugs. This is especially surprising, and troubling, because there is little empirical evidence to support their view.

When we consider adoption as a way to parenthood, voices of prejudice hiss at us and discourage us. And because adoption is still not the norm for parenting, we have few positive cultural images of adoption. Recently, several books have chronicled the disconnect between the media images of cozy, rosy-cheeked motherhood and the sometimes frazzling reality of 24/7 parenting. Even so, most images are of *biological* mothers. How many stories can you think of with adoption as the focus, or with adoptive families as the stars? The exceptions tend to be stories of celebrity adoptions, disrupted adoptions, custody contests with biological parents, or scary, out-of-control adolescents with reactive attachment disorder—all despite the fact that these are as rare as paid parental leave.

The lack of cultural models means that we must make our own models. We have to create our own mental pictures of ourselves as adoptive parents, of our children to come as *our* children, and of our own goals and benchmarks for the process. Unlike in pregnancy, when you can imagine a point when your clothes will be too tight, when you should tell family and friends, or how soon the nursery should be ready, there are no simple milestones for the adoption process and becoming an adoptive family. Because we don't often know when the baby will come to us, how old he will be, or even where she will come from, it's difficult to imagine the homecoming.

One reaction to the changing possibilities of parenthood might be fear. When we have to change our mental picture, or dearly held emotional myth, it is frightening. The streets are still laid out as before in Missouri or California or Vermont. We still see the same people at work or school or home. There are still red leaves in the fall, flowers in the spring. But the emotional landscape in our heads has changed completely. We suddenly aren't who we thought we were. We know we aren't going to become the people we once imagined. Eleven months before we adopted our daughter, I wrote in my journal:

> My agony about motherhood stems partly from grief and partly from this kind of myth shift. In my personal myth, I would birth a child and raise her. I don't want to leave that movie, that myth. It really does have all the qualities of myth, with specifics, concrete details, and archetypes. I don't know what myth I'm moving into. I'm between myths.

ADOPTION MYTHS, FAMILY, AND FRIENDS

At the other extreme, some people have an idealized vision of adoptive parents. When we told our extended family about our plans to adopt a baby from Vietnam, one of my dear cousins said, "That's wonderful! You are such a saint! You're saving a child from poverty and ignorance and giving her a loving home."

I love my cousin, but the only part he got right was the "wonderful." Adoption *is* wonderful. But my husband and I will never reach sainthood, and we didn't adopt our daughter to "save" her. Our motives were as selfish as any parent's. We wanted to be parents, and adoption was our way of bringing a child into our family.

We adoptive parents confront many odd stories about ourselves that well-meaning people tell us. It's part of the transition to adoptive parenthood. We change according to how other people treat us, and people treat us according to how they see our roles in society. We grow into the roles we want to take on, partly by meeting other people's expectations of what that role should be and how we should act. So another hard part of the transition to adoptive parenting is that, because it is so rare, very few people in our families or our workplaces will know how to act toward us, or what they should expect us to be doing. Because the expectancy period of adoption is invisible, people don't treat us as if we're about to become parents. That creates yet another task, with its resulting stress, for adoptive parents: getting the kind of support we need from the people around us. As we'll see later in the chapter, social support is important in most phases of adoption, and there are *many* ways to get it.

People Are Not Hard-wired for Adoption

Mother and Father Nature wired us so that the decision to have children would be nearly out of our control. Our non-thinking biology says, "Have sex. Get pregnant. Have babies." New technology from contraception to *in vitro* fertilization makes planning and decision-making possible, but it doesn't make it easier. The concept of bringing a child into our family without sex and passion is contrary to our biology and to current cultural myths.

For some people, adoption is so contrary to biology they even think it's unnatural. But Mary Landrieu enjoys contradicting them. She said, "I like to tell people that adoption has been practiced from the beginning of time, and it's as natural to the human family as any other kind of parenting. When a parent was deceased, children were adopted by aunts, uncles, older siblings, cousins. This has always been done. People today make it out to be so unnatural but it's the most natural thing in the world."

The parenting is "natural," but the process of bringing a child into the family through paperwork isn't. Neither are the decisions about the children we bring home. But the decisions are not impossible, and when we make them, we learn that love and commitment are independent of biology and every bit as strong.

After infertility, this decision means acknowledging that the quest for a biological child is over. Joan, a medical researcher, said, "It took me a long time to get to the point of knowing I wanted a baby and child, not just a pregnancy, a birth, and breast-feeding. I had been a labor and delivery nurse, and had taught breast-feeding. I really wanted that for myself. We had eight years of infertility treatments, from Boston to Virginia. Then we decided not to borrow any more money, unless we knew there would be a child at the end of the process. That meant no more *in vitro*. It meant adoption."

Many parents struggling with the decision to adopt are haunted by the general Western notion that you can't *really* love a child who's not your own flesh and blood. Unfortunately, this idea is ensconced in most media stories about families, and also in family law, which often gives biological parents precedence over adoptive ones in contested custody cases. But you don't have to look far to see that simply birthing a baby or fathering one doesn't guarantee good parenting, love, or even basic safety. I remember a little boy in foster care, whose family came to the Child-Parent Attachment Clinic where I worked. His birth mother had broken his arm when he was six months old. In a famous case in Maryland, an infant boy entered foster care after his biological mother was convicted of murdering his sister.

Still, the general cultural bias is that biological is better. Many people believe that biological parents somehow feel more entitled to be their children's parents. Dr. Nancy Cohen (1993, 1996), a Canadian psychologist, was surprised to find that adoptive parents actually felt more "entitled" to their children than did biological parents. Dr. Cohen defined "entitlement" as having few doubts about their parenting and feeling close to their children. Feeling entitled to be our children's parents makes us their "real" parents. And having a child through adoption instead of birth doesn't mean you won't love him or her. The key ingredient is *commitment*: a commitment to be the best parent you can possibly be to a particular child.

Commitment is a conscious choice, and you will have to make that choice, over and over, during the process of adoption. This series of decisions creates a very different experience from biological parenthood. For birth parents, after the first trimester with its legal option of termination, parenthood is almost (but not always) guaranteed. The biological window of choice in an established pregnancy is small, and short. But in adoption, that window is large, and long. You will spend months, and possibly years, in the process. You can stop at any point along the way. Each time you decide to proceed—with another education session, another fingerprint check, another home study session—you reaffirm your commitment to becoming a parent. This developing, deepening commitment is a great asset for adoptive parents.

Four Emotional Challenges for Adoptive Parents and Four Ways to Cope

We're supposed to be optimists in America: happy all the time, in the land where never is heard a discouraging word. But parents adopting after infertility will need to cope with at least the big four negative emotions of grief, anger, fear, and guilt. You will almost certainly cycle through them many times before the emotions begin to resolve. Each time you go through the cycle, the feelings will be less intense, less overwhelming. After a while, you'll remember them as part of a landscape you left behind.

Meanwhile, the new movement in positive psychology is reframing sadness and guilt. Most studies of depression use a psychiatric or medical model, which defines depression as a disease. But two components of depression—sadness and guilt—are basic human experiences, not necessarily symptoms of pathology. There can be personal, social, and moral meaning in these emotions. Depression's social stigma can complicate our experience of sadness and guilt, which we must live through not only to transcend depression, but also to heal its roots successfully. Psychologists have found the potential for personal growth after successful coping with an important loss. The resolution of loss can include increased self-understanding, maturity, better coping skills, and the ability to regulate one's emotions.

Toni Ayers knew loss firsthand. Now an adoptive mother, she herself was adopted into a multiracial family of fourteen. She and her husband had a stillborn daughter, and then a series of miscarriages. "We had always assumed adoption would be part of our family. And we always assumed we'd have a lot more kids than we have. But when adoption is chosen for you, it's a different emotional journey."

It's vitally important to begin this process before your child comes home. Many psychologists have researched the path adults take to resolve their childhood losses and the way their resolution later affects their parenting. The research rests on a couple of main ideas: We create an emotional blueprint or working model in our minds of how relationships should be, and then we act them out with every important person in our lives. We create our family relationships in millions of small, daily interactions, not in one grand illuminating moment, as storytellers from the front porch to Hollywood might try to make us believe. The interactions are with each other, parent to child, at home, and with the society outside, in stores, preschools, churches, schools, at the soccer field, in the museum. If our interactions as parents come from a position of strength and resolved negative emotions, we will promote healthy attachment for our children. If we have reached a point of comfortable acceptance of ourselves, our past, and our identity as adoptive parents, we will be able to create our families in our own ways, in our own image—not struggling with the image of someone else's family or with a cultural myth.

The ways we respond to our children's negative emotions will determine their attachment to us and their eventual psychological health. Our children will see us as models for dealing with their own negative emotions. The way we resolve infertility now can forecast how our children will resolve the loss of their birth parents and/or culture, and will teach us to teach them. The process will continue throughout our children's lives, as events occur that are outside of their control and ours—such as, for example, a birth parent's decision to sever contact in an open adoption.

Another reason to begin working with all emotions now is that after the baby or child arrives, there won't be a lot of time for self-reflection. But unresolved emotions will still be there, hovering over interactions with your child like a mean storybook witch. The more aware you are of your emotions *now*, and the more resolved they are, the better equipped you'll be to help your child be aware of his. This is a crucial part of teaching your child emotional awareness, because he or she will not only watch you and learn how you handle anger and sadness but will also copy what you do. When you demonstrate self-reflection and handle your own emotions calmly, your child will learn by your example.

• • •

The next sections describe one by one four emotions and four positive ways to cope, from the point of view of adoptive parenting. The figure on the next page shows these feelings on a circle, because we often go around and around before we resolve them. The exercises at the end of the chapter suggest specific methods for working with each emotion for positive outcomes.

EMOTIONAL CHALLENGES

Sadness and Grief

If the decision to adopt arose from infertility, adoptive parents experience sadness when they find that they cannot have the biological child they imagined, even if they already have a biological child or children. For some people, sadness expands into acute, debilitating grief for the child who never was or could be. Psychologists call this "ambiguous loss," because the

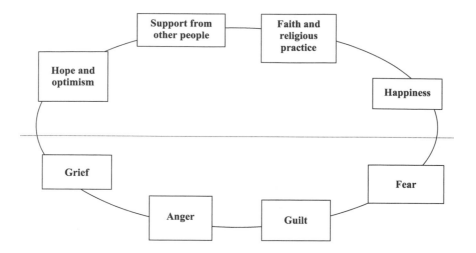

person for whom we grieve did not exist, and so could not really die. But the loss of an ideal is nevertheless very real and deserves full mourning.

Natalie told me, "I grieved a lot for my lost pregnancy and birth experiences, and still do. I recently saw the *Vagina Monologues*, and when she talked about labor and birth, I teared up. It'd been how many years since I stopped trying?" She paused, then answered her own question. "Eight. Seven since we adopted our older daughter. I traversed an awful, dark place but had the sense that if I persevered, I'd have a child."

The "awful, dark place" of grief contains two traps for adoptive parents. First, research on bereaved people shows that they do not cope with life as well as do people who are not grieving. Poor coping can mean poor decisions. Poor decisions in adoption can have lifelong consequences. Second, the grief related to children can set someone up for no-exit thinking. The mental message might be something like, "I can't have the baby I want, and I don't want the baby I can have." This kind of thinking creates a merry-go-round of feelings—a sense of helplessness victimization, and depression. If this sounds familiar to you, it might also show you that you have more work to do with grief and with the reorganization of your mental models of parenthood.

Psychologists have long known that adoptive parents who use denial to cope with infertility will have a much harder transition to parenthood, and that their children will have more negative outcomes. These parents might say, or think, something like, "It's okay that I can't give birth. . . . Adoption is really just like having a birth child, except that somebody else went into labor." That might be a comforting thought for a little while, but it is not true. Back in 1964, Dr. David Kirk proposed that adoptive families who denied the differences between their reality and that of biological families had less positive adjustment than those who fully acknowledged all aspects of adoption.

Anger

Anger and sadness go together like peanut butter and jelly. Sometimes we flip-flop between them. Some of us find it a little easier, or safer, to be angry than to be sad—anger helps us feel powerful instead of vulnerable—but for others, especially women, anger is not nice. It gets denied and stuffed, and stuffed some more, until the woman either explodes in a rage or implodes in depression. Toni Ayers knows trauma and anger. She said, "Over all, there's not enough education or support or emotional protection for adoptive parents. You have people who've gone through God knows what for ten years, and then you have the trauma with lawyers and counselors who're worried about the birth mother. You can't sacrifice emotional stability to create a family."

Trauma can lead to anger, which can pop out in a variety of ways, including in marital discord. Adoptive parents often find themselves angry with their spouse or partner, as if the infertility were the partner's fault. Sometimes, one spouse or partner isn't as eager for adoption as the other one. This situation can lead to anger, blame, and resentment. These emotions can erupt openly, or they can bubble like lava under a calm surface. Some partners might fight about stand-in issues, like sex or money, when their real conflict is about having children.

Some adoptive parents get angry with God, or the universe, or fate, for not sending them the baby they think is the "right" one, or for the unfairness of who gets to have biological children. For devout people, this can create a crisis of faith.

Most adoptive parents experience anger and frustration about the expense of adoption compared with biological parenthood. Joan said money issues caused stress for her and her husband. "I was angry about having to spend the money for fingerprints, and a police background check, and all the other expenses that biological parents don't have to even think about," she said. "And all of it on top of medical expenses not covered by insurance."

Most of us have felt frustration at government bureaucracies, adoption agencies, and all the impersonal systems that seem to be keeping our children away from us. The process of adoption is tedious and arouses anxiety and frustration for many parents.

Ten months before we adopted our daughter, I drove our dossier—the three-inch-high file of everything from our 1040 tax form to photos of our house—seventy miles to the state capitol to have them certified by the secretary of state before they could go to Vietnam. I wrote to a friend, "It's a relief to have this over. I've felt really helpless and out of control to have the fate of my motherhood resting on a notary's stamp or a signature in the wrong place. Sometimes my husband and I can laugh about how pointless this is—as he said, all the gold seals and state folderol are just to reassure bureaucrats that they aren't going to screw up by letting us adopt a baby. But other times, I'm really pissed that we have to go through all these hoops which are purely clerical and have nothing to do with parenting."

Guilt

Adoptive parents who are especially religious might feel guilty about being angry with God. We have also felt guilty about real or imagined sexual "sins" of the past, as if they somehow caused our infertility. Many of us have felt absolutely green with envy of friends' pregnancies or children. And, of course, we feel guilty for envying their happiness.

Guilt is often considered a religious or legal notion. Psychologically, it's a close cousin to shame and anxiety. Shame is extreme, toxic guilt—a sense of being "guilty until proven innocent." It tells mean lies, like "You're no good and don't deserve to have a child." Shame can be rooted in childhood messages from insecure parents. It can also be reinforced by the process of an adoption background check and home study, which requires parents to be fingerprinted, and cleared by the FBI and their state's Child Protective Services branch. The process implies that everyone who wants to adopt is assumed to be unfit, or guilty of *something*, until they prove otherwise.

Guilt and shame arouse anxiety, the basic fight-or-flight response hardwired into us from prehistory. This response stresses our bodies, especially if it occurs regularly, so it's vital to reduce our anxiety. There are two basic ways to do this which don't involve drugs. The first is through cognitive, or thought-based, therapy. Many studies have found that the way we think about a situation predicts how we react to it and how we feel about it. This is good news—it means that we can talk back to shame and guilt and the lies they tell us. When we do, we have the chance not only to think differently but also to feel differently. The workbook section at the end of this chapter suggests ways to work through cognitive change on your own, and of course a good therapist can help you with it. The second way to combat anxiety is through meditation. There are many variations, from Eastern Zen-based techniques to Western centering prayer.

Fear

One of the effects of social stigma toward adoption and adoptive families is fear—fear that an adopted child cannot be the child we really want. On top of this concern, adoptive parents also have all the same fears as biological parents. We might fear that the child or children we adopt won't be healthy, or that we won't be able to cope with whatever disabilities they bring home. If we have any inkling of how hard parenting is, we will fear that we can't meet the challenges. Some fear of new situations is normal, but fear can escalate until it paralyzes us with anxiety.

In adoption there are many more unknowns than in biological parenting—and many unknowables. These might include the process itself, the birth parents, the foreign country where your child might be born, your child himself or herself, and your fears about your ability to love and nurture a child not born to you.

Joan described adoption as "a continuum of anxiety and fear that lasts way longer than a pregnancy." We might revisit this fear when we face a major decision at each step of the adoption process, such as choosing an agency, deciding to advertise for birth parents, or picking a country. These decisions are discussed in detail in chapters 2 and 3.

At the beginning, though, it helps to remember that there are always risks in bringing children into a family, whether through birth or adoption. It might seem a little easier to deny the risks of a birth, because we have the illusion that we are in control of most aspects of it. We might think, "If I were pregnant, I would eat well, have perfect prenatal care, make the best birthing arrangements, and be assured of a pediatrician's care for the baby at birth." As Joan points out, "No one gets pregnant thinking, 'I have a 27 percent chance of having a baby with Down syndrome.'" Our illusion of control—our denial—might help us to feel less fear. But in adoption, most of the risks are out of our control. That makes us feel more at risk, even if we are not.

WAYS TO COPE

Reading the words *fear, guilt, anger,* and *grief* might make you feel uncomfortable. That's normal. Allow yourself to feel, and call the feelings by their true names. Know that you're safe enough to come out of this a whole person. You will also be a much stronger person, and a more committed parent, as a result of doing this emotional work now. Hope, faith, and social support all help us to overcome most of the fears that go with parenthood—in all forms, and especially adoptive parenthood. Eventually, as we do the emotional and spiritual work of preparing for adoptive parenthood, we will spend more time on the top side of the circle, and we will have less intense experiences on the bottom side. When that happens, we can safely say that our feelings have been resolved. Resolved means that you can make sense of them cognitively, explain them clearly to yourself and to another person, and understand yourself and your reaction to the situation you were in. We can still feel the feelings, even if they're resolved, but they no longer have the power to overwhelm us or blow us around like a Category 4 hurricane.

Natalie put it this way: "I re-read my journal from that time [before her first child's adoption] recently, and realized how much I was in crisis." Now, though, she's the busy mom of two, juggling her younger daughter's kindergarten schedule and her older one's middle school activities.

Hope and Optimism

Hope is the spiritual-sounding word for great expectations, or optimism. Dr. Levy-Shiff's research found that adoptive parents who expected a positive transition to parenthood reported more satisfaction with their family life after their child came home. She says that high expectations could be irrational, or they could come from parents' good intentions and high hopes. This finding confirms work in other areas of psychology. For example, AIDS patients who expect to get better actually have stronger immune system activity, even when their expectation is not based on medical facts.

Hope can be a healer, but it can be in very short supply during the process of adoption. Allowing yourself to hope for the child you want, especially if you've gone through years of disappointing infertility "treatments," can seem as risky as hang-gliding. But hope and optimism come in many bright packages. I am eternally grateful to all the women who hoped and believed for me, when I could not, and to the wise visionaries who kept reminding me that they saw me with a child.

Sometimes hope and optimism come in the form of other adoptive families. "I went to an infertility support group and it was so depressing," Natalie recalled. "Then, when we began to consider adoption, we went to the adoptive families support group. Everyone there was happy; the kids were playing and *they* looked happy. It was where I wanted to be."

For some people, religious faith provides optimism. A study of patients facing a major medical crisis found that people who prayed regularly were more hopeful and optimistic about their outcomes than people who didn't. Another found that no matter how dire a doctor's predictions were for people with various types of cancer, those with a high degree of spirituality and religious well-being were less distressed and experienced better quality of life.

Take note of the moments when you do allow hope into your life, and accept the happiness of allowing yourself to dream about your child.

Support from Other People

An important part of social support in adoption will come from other adoptive families. They have been through some of what you're experiencing right now. An enriching part of the adoption process is that other adoptive parents, who you don't yet know, will become your close friends. Just as your child is waiting for you, so are these friends.

Joan said, "Talking to other families and seeing them was most helpful early in the process. They all looked so *normal*. They made adoption concrete and normalized."

Natalie agrees. She used social support throughout her grieving and her adoption process. "Being supported by women sustained me through the grieving," she said. "My friends were a great support. My husband is wonderful, but he never understood that deep pain and loss of the biological child. I remember once I had to stay in bed all day, after a failed IVF. I just couldn't go out into the normal world."

Maureen recalled that her family didn't understand the choices she and her husband made when they adopted two girls from foster care. "The girls' foster families and the adoptive families of their [siblings] are our strongest support now," she said.

Dr. Cohen and her colleagues found that adoptive families at their clinic had significantly more social support than did non-adoptive families. Adoptive mothers were closer to their extended families, and reported less adversity in the families in which they grew up. Adoptive fathers were also closer to their families and had more contact with friends. Other studies of social support found that, of a sample of people who had recently lost a close loved one, those who received more social support were more spiritual and less depressed. The authors speculated that spiritual communities were providing important support.

As you go through your adoption process, you might decide that you'd like a special person to hold your hand, physically and emotionally, from your first phone calls to agencies until your last post-placement visit. This person can act as your adoption *doula*. *Doula* is a Greek word for a very important woman in ancient households—the person who accompanied other women through labor. The *doula* is like a lay midwife, friend, big sister, and mother, all in one body. There are associations of professional *doulas* who work in childbirth; your adoption *doula* can be anyone you choose.

How does ideal support work? Sometimes the last thing an adoptive parent-to-be needs is more advice. Instead, we long for someone to understand us deeply, to pay attention, to empathize. This can feel like a balm to a hurting, angry, fearful, guilty, anxious person. Everyone deserves this kind of support. The ideal social support person listens without judging, and sometimes without even giving advice.

Social and clinical psychologists say that there are two major types of support. The person being supported (maybe you, if you're an adoptive-parent-to-be) must *disclose* her secrets—in other words, tell her story to someone. You can do this in person, such as when you're talking to your best friend or to a therapist. The listener then shares your emotion in some way, such as by restating what you've said or mirroring your speech patterns or your facial expressions.

Writing about trauma and loss has great benefits, too (Pennebaker, 2002). You don't necessarily have to disclose your inner feelings to another person directly; just get them onto paper or into the computer. One mother says that she writes to God about everything that troubles her deeply, and she keeps writing until God writes back, through her hand.

Faith, Religious Practice, and Meaning

Two kinds of faith may come into question after infertility: faith as a belief that doesn't need logical proof, and faith as a belief or trust in God, or a higher power. If we put our faith in medical technology and have had failed *in vitro* or other procedures, we have lost that faith. If we prayed for a child and didn't get pregnant, does that mean God has abandoned us? Should we now have faith in adoption agencies, or private adoption attorneys, or birth mothers?

For psychologists, the scientific study of religious faith and practice as a way of coping is relatively new. There are no studies of adoptive parents and the role that religion plays in their transition to parenthood. But in my own research, I have found that adoptive parents are more religious than non-adoptive ones, and the adopted adolescents in one of my studies were more religious than those who were not adopted. "Religious" meant that they attended more services, said that their religion was more important to them, and prayed more often (Whitten, 2002). Natalie's struggles with what she called the "awful, dark place" led her to a church. She found support, and a better sense of perspective—that most of her life was really good. She also came to believe that if she persevered, she *would* have a child.

Many adoptive families are sustained by religious faith that never wavers. Senator Mary Landrieu said, "I could not have two more beautiful, remarkable children. They are all that I prayed for."

Some explore other religions. One psychologist who studies bereaved people suggests that they can find new meaning through the Buddhist Eightfold Path with its emphasis on ending craving and attachment. Buddhism also affirms the universal nature of suffering.

But no matter what condition our faith is in at the beginning of the process, in the end, when the child comes home, many of us come to believe that the child or children we have are the ones God or the universe intended us to have, as if a divine hand guided the adoption agency, the birth mother, and all the decision-makers involved in the process.

Happiness

With all the focus on the negative, in this chapter and possibly in your home study, it's important to think about what happiness means to you. Only then can you know when you're happy. Sometimes, the paper chase for adoption and the angst over infertility overwhelm us to the point that happiness could hand us a balloon and a giant bubble wand, and the only thing we'd feel would be annoyance. It is easy to concentrate so much on "what's wrong" that we forget to ask—and answer—the question, "What's *not* wrong?"

It's important to try for two reasons. First, when you do get good news, you can be as happy as you allow yourself to be. Natalie said, "When our daughter's birth mom chose us, we were ecstatic! We lived in St. Louis then, and we were on vacation in Utah when we got the call. It was the best vacation we ever had! It was an incredibly positive, wonderful feeling." Second, if you cannot be happy until your child comes home, your child is carrying the burden of making you happy. That's too heavy a load for a little one— or even a big one. Some aspects of your child's life with you, and your relationship, will delight you and thrill you. Others will challenge you more than you ever imagined. Now is the time to practice finding your own contentment and happiness, whether your child is with you or not.

Special Advantages of Adoptive Parents

When the emotions are on their way to being resolved, adoptive parents can begin to enjoy the extra resources they bring to parenthood. They can also begin to appreciate two positive aspects of the different transition to adoptive parenthood.

An obvious plus factor is that both partners can share the work of bringing the child home. Adoptive fathers and mothers are equally able to fill out forms, order birth certificates, schlep papers to the notary, make photocopies, schedule appointments with professionals, research information on the Internet and at the library, and attend adoptive parent group meetings. Sharing the work means sharing the burden, and an opportunity to become closer. If you're a single adoptive mom- or dad-to-be, a friend or family member can share the paper chase with you.

Sharing the pre-adoption work can help buffer your marriage against post-baby stress. If you're married, you might be concerned about the change in your roles after the child's arrival. Married psychologists Phillip and Carolyn Cowan (1988) found that in general after a child's birth, mothers are less satisfied with their marriages than before, because they feel that they do an unfairly large amount of the child care and housework. Their research showed that the more aspects of parenting the women were responsible for, compared with their husbands, the more dissatisfied they were with their marriages.

These couples, maybe unconsciously, split roles the way their parents did. Think Donna Reed and June Cleaver: decades of TV moms at home baking cookies and wiping bottoms while dad's out winning the bread. The change in roles happens before birth, because the woman, of course, is the only one pregnant and doing the work of bringing the baby into the world and into the family. Adoptive parents have a golden opportunity to avoid this subtle but powerful trap, if they collaborate well before the adoption and continue to collaborate afterwards

Adoptive parents also have other advantages. Many psychologists have noted that adoptive parents tend to be older when their first child arrives. This is a source of angst for many of us, who do endless calculations even if we're math-phobic: "When he's 6, I'll be 52; when she graduates from high school, I'll be ready to retire." However, most research confirms that older parents tend to be more mature psychologically as well as more resourceful. Maturity and resourcefulness make them better able to cope with the stress and difficulties of parenthood. They are usually settled in careers or jobs, and therefore earn more money than younger parents.

Finally . . .

The transition to adoptive parenting is demanding and difficult, and filled with wonderful opportunities to develop skills that will help you to be a better parent when your child arrives. It might be as different from your first picture of parenthood as a Rembrandt from a Picasso, but it will be the right picture for your family. Your family and friends might not know how to help you or even how to talk to you about it, but you can teach them—as you will have to teach others how to help your child later. You might see few positive role models, or none at all, but you can create your own with the help of other adoptive parents. Although you might face sadness, anger, guilt, and fear in the process of infertility treatments and the home study, these negative emotions give you the opportunity to employ optimism, support from other people, and faith and religious practice to deal with them. In time, your children will watch you coping successfully with life's challenges and will benefit from the type of parent that you have become.

An old friend from high school recently said to me, about becoming a mother, "Don't you wish you'd done this a lot sooner?"

"No," I said. "If I had, I wouldn't be my daughter's mother."

These exercises are a way to explore your feelings about adoptive parenthood, and to make them conscious enough to cope with effectively. They are not intended to be psychotherapy, or to take its place. Not all of them will apply to you. Feel free to take what is useful and ignore the rest.

These exercises also will not take the place of your home study. If you decide to use an adoption agency, you can expect that your social worker will ask you some of these questions or similar ones. A little familiarity with the questions will help you to prepare. At the same time, they are private, and you can keep them private if you choose. You don't have to tell your social worker everything.

You can do these exercises in any order, of course. I recommend that you start with number 1, though, because this is your North Star. It also gives you a way to begin "trying on" the life of an adoptive parent. You will probably try on more than one life during this process before you find the one that's the right fit for you and your family.

1. Your favorite fantasy for adoptive parenthood

- ❏ Write a story about this, draw a picture with crayons or markers, or both. (You will need craft supplies when your children arrive, so you can stock up now.)
- ❏ What do you look like? What does your child look like? Boy or girl? How old? What color hair, eyes, skin?
- ❏ When and where do you first see your child? How do you feel? What do you do first? What do you do after that?
- ❏ Feel free to steal good ideas from stories of biological parents, but adapt them to adoption.

2. Sadness and anger

Anger and sadness can dissipate only if they're felt and experienced. How do you know whether you're experiencing them in a healthy way?

- ❏ Name the emotion and feel it. React to it.
- ❏ Cry, or scream, if that's your style.
- ❏ Realize that, sometimes, anger is a cover for pain. After you go through the anger, pain might be underneath.
- ❏ Find someone to hold you when you cry. This might or might not be your partner. Each of you might also need another friend or relative to share part of this experience.
- ❏ If you have negative voices in your head, write down what they say about you as an adoptive parent, or about your child, or about when your child is coming. Skip a space between each one.

- Now, go back and write in a positive response from your strong, nurturing self to each one. Remember that depression lies. One of the meanest lies it might tell you is that it will never go away and that you will be miserable forever. Depression needs to tell itself this lie in order to keep itself alive.
- If you feel sad all the time, or think that you will never be able to stop crying or feeling sad, consult a professional counselor or psychotherapist. If you are depressed, your depression and anxiety will tell you that all of these activities are hogwash.
- If your anger makes you feel physically tense, find a physical way to release it—run, race-walk, bicycle as if you're in the Tour de France, hammer a fence, pound dough, chop down trees, prune your hedge, dance.

3. Guilt

There is a three-step process for giving up guilt. First, make a list of the things you feel guilty about. When you are sure that the list is complete, write each item on an index card. Then, do a reality check with someone you trust. Which of these things were really and truly your fault and are really and truly related to the present? For example, you might feel guilty about early sexual experiences when you were a teenager. But that didn't cause your infertility, and you don't owe anyone an apology for that, except maybe yourself. You can put that card aside. On the other hand, did you say something hurtful to a pregnant friend because you were jealous? If so, then you owe her an apology. On that card, write her name, and write out how you will make your apology.

When you finish, you'll have two stacks of cards. One is your "Action" stack, and you will need to make amends to the people in that stack. But if you think that apologizing or making amends might be detrimental to you or to the other person, put it in the other stack.

The other stack is for God, or the universe, or your higher power. Give them to God in a symbolic way, either by putting them in a box with God's name on it, or burning them and letting them, and the guilt they carry, turn into smoke.

4. Fear

- Make a list of your five worst fears about adoption and adopted children. As in the exercises for anger, write down what negative voices in your head say about adoption and about adopted children. Skip a space between each item.
- Now, go back and write in a positive response from your, strong, nurturing self to each one.
- Talk to adoptive parents and visit adoptive families. Seeing the realities can reduce your fear, because the unknown becomes the known, and the known is always more manageable than fearful imaginings.
- Ask adoptive parents and families about your fears and get a reality check.

❏ Also, read chapter 4, "Fire-setters, Egg-suckers, and Oreos: Scary Myths and Reassuring Realities about Adopted Children." Use this information to re-do your list above.

5. Hope and optimism

❏ If you fear that you will never have a child in your family, and if you find hope impossible right now, ask a few trusted people to believe in your child for you. They will do the hoping and believing until you are ready to do it for yourself.

❏ List three things that symbolize hope for you. These items might include a piece of children's clothing, an object from your own childhood, or a quotation from a favorite poem or sacred text.

❏ Choose one item from this list and make it concrete. Draw it, paint it, or sculpt it in Play-Doh. Or, if you aren't drawn to any traditional symbol, pick up a special stone from a river or shell from a beach. Put it in an important place where you can see it every day, or carry it in your purse or pocket. It will remind you that you really are expecting a child.

6. Support from others

❏ List three people whom you can tell that you are considering adoption. Will they be encouraging and supportive? If not, list three other people who will be.

❏ List one person who is an adoptive parent. If you don't know any, ask your local Department of Social Services for parent support groups, or check the Internet for groups in your area. If there are none, join on-line adoption groups and find support that way.

❏ You can support yourself, too. Write in a journal (preferably a new one in a hopeful color) about your adoption ideas. Try to write three pages really quickly, without stopping and without censoring or editing yourself. Do this for six days straight, every morning. On the seventh day, rest, and read what you've written. Are there any new insights?

7. Faith, religious practice, and meaning

❏ If you are a religious person, have you had a crisis of faith because of infertility? List two people with whom you can discuss this. Only supportive, sympathetic people, please.

❏ Complete these statements if they apply:

"I'm angry with God because _____."

"I don't believe in God any more because_____."

"I don't think God loves me because _____."

"I want God to _____."

- ❏ What does your religion say about parenthood and adoption?
- ❏ Write to God, or your higher power, or the universe, about your adoption plans, hopes, and dreams. What does He or She or It write back?

8. Happiness, and loving yourself while you wait

- ❏ List five positive things that you can do to make yourself happy today.
- ❏ Do one of these things now.
- ❏ Then do another one before you go to bed tonight.
- ❏ Every day, ask yourself, "What's not wrong today?" Come up with at least one answer.
- ❏ Every day, look for at least one happy surprise outside of your control—the blue sky, a perfect daffodil, a shorter commute, clean water coming from your faucet.

References and Resources

GENERAL INTEREST

Gottman, J., & DeClaire, J. (1997). *The heart of parenting: How to raise an emotionally intelligent child.* New York: Simon and Schuster, 1997. Includes excellent self-tests for assessing your own emotional intelligence and gives suggestions on how to work on weaker areas.

Johnston, P. I. (1996). *Adopting after infertility.* Indianapolis: Perspectives Press. The book includes two chapters on medical treatments (current in 1996) for infertility and how to make an "infertility plan."

Pertman, A. (2001). *Adoption nation.* New York: Perseus Books Group. This general-interest history of modern adoption in the United States provides valuable background for anyone considering adoption.

FROM THE PROFESSIONAL LITERATURE

Cohen, N. J., Coyne, J., & Duvall, J. (1993). Adopted and biological children in the clinic: Family parental and child characteristics. *Journal of Child Psychology and Psychiatry, 34*(4), 545–62.

———. (1996). Parents' sense of entitlement in adoptive and non-adoptive families. *Family Process, 34*(4), 441–56.

Cowan, C. P., & Cowan, P. A. (1988). Who does what when partners become parents: Implications for men, women, and marriage. *Marriage & Family Review, 12*(3–4), 105–31.

Hall, E. J., & Stolley, K.S. (1997). A historical analysis of the presentation of abortion and adoption in marriage and family textbooks: 1950–1987. *Family Relations, 46*(1), 73–82.

Kirk, H. D. (1964). *Shared fate: A theory and method of adoption and mental health.* New York: Free Press.

Leon, I. G. (2002). Adoption losses: Naturally occurring or socially constructed? *Child Development, 73*(2), 652–63.

Levy-Shiff, R., Zoran, N., & Shulman, S. (1997). International and domestic adoption: Child, parents, and family adjustment. *International Journal of Behavioral Development, 20*(1), 109–29.

Pennebaker, J. (Ed.) (2002). *Emotion, disclosure, and health.* Second ed. Washington, DC: American Psychological Association.

Wegar, K. (2000). Adoption, family ideology, and social stigma: Bias in community attitudes, adoption research, and practice. *Family Relations, 49,* 363–70.

———. (Ed.). (2006). *Adoptive families in a diverse society.* New Brunswick, NJ: Rutgers University Press.

Whitten, K. (2002). *Healthy development of adopted adolescents: The role of family, school, and community.* Doctoral dissertation, University of Virginia.

2

The Life-changing Decisions in Adoption

. . . and parents were born to bring the children home.
WENDY SALINGER, *Folly River*

The decision about which child to choose is almost too big for humans to make, and that's one reason that decisions around adoption are so hard. If you reach this point in the process, though, you have probably chosen to build your family through adoption. That's already a huge decision. Let yourself sit with it for a while, as long as you need to, and celebrate your commitment to becoming a parent. That little respite will nurture and strengthen you for all the decisions to come.

This chapter is designed to help you with them. There are five major considerations in choosing the type of adoption. First, think about your child's age, ethnicity, and health status. You will also need to consider whether you could be comfortable having a relationship with your child's biological family. Finally, decide how long you think you can stand to wait. Each major decision section has three parts: one for the heart, one for the brain, and one for practical considerations.

Decisions about bringing any child except a newborn into the family are foreign territory in human evolution. We're hard-wired with sex hormones that whisper or scream this simple message: "Have sex. Make babies." We can make a decision about sexual activity and contraception. That decision is really about whether to become pregnant, or how to become pregnant, and to have a baby or child. It's not a choice about our child's ethnicity, age, or, usually, health. Adoption, though, presents us with just those choices. It requires us to think about issues that wouldn't come up in the decision to get pregnant and have an infant. While we think about the choices that we face in the process of adopting, we are feeling our

Adoption professionals have developed a set of specialized terms for the people and processes in adoption. These might sound odd when you first read or hear them. You can use the decoder below to translate.

Adoption Term	Plain English
Triad, as in "members of the adoption triad."	Usually means the three people most closely involved in adoption: the child, the birth parent, and the adoptive parent. Of course, this assumes only one parent per set, and there are often two—a mom and a dad.
Referral, as in "get a referral," or "time to referral."	Referral usually refers to the child who is being referred to the adoptive parents. This is the first step toward bringing a child home. After paperwork has been processed, and a parent-child match made, adoptive parents are notified that there is a child available for them. Adoptive parents then have a short period of time to consider whether that child should be part of their family. This process is discussed in depth in chapter 3.
Placement, as in "I have a placement."	Can mean (1) the child placed in your (foster) home waiting to become eligible for adoption, or (2) the family or institution where a child lived or lives.

way through a bramble of thorny issues while wearing short sleeves. Ultimately, we're loving our child-to-be through our choices of the heart.

Each of those choices will involve your brain and some practical issues. This chapter's section designed to help you with the brain part contains information that you need, which comes from peer-reviewed, published papers in medicine, psychology, and social work. The age divisions are based generally on those used by researchers, but—in adoption issues, there's always a *but*—there are no absolute age limits on any of the research reported here. Also, as you read, keep in mind that studies generalizing to all adopted children might not apply to your child. This might be good or bad, depending on the findings.

The parts of this chapter designed to help you with practical issues tell you why each decision in the process is important and what implications

The Children of My Dreams

A Toddler Girl

Julie said, "We both wanted a girl. From there, we began a journey of trusting our instincts. I'd always liked toddlers and was thinking about an older child, so we thought we'd ask for a twelve- to twenty-four-month-old. That gave us primarily Russia and China."

Two Infants Who Have Contact with Birth Parents in the United States

Natalie said, "We decided on an open, domestic adoption. The most important thing for us was that our children know as much as possible about their birth parents. We also wanted to know as much as possible about our daughters' medical history."

Two Older Girls from U.S. Foster Care

Maureen said, "We knew from the get-go we wanted to have a large family. My husband and I actually met in a residential treatment center. I was the recreation therapist and he was a childcare worker in charge of the more aggressive adolescent males. He was a gentle giant with a big heart. We both knew we could work with special needs kids."

A Five-year-old Boy from Kazakhstan

Lorie said, "I'm single and I have a career. I'm on the go a lot, so from the beginning I knew I wanted an older child. I also wanted to meet the child first, to make sure we connected. After a year of searching the Internet for waiting children, another adoptive mom told me about Kidsave, which brings children to the United States from abroad, and arranges for them to spend six weeks with potential adoptive families."

---

your choices can have. Your decisions about your child's age, ethnicity, and health will determine which adoption agencies you will work with, and whether you choose domestic or international adoption. Once you have answers to the questions in this chapter, you will be in an excellent position to decide on the best agency for your family. You will also be ready to respond to questionable "sales pitches" for adoptable children who might not be right for you and your family. And speaking of sales, a word about money. Adoption can be expensive, but prices vary widely—from state governments paying you to parent a child from foster care, to your spending many thousands of dollars in domestic adoption. But even in private U.S. adoptions, there are different types of adoption to fit many budgets.

The myth or story that you created in the exercises at the end of chapter 1 will help guide you through the process of making decisions. Different families, of course, come to their children through different decision routes that start at different points of the family compass. The stories from adoptive parents show some of those different possibilities.

Regardless of where you start creating or adding to your family, you do not have to do this alone. It's better for you and your child-to-come if you don't. Use your adoption *doula* or *doulas* as much as possible to help you. Also remember these wise words of Maureen: "There's no rule book" for making these decisions. The good news is that you can't do it wrong, but you will find it much easier with the help of others who've gone before you.

Five Important Decisions About Your Adoption

AGE: DO YOU SEE YOURSELF WITH AN INFANT, A TODDLER, OR AN OLDER CHILD?

In adoption, as in biological parenting, there are always surprises. You might envision an infant in your arms, gazing up into your eyes. But you might have an infant "referred" to you, and then learn that you have to wait—for her country's government to negotiate an agreement with the U.S. State Department, or for your birth certificate to be re-certified. While you wait for her, she will develop into a toddler, without you. But you will still be her parent. Or you might envision a toddler, and be on an agency list for a little one, only to get a call that there's a five-year-old ready for a parent—and somehow you'll know that you were meant for him, and he was meant for you.

 The Heart Part

In your parenthood fantasy from chapter 1, how old is your child? How does it feel to imagine parenting a child older, or younger? Are you comfortable with that new image, or anxious? Feeling comfortable is a good signal that you should seriously consider children of different ages. And remember that some anxiety about this is normal, not a signal to abandon the process. There are questions in the workbook section at the end of the chapter to help you tune in to your heart.

Adoption Decisions: Using Your Heart and Brain

Adoption Decision	Heart Part	Brain Part	Practical Considerations
Age: What age do you want your child to be on arrival? What age child can you parent?	You long for baby love, toddler cuddles, or soccer games with an older child.	The younger the child at adoption, the best chance they have for growing up healthy. Older children might come with attachment issues or other behavioral or emotional problems.	Older children are waiting for adoption in the United States and abroad; U.S. infants are placed through private agencies and attorneys; international infants are more easily available.
Ethnicity: Can you parent a child of a different race?	Any child can fill your heart—or do you need a child who looks like you?	Having a mixed-race family is a life-long challenge; different ethnic mixes present different issues in different communities.	More non-white children are available for adoption.
Health: Are you willing to care for a child with medical problems?	Your heart goes out to children who need extra physical care.	Many conditions are treatable or manageable with love and advanced medicine.	"Special needs" aren't always serious medical or developmental issues, but sometimes they are. Do you have the resources to take care of a child with special needs?
Relationship with birth family: What kind of relationship do you want with your child's birth family?	You would welcome a relationship with birth parents—or you would feel threatened by competition for your child?	It's important for a child to know as much as possible about her birth family if she wants to.	Some domestic adoptions require openness, but some international ones lack information about birth families.
The wait: How long can you wait until your child comes home?	Do you, like most parents-to-be, feel that you want a child NOW? Or can you wait for years?	Only you can decide how long to wait, and how important this factor is for your family.	Progress in the adoption process often moves at a snail's pace, unless you are adopting older children from the United States who are already eligible for adoption.

THE BRAIN PART: WHAT YOU NEED TO KNOW

Infants, newborn to about six months, can attach to an adoptive parent more easily than older children, so their emotional transition into their new family is smoother. They have only just begun to learn a language, so if they're adopted internationally, they will learn the adoptive parents' language on about the same schedule as non-adopted children. With an infant, adoptive parents have the longest possible time to influence their development. Research shows over and over that children adopted as infants (before one year of age) are most like non-adopted children in all outcomes: parent-child attachment, school achievement, peer relationships, and behavior. Dutch psychologist Femmie Juffer, herself an adoptive mother, found that internationally adopted children's age at placement had the greatest effect on their attachment to their adoptive parents, regardless of their birth weight or country of origin. So it is better for a child psychologically to be adopted as an infant.

On the other hand, infants adopted from orphanages might have medical or emotional conditions that will not become apparent until they are older. Also, babies don't sleep through the night. Infants need calm, warm, responsive, 24/7 care from you or from another sensitive, caring adult. When you hit your tenth night of 3 a.m. feedings, and you are jet-lagged from two weeks abroad, giving calm, warm, and responsive care might be the hardest thing you can imagine or manage.

Older babies and toddlers, seven to thirty-six months, who have been securely attached to their caregivers in a foster family or orphanage can form another secure attachment to adoptive parents who give them sensitive, responsive care. Children are able to attach to more than one adult—for example, to a mother as well as to a father, grandparent, nanny, and/or day care teacher. Attachments can change over time, and a secure attachment to one adult gives the child the emotional memory to form another secure attachment. My research with children adopted from foster care shows that the majority of them do form secure or ordered attachments with the adoptive families, even after a history of abuse. In addition, toddlers who are adopted into a "rich" educational environment—with toys, books, and a lot of talking—can overcome early deprivation and catch up to their early-adopted or non-adopted peers in cognitive development and school achievement.

Children adopted from abroad experience a wide variety of pre-placement care. You might remember the world's shock at the conditions in Romanian orphanages at the fall of the Nicolae Ceauçescu's regime in 1989. The children adopted from those orphanages have been followed in an excellent series of studies by Dr. Michael Rutter in Great Britain and his colleagues in other countries. Not all of the children are thriving, but some are doing very well. These findings should be encouraging to all adoptive families. When the Romanian children were four years old, 38 percent of those adopted after the age of seven months were securely attached to their adoptive parents. Among non-adopted children in general, about 70 percent are securely attached.

Cognitive development presents an even rosier picture. According to Rutter, even children adopted after six to twenty-four months in the Romanian orphanages achieved "spectacular" cognitive catch-up by age four. Those adopted before six months of age were similar in IQ at age four to a group of children adopted in the United Kingdom as infants shortly after birth. Researchers looked at both groups again when the children were six years old, and they found that families with children who had started with low scores but had made marked gains in ability between assessments showed more positive interactions than families whose children had not made gains. The authors think that this is because parents were reacting well to their children's improvements. At age eleven, there was no overall cognitive difference between children who had spent six to twenty-four months in an orphanage and those who had lived more than twenty-four months in an institution. However, at age eleven, children who had been in the most deprived orphanages longer than six months had IQs that were on average fifteen points lower than those of children who had spent six months or less in those institutions. Children adopted from orphanages with more enriched environments and more conscientious care are likely to fare better in their adoptive homes. Doctors estimate that children have one month of growth lag for every five months in an orphanage (Albers et al., 1997).

In adopting an older infant or toddler (seven to thirty-six months), it is also important to consider that, by toddlerhood, many medical conditions that are not obvious in infancy can be more easily observed. These include autism and autistic spectrum disorders, deafness and specific language problems, and fetal alcohol syndrome. However, toddlers might also come with the effects of untreated illnesses or the malnourishment common in many children from orphanages. When children are fed on an institutional schedule instead of when they're hungry, they don't learn to recognize signs of hunger or of being full. They keep eating until all the food is gone or the bottle is taken away. If extremely deprived of nourishment from infancy, children might learn to hoard food. Even in more nurturing situations, such as a foster family, a baby might learn that when he finishes eating, the parents put him back in his crib. In that case, the baby may become used to eating past the point of fullness to prolong contact with the caregivers.

Compared to younger children, toddlers will have a longer transition into their adoptive families. This might require more time off from work for the main caregiver. For internationally adopted children, one challenge of the transition includes a language barrier. Most children begin their "vocabulary spurt" at around eighteen months of age. At this time, they begin speaking in phrases of two or three words, and each day they speak one or two new words. Imagine a Chinese two-year-old, running through your house on her little legs, trying to tell you something important with a stream of her new—Chinese—words.

The normal emotional difficulties of the transition are sometimes complicated by poor pre-placement care, which means moving from one foster home to another, or from an orphanage to a foster home, or from an orphanage to another orphanage. It could also mean neglect in an orphanage, benign or otherwise. You should be able to find out from your agency or social worker how many moves your child has had, and what the care was like. If your child has had many moves, and/or less than ideal care, what should you expect?

My best advice is always expect the best and at the same time prepare for anything. Most children adopted from orphanages or foster care do very well. However, some children adopted from foster care and from orphanages at older ages have abnormal ways of showing that they're upset. For *abnormal*, read *uncomfortable for parents and hard to interpret if you're accustomed to children's usual reactions.* These children may show sadness and hurt in quick-trigger tantrums that parents might interpret as acting out or as disrespect. Alternatively, the children might hurt themselves by hitting or biting or scratching themselves. Such ways of dealing with an emotional upset are classic miscues. Children who react in these ways actually need comforting and reassurance from parents—which they didn't get from orphanage caregivers or the birth family. Unlike children raised from infancy by loving, responsive parents, these children try to relieve their distress by blowing off emotional steam through tantrums or by turning it into physical pain through self-harm. Their adoptive parents can help them to learn that they will be cared for. But tantrums and self-harming behavior can be unnerving to parents who aren't prepared for these possibilities.

Preschoolers and older children (thirty-seven months and older) might also come with risk factors for difficult outcomes. However, in this discussion about children at various ages, remember that the addition of one month of age doesn't magically change a child. Rather, age groupings are a convenient way to talk about various stages of development. The particular child you want to adopt might or might not fit into the relevant age group generalizations.

In general, the older the child at adoption, the greater the challenges—and possibly the greater the rewards for their families. For example, the strongest predictor of cognitive achievement at age four for the Romanian orphans was the child's age at adoption. Late-adopted Romanian children were more likely than those adopted younger to have unusual patterns of attachment.

Children with clinical levels of oppositional defiant disorder (ODD) or attention deficit hyperactivity disorder (ADHD) symptoms were more likely to have been adopted after age two, to have had multiple foster home placements, and to have experienced abuse or neglect, compared with adopted children with lower symptom levels (Simmel et al., 2001). Many studies have found that an older age at placement is associated with more aggressive behavior in elementary-age children and with more problem behaviors in adolescence.

Like toddlers, some older children can have a hard transition into their adoptive homes. If they are internationally adopted, they have the difficulty of learning English—and adapting to an entirely new culture, school, and family—at the same time that they're grieving the loss of the caregivers and friends whom they left behind at the orphanage or foster home. Their parents might need to plan for a much longer adjustment period than that required for parents of babies and very young children.

Almost all older children adopted from the U.S. foster care system have experienced abuse or neglect. This makes them more challenging to parent. Some parents might decide to pursue this type of adoption out of altruism—certainly a worthy goal—and might imagine that all the children need is love. This is true, but proceed with caution: *Love* must be defined not only as starry, soft-focused hugs, but also as warmth, unfailing kindness, mature parental strength, and consistently firm but always gentle limit-setting. You can learn the special kind of techniques to put love into practice for these children, but be at least 99 percent sure of your commitment. (See chapter 5 for information about the importance of commitment to your child.) As Maureen says, "People think there's a formula, that if a child's been in your home longer than out of it [in foster care], they should be okay. But the hard part is parenting a child who's like a porcupine. I'm so clear that my older daughter's a hurt child. The *I hate you*'s are meant for her birth mother, not for me." Parenting children with emotional issues like these is a challenge, but it brings rewards, too. Maureen said, "If I'd known before what I know now, would I do it again? Absolutely."

We don't know all of the factors that lead to problems in children adopted at older ages. We do know that empathetic, responsive parenting can help children overcome many emotional difficulties. And we do know that many of the so-called special physical needs in children from abroad are easily correctable with Western medicine.

Kyle, whose mother Lorie knew that she wanted to adopt an older boy, is a perfect example of a child with a physical impairment that could be fixed. I first met him five years ago at a picnic for adoptive families. He had been with Lorie for two weeks on a summer visit arranged by Kidsave. She stayed close to him as we chatted and our children played, and we walked back and forth under the monkey bars, around the slide and ladder. When the children paused for breath, she introduced us. I said, "Hi, Kyle." He smiled at me and said, "Hch." His cleft lip parted vertically as well as horizontally.

Kyle was a little smaller than some of the other six-year-olds, but he was strong and getting better by the second on the monkey bars. And he wanted his new mom to notice. Before he began each run on the bars, he'd look down at us and say, "Ma." She'd smile up at him and say, "You can do it!" She said that he'd already learned some English, and that she hoped to learn Russian.

Five years later, Kyle is totally fluent in English. Surgeries—three easy ones, according to Lorie—have corrected his cleft lip and palate. He continues to look securely attached to his "Ma." There are many other children like him, who also need families.

Senator Mary Landrieu said, "As an experienced mom, I'd add my voice to those that say that not only is infant adoption a wonderful choice, but adopting older children as well. At first I was hesitant about the idea of adopting children over five years old, but having experienced adoption, and seeing the need, I'd encourage people to think beyond infant adoption. I've met hundreds of families who've chosen older children with special needs and almost every adoption has been happy and rewarding."

 ## THE PRACTICAL CONSIDERATIONS

In general, healthy infants can be more easily adopted from other countries than from the United States. In the United States, only 1 percent to 2 percent of infants born out of wedlock are placed for adoption. Infant adoptions are often private, arranged between birth and adoptive parents by an attorney. In this type of adoption, adoptive parents frequently pay expenses for birth parents, who decide after the baby is born whether to proceed with the adoption. Private agencies also arrange adoptions for U.S.-born infants. Agencies differ in their requirements for adoptive parents of infants, with some requiring a religious statement or commitment. Waiting times for a completed adoption can range from months to years.

Foster-to-adopt programs are now more frequent in the United States through local departments of social services. Infants and toddlers are sometimes placed with a foster family interested in adoption, but usually children who enter foster care are older. In 2004, the most recent year with solid data available on the U.S. foster care system, children who entered the system were an average of eight years old. About half were older and about half were younger; 14 percent were infants.

In addition, in most states, some foster parents are approved to adopt at the same time that they are approved to be foster parents. This means only one home study, and the possibility of adopting a child placed into your home as a foster child. The practice was once discouraged by social workers, and because it is a new method of forming families, it has not yet received wide acceptance. As of August 2006, only nine states had formal concurrent planning policies, and only eight had provided specialized training on concurrent planning to social work staff, according to the Federal Child and Family Services Reviews (2006). However, eight states reported that concurrent planning had led to reduced time in foster care and a shorter time to adoption for some of their foster children. If you are interested in this type of adoption, contact your local department of social services. This program really is a win-win situation, especially for the children who have continuity with the foster parents whom they have grown to love.

Some agencies have policies about the age difference that they will allow between parents and children. These policies may mean that older parents must adopt older children. Some countries have similar regulations or laws. For example, the Russian Federation requires that age differences between unmarried adoptive parents and their adopted child should be at least sixteen years; also, some countries impose a maximum age. Be sure to check for your particular situation.

Many families pursue international adoption, as we did, because they decided that it was most important to them to adopt a child as young as possible. Of course, children of all ages are available for adoption from overseas, too. We don't know how many children in each age group are adopted from overseas, because data on ages are not collected.

The possibility of international adoption from many countries leads us to your next major decision: how important is it that your child look somewhat like you, or share your ethnic background?

ETHNICITY: DO YOU AND YOUR CHILD HAVE TO MATCH?

You might think that you should feel a certain way about this question, but political correctness has no place here. Allow yourself to be absolutely honest in the privacy of your heart. Think about, and feel, whether you are comfortable with children of a different race. Then, imagine going outside of your comfort zone. Also, educate yourself about the history of transracial adoption in the United States and Western Europe, because it isn't all liberal sweetness and light—there is a long and controversial history.

 ### THE HEART PART

The heart part of transracial adoption has two sections. One relates to the child, while the other is connected with some people's idealism about a multicultural society.

The child. If you're adopting after infertility, you might have spent time during your attempts to get pregnant imagining your baby. That ideal baby is the one who would look like the best parts of you and your husband or partner. For me, I picked out my husband's blue eyes and curly hair, my small nose and strong chin. Of course, I did not imagine my thin hair or his "majestic" nose. Sure, in my brain I knew that the chances were equal that a biological child would have any of those characteristics, but in my heart I didn't believe it.

Looking back now, I know that I found it hard to imagine a baby in very specific terms. When we made our final decision for an international adoption because we wanted a young baby, I couldn't visualize her, especially at first. This process was easier for my husband, he said, because he had spent three years teaching on remote islands in Micronesia, where he was the only Caucasian within two hundred miles.

What helped me to get specific in my imagining? Going to visit babies, toddlers, and older girls from China, where we'd originally planned to go for our daughter. Spending time with other multiracial families in our community, especially at our local support group for adoptive families. This last part is important, because different cities offer different social and political environments for adopted children and multiracial families. Some aspects of your local environment might be welcoming, and others might not be. In the university town, with its diverse faculty and students from around the world, we were sure to find groups of almost all ethnicities and nationalities. We have felt welcome in most situations. However, I do remember a distinctly uncomfortable afternoon, in which a group of white women in a garden club directed cold stares at my daughter and me.

Theresa King, an adoption social work supervisor, began her career in Philadelphia thirty years ago at a private agency whose express purpose was placing African-American children in same-race homes. For the past three years, though, she has worked with some transracial placements. "I feel good about the families who're taking on this challenge through our agency, and they're very open about what they need to do to be successful. They've been reaching out to the community to get help and to get the resources they need."

Still, she has strong feelings that parents should receive solid preparation for transracial parenting. "To think you can do it with love alone—that's just crazy, because racism is too deeply entrenched in American society."

Ms. King recommends a hard, searching look at three areas of your life. First, consider the extended family. Family reactions can be important and are not always welcoming. Some grandparents have a difficult time imagining a grandbaby who is darker than they are. Extended family members who served in the military in World War II, the Korean War, or the Vietnam War might be challenged to overcome years of negative feelings—and propaganda—about people from Asia. Some folks, like my originally Southern family, grew up with generations of prejudice against African-Americans. You might decide to ignore their reactions, but they will still be there after you bring your child home. Think about how you will deal with your relatives for the next eighteen Thanksgivings and other family occasions, and how they will react to your child.

Maureen ruled out transracial adoption almost without thinking about it. "If we'd brought a child of color into our home, it would've alienated my family," she said. "Some of my brothers are like Archie Bunker. It was a blessing to grow up in a diverse area of New York, but racial jokes are more accepted there. Now, as soon as we cross the Verrazano Narrows, I tell my daughter to put on her listening ears and don't repeat anything she hears!"

After the family, Ms. King says, think about your neighborhood. Many of us, especially white people, take a mostly white neighborhood for granted and do not see it through the eyes of a person of color. Also consider your church or religious institution and the local schools. How diverse are they? How do people of different ethnicities get along in these places? Is yours a truly blended community, or are different groups "separate but equal"? If your local environment includes almost no people of your prospective child's race, how willing are you to seek out other settings where the child might see herself reflected in others?

It might be hard to imagine that you will need the answers to these questions if you are adopting a baby. I felt that way—but then it seemed that just a few minutes after our adoption, I was dropping my baby off at the neighborhood public school for first grade. (Actually, five and a half years had passed.) This lovely, diverse school turned out not to be ideal for my daughter. She was the only Asian child in her class of many African-Americans, Caucasians, Afghani immigrants, and recently arrived African refugees. There was little mixing, and she was hurt when an African-American friend said that she would invite "only brown girls" to her birthday party. I asked, "What color does your friend think you are?" She answered, "Sorta brown, sorta white."

On a personal level, think about what characteristics you associate with people of different races. Toni Ayers says that all ethnic groups have a certain stereotype in Western society. These are usually so woven into the fabric of our cultural myths that we're not consciously aware of them. However, living in a multiracial family makes us aware of stereotypes, and our dawning awareness is part of becoming a multiracial family. Once we are aware of the stereotypes, we also become aware of the racial hierarchy in the West. Our non-white children will fit into that hierarchy, and our job as parents will be to help them deal with that.

Toni Ayers says of transracial adoption, "Think about what this means for your whole family: If you're white, you're no longer a white family, you're a multiracial family." Even though there are some African-American and mixed-race parents who have adopted children of other races, most adoptive parents are white, and many adopted children are not. Until this mix changes, the advice of Toni and Theresa will hold.

Also consider how you will raise your child. Experts in transracial adoption recommend the following ways to promote healthy adjustment for children. As you read them, imagine what it would be like, and how you would feel, doing each one:

Become part of a community with people from your child's ethnic group. That means making friends with people of other races and ethnic backgrounds, spending time with them, having them over for dinner, attending their children's school performances, and all the things that friends do for and with friends. It also means finding communities or places where adults of your child's race or ethnic group are engaged in a variety of occupations. On one Internet site, an adult adoptee said that the only people of his race whom he saw growing up were waiters and convenience store clerks. The message he got? People of his race are supposed to serve white people.

Learn about the experience of transracially adopted adults from your child's ethnic group. Not all of the stories will have happy endings. You will encounter anger and resentment, but try to remember that the adopted adults who post to Internet lists or blogs are more likely to have an extreme position than to represent all adopted people. Still, they do represent some adopted people, so imagine that your child may encounter some of the same difficulties. How would this affect you and your relationship to your child?

Confront racism head-on. While the fun part of adopting your child's culture might be eating great noodle dishes, celebrating Asian New Year, learning your birth animal, or having a great collection of matrioshka dolls, the hard work comes in learning what it means to live as a racial minority in a white society, especially as a young adult facing prejudice, stereotypes—and sometimes even violence—on her own. Your contacts in your child's ethnic community can help you to understand the implications of racism. So can reading and research. See the relevant list of suggested reading at the end of this chapter.

Idealism about a multicultural society. Some parents who consider transracial adoption are motivated by a desire to help a less-fortunate child. This motivation raises the specter of a stereotype: that of the well-coifed "church lady"—almost always a white church lady—in a pastel suit who takes food to The Poor, or, in this case, adopts a poor brown child out of charity. Here is a hard question: Is your desire for a transracial adoption a heart-felt desire for a child? Or is there some part of you that wants to see yourself as enlightened and altruistic? Do you want others to see you as enlightened and altruistic? There's certainly nothing wrong with enlightenment and altruism—but they don't provide a strong enough foundation for a family.

At the same time, be aware that if you adopt a child of a different race, your family becomes multiracial, as Toni Ayers said. Your family will continue to be multiracial or multiethnic through the next generations. I firmly believe that multiracial and multiethnic families lead the way for others to envision relationships based on love, acceptance, and true family values, not on matching skin tones.

While having a multiracial or multiethnic family is generally a great thing, your family will encounter people who are totally mystified by the idea that you can even be a family if you all look so different. Every multiracial family has at least one such story. The stories are not all pretty, but every parent has the chance to model tolerance and compassion, even to the ignorant and uninformed. Your children will watch you deal with these people, and they will learn from your example. Chapter 8 describes some of the emotional and spiritual opportunities that adoptive parents have found when faced with others' lack of understanding.

 ## THE BRAIN PART: WHAT YOU NEED TO KNOW

Prospective adoptive parents should be informed about three major issues in transracial adoption. First, there is a long and controversial history of transracial adoption in the United States. Second, ethical issues in international adoption have made transracial adoption from other countries potentially problematic. Third, there is the question of how you will parent a child of a different race. The answer depends partly on your ethnicity and your child's, as well as on your community. A fourth important question, that of how well children develop in transracial families, is covered in chapter 4, which explores myths about adopted children. Quick preview: most transracially adopted children do extremely well.

The controversial history of transracial adoption. Transracial adoption has become more common in the United States and Western Europe in the past twenty years. Before about 1980, adoptive placements in the United States were made so that children could "pass" as biologically related to their adoptive parents. This practice reinforced secrecy in adoption. Parents and social workers worked hard to keep children from knowing that they had been adopted.

The first documented adoption of an African-American child by a white family was in 1948 in Minnesota. Shortly afterward, children from Korea began to be adopted by U.S. couples, primarily white, through Holt International, a pioneering adoption agency. At the same time, white couples were also adopting Native American children. By the mid-1970s, about twelve thousand African-American children had been adopted by white couples. More recently, though, there has been an increase in the number of Asian and South American Native children adopted by white parents in the United States, Canada, Israel, and Western Europe. The 2000 United States census discovered that 17 percent of adopted children under the age of eighteen were of a different race than the "householder," who was the adult answering the questions.

Not everyone has welcomed transracial adoption, especially in the United States, which has a history of slavery and racism. Opposition to transracial adoption in the United States came from two main sources: from institutionalized white prejudice against people of color, and from the National Association of Black Social Workers (NABSW), which opposed placing children of African descent with white parents. In addition, Native American tribes began to oppose placement of Native children off the reservation with white families. Barbara Kingsolver's superb novels *The Bean Trees* and *Pigs in Heaven* describe this dilemma eloquently and emotionally.

The NABSW argued that transracial adoption results in "cultural genocide," because parents cannot foster positive racial identity in a child of a different race. However, the emphasis on ethnic identity assumes that a child cannot be psychologically healthy without it. This idea was an important reason that a judge awarded custody of an African-American preschooler to his biological mother, who had previously been convicted of murdering the boy's older sister and of neglecting him (*In re:* Adoption No. 12612 [Md., Feb. 17, 1999] NO. 83 SEPT. TERM 1998). The judge's decision was later overturned, and the boy was allowed to remain with his white foster mother, who adopted him. The family court judge had been strongly influenced by conventional wisdom. But twenty years of research in this area contradict this prejudice: most transracially adopted children in the United States and Western Europe develop as well and as healthily as those in "matching" families.

One outcome of opposition to transracial placement was an increase in the number and proportion of non-white children in foster care during the 1980s. To remedy the problem, the Multiethnic Placement Act of 1994 and its later amendments prohibited the consideration of race in adoptive placements. Departments of social services are now required to document that "All families have been considered" for children eligible for adoption, "regardless of race, color, and national origin." There is still debate about the wisdom of this policy, and actual practice differs from county to county and state to state.

Just recently the supervisor of my county's department of social services told me that her agency had placed an African-American baby with a white couple because he was in imminent danger in his birth family. The couple was already approved for adoption, and when his birth mother's parental rights were terminated, the couple wanted to adopt the little boy. However, his guardian *ad litem* filed a petition to prevent the adoption, because she thought that the boy should be adopted by an African-American couple. The family court judge ruled in favor of the white family, and they were allowed to adopt him.

Ethical issues in international adoption. The economics of international adoption show that children from impoverished developing countries are often adopted by parents in the developed—read *wealthy*—countries. You might not consider yourself wealthy, but in contrast to the government worker in, say, Vietnam who earns six hundred dollars per year, you are. The potential for unethical adoption exists in all developing countries. Because Westerners have money in hard currency, they are willing to spend it on an adoption, and agency facilitators and attorneys are willing to take it or to pay government authorities a "little extra" for whatever they want. In some countries, facilitators have even paid birth parents.

Two countries in which birth parents have been paid openly and flagrantly, Vietnam and Cambodia, were closed to international adoption for over a year. Several families were stranded in Cambodia after adopting their children there, because the U.S. embassy would not issue a visa for the children to enter the United States. The children's status as orphans could not be verified, because of the suspicion that the adoption agency's facilitator had paid the birth families for the children. Similar scandals in Guatemala prompted the U.S. State Department to issue a warning that adoptions from that country would be scrutinized more closely and that the department did not recommend beginning an adoption from Guatemala in the summer of 2007.

In the Russian Federation, a popular country for U.S. adoptions, the federal government passed a set of regulations governing adoption. These rules include specific punishments for illegal actions related to adoption, such as the selling or buying of children, assisting in the illegal placement/ possession of a child, and substituting one child for another. Sentences include "limitation of freedom" or forced labor. However, enforcement may vary widely from one province to the next. There is no guarantee that local officials honor all the laws of the Federation.

In 1993, a group of countries passed the Hague Convention on Protection of Children and Cooperation in Respect of Intercountry Adoption (usually shortened to *the Hague Convention*). The United States ratified this agreement through the Intercountry Adoption Act of 2000. Six years later, the U.S. State Department published regulations to implement the act. The goal is to create safeguards to ensure that intercountry adoptions take place in the best interests of the child. The laws prevent abuses against children, birth families, and adoptive parents involved in adoptions in countries governed by the Hague Convention. They also stipulate that all agencies and all individuals providing adoption services in countries governed by the Hague Convention must be licensed or accredited. The U.S. Department of State is responsible for keeping a list of licensed agencies, and you can access it on their website. Because this list is fluid, changing as new agencies open or existing ones become licensed in additional countries, I will not include it here.

You would think that the question of whether an agency is licensed could be answered simply with *yes* or *no*. You would be wrong, though, because of the three *c*'s of international adoption: complication, complexity, and convolution. The fourth *c* is *caveat emptor*, Latin for *let the buyer beware*—the buyer not of children, of course, but of adoption services.

When Vietnam reopened to U.S. adoptions in 2006, all agencies that wanted to resume working there quickly began the licensing process. Some were licensed rapidly, but others were not. A few unlicensed agencies tried to resume work anyway, under an "umbrella" or "partner" agreement with a licensed agency. Prospective adoptive parents realized through Internet questioning that this kind of arrangement could lead to potential problems. For example, if a prospective parent works with an unlicensed agency, is that agency responsible for correcting any problems if something goes wrong? The unlicensed agency may have passed on the parent's money to the licensed agency. Do the parents have any contact with the licensed agency, or do they only have contact with their unlicensed agency? Do the agencies blame each other for the problem? In the days before the Hague Convention, in similar situations there was always plenty of blame but, sometimes, little resolution. In these cases, adoptive parents lost money and gained heartache. Chapter 3 offers extensive information on choosing an ethical agency.

 THE PRACTICAL CONSIDERATIONS
In domestic adoptions, there are still barriers to transracial adoption. Like the guardian *ad litem* mentioned above, many social workers still oppose transracial adoption. Julie recalls, "We felt really . . . unencouraged . . . by our agency to consider an African-American child." Even though federal law forbids agencies to consider race or ethnicity in making adoptive placements, many social workers try to make end runs around the regulations.

International adoption agencies are obviously more open to transracial placements because most Western adoptive parents are white and most children to be adopted are not. This generalization applies to Russia, where some orphans are Roma or Asian. Lorie, mother of Kyle, says that about half of the children in his orphanage are Kazakh (Asian), while the others come from Russian Slavic or Caucasian ancestry.

Practical considerations related to ethics in international adoption mean that adoptive parents must do very careful homework to make sure they're working with agencies that not only are licensed but also are very reliable and ethical. How? Check with other adoptive families, ask for their recommendations of agencies, and narrow down your list to three or four. Then post to e-mail lists and ask for people's experiences with each agency. Different lists treat this process differently; for example, some allow agency recommendations or criticism only privately between list members, not publicly posted to the Internet. The next chapter gives more specific recommendations on how to evaluate information about an agency.

HEALTH: CAN YOU TAKE CARE OF A CHILD WHO IS NOT PERFECTLY HEALTHY?

Your answer has to be *yes*, at least part of the time, because all children get sick. However, some have chronic conditions that require more parental involvement and vigilance. They may be mild and easily managed, such as my daughter's asthma, or they might be severe and challenging, such as spina bifida. When you think—and feel—through this issue and the questions below, put all your *should*'s on the shelf. Don't say to yourself, *I should be able to parent a child with any condition*, or *I should love and be open to even the most challenging child*. It's true, up to a point—we *should* be able to be supermom or superdad and do anything. But we can't. Some people are more equipped to positively parent disabled children than are others. The only potential wrong step here is not being truthful. Dishonesty could inflict long-term damage to an already vulnerable child.

THE HEART PART

I remember reading newspaper features on older children waiting for adoption from foster care, and wishing in a part of my heart that I could bring them all home. However, after thinking over the brain part (see the following section) with my husband, we decided that we were best suited to raise a basically healthy baby.

Julie and her husband adopted a Chinese toddler with a heart defect just three months before I met them. Julie said, "I started looking into waiting child programs. I'd met people who'd given birth to children with heart problems and with the teaching hospital in our area and its great pediatric cardiology department, it seemed manageable. One thing that helped was, that I could daydream about special needs kids because there are [Internet] photo listings."

Like Julie, Lorie planned to rely on her local university's medical system, as well as her own training. "I'm a nurse, and the plastic surgeon was a friend," she said. She knew that her son's cleft lip and palate could easily be corrected, and she had the resources close by to make that happen.

As you consider risks to your child's health, think about the questions in the Adoptive Parents' Workbook at the end of the chapter.

THE BRAIN PART: WHAT YOU NEED TO KNOW

In international adoption, it's important to remember that different countries have different rules on what constitute "special needs." In some countries, laws prohibit "healthy" children from being adopted by foreigners. Therefore, many basically healthy children in orphanages will be diagnosed as having significant medical conditions. However, all countries governed by the Hague Convention require pre-adoption medical exams to find "excludable diseases" which mean that a child could not be admitted to the United States.

An interesting study compared the pre-adoptive medical reports of fifty-six children adopted from the former Soviet Union and from Eastern Europe with the children's actual health status as determined by U.S. physicians (Albers et al., 1997). The pre-adoption reports included many unfamiliar neurological diagnoses, but none of them were confirmed by the U.S. physicians. The pre-adoption reports mentioned developmental delays for half of the children, and U.S. medical check-ups found this to be correct: 70 percent of the children were delayed in gross motor functioning, 82 percent in fine motor functioning, 59 percent in language, and 53 percent in social/emotional development. In addition, the U.S. doctors showed that 44 percent of the children had growth delays in weight, 68 percent in height, and 43 percent in head circumference, often a measure of intellectual potential.

You should also know that not all countries do routine screening of newborns for the same conditions that U.S. hospitals' tests cover, such as phenylketonuria, hemoglobin, thyroid function, and others. Pediatricians specializing in international adoption recommend newborn screening for all children five and under as soon as they return home.

If you adopt a child in the United States, you will have access to more complete and accurate medical records. On the other hand, an adopted infant might have conditions that cannot be diagnosed until she is older.

Again, consult the Adoptive Parents' Workbook at the end of the chapter. There you will find some practical questions to ask yourself and to explore with your family

Adoption agencies will ask you to complete a very detailed application for a waiting child with special needs. Julie, mother of the little girl from China with a heart defect, explains: "We did a very specific application for waiting children. The application is much more specific than the general list of conditions that all agency applications include. It was hard; I felt like I was turning down a child with each *no* box we checked. But we both knew we were willing to deal with heart conditions. My brother-in-law has a seizure disorder and autistic spectrum disorder, so my husband knew he didn't want to deal with disorders like those or with severe developmental delays." Other prospective parents, of course, might feel differently.

THE PRACTICAL CONSIDERATIONS

There are five practical aspects to consider in your decision about a child's health status.

First, you should meet with a health care professional early to ask about what is really involved in raising children with certain conditions. If you think that you could raise a child with, for example, Down syndrome, visit with families of children with Down syndrome to observe their care. Interview parents, and be as thorough in your own education as possible.

Most parents' views of what works for them will change. As Julie put it, "One of my post-adoption insights is that the stuff I said I didn't want just don't matter a lick. She has a need to catch up? Big deal."

Second, some agencies, especially public ones in the United States, discount their agency fees for special needs children. *Special needs* can mean many things, from being older than twelve months of age to having multiple handicapping conditions.

Third, in international adoptions, you might need to specify that you will accept some conditions which seem more serious than they really are, given the realities of foreign laws governing which children can be adopted, and the sometimes fictional diagnoses. Your international agency and the pediatrician whom you consult can give you guidance in this matter.

Fourth, your adoption agency should give you as much information as possible about your child's health. Domestically adopted children will come with fairly extensive medical records, but internationally adopted children usually do not.

As more parents adopt children from abroad, international adoption medicine has become a subspecialty in pediatrics. The American Academy of Pediatrics has a group of adoption professionals who meet annually and keep in contact with each other through an e-mail list. This list includes physicians in various countries, including some practicing in China and the former Soviet Republics and some who read Russian. These doctors therefore have access to the most complete and up-to-date information about adopted children's health. The list also includes physicians with expertise in interpreting foreign diagnoses and pseudo-diagnoses.

Prospective adoptive parents should find a pediatrician before a child is referred to them. International adoptions will require a pediatrician with experience in international adoption, preferably a member of the Adoptmed listserv. This expert can help in three important ways. First, she can give you general guidance on the types of care that will be needed for children with various conditions. A nurse can do this, too. Second, a specialist in adoption medicine can review the child's photo and pre-adoption medical or health report and interpret it in terms of Western medicine. Pre-adoption consultations are not covered by most health insurance policies, though, so check with your pediatrician about costs ahead of time. Ask whether you can contact the pediatrician during your stay in your child's country, too, for any health concerns or especially for health emergencies. Third, the international adoption pediatrician or clinic can care for your child immediately after you return home.

As mentioned above, health insurance is a consideration. Some agencies require you to take out coverage on your child, regardless of health status, before the adoption. The Health Insurance Portability and Accountability Act of 1996 (HIPAA), Public Law 104-91, stipulates that health insurance coverage for adopted children must be available to all families covered by group health plans as soon as those families assume financial responsibility for the child. It also requires group health plans to offer employees the right to enroll their new child in the plan immediately, not just when "open enrollment" season rolls around. If you are self-employed and have an individual insurance policy, yours will not fall under the requirements of HIPAA, so be sure to check its provisions.

If each member of your family is covered by an individual policy, then obtaining coverage for a child with handicapping conditions can be very difficult. Sometimes the child will be eligible for Medicaid, or state-run Children's Health Insurance Programs (SCHIP). Requirements vary by state. Be sure that you understand the information that applies to your situation.

YOUR RELATIONSHIP WITH YOUR CHILD'S BIRTH FAMILY

Your first thought might be, "What relationship? He'll be mine, all mine." He will be all yours, but he will always be part of his birth family, too, and they will be a part of him. Because they are his relatives, they will be yours, too. If you are married, your husband's or wife's family became your in-laws—for better or for worse. (Just listen to all those mother-in-law jokes!) The same is true in adoption, but there are vast differences in the degree of closeness and the frequency of contact, depending on the type of adoption. The way your child thinks about it, and feels about it, can be strongly influenced by you.

THE HEART PART

Natalie and her husband decided to pursue an open, domestic adoption because they wanted to know as much as possible about their children's medical history. Both of their girls were adopted in the United States. "But most important," she said, "we wanted our children to know as much as possible about their birth parents."

Toni Ayers also wanted an open adoption, but for different reasons. "I have a relationship with my birth mother," she says. "My parents helped me search, and I was in my mid-twenties when I found her. She's like a distant aunt. I have a close relationship with my birth sister who's sixteen years younger and my maternal grandparents. I wanted an open adoption because the relationship with siblings is so important. Having the information is a gift."

Adoptive parents' worst fear is that biological parents will decide that they want their child back. Media horror stories throw gasoline on that fire, although such problems occur only in a tiny fraction of adoptions.

Natalie said, "I'm a nurse and used to work with young women at Planned Parenthood. I know the young women making adoption plans did it out of love. They knew they couldn't parent. I felt an intimate connection to them. I didn't have any fear that the birth parents would show up on our doorstep years later and try to take our children away. We knew if we could meet a birth mom, we could win her trust."

Many people have an idealized picture of a relationship among birth parents, adoptive parents, and children—like an all-inclusive, Norman Rockwell–depicted Thanksgiving dinner, with some extra folks related by adoption to dig into that turkey. In some cases such a harmonious relationship works forever, in some cases only for a while, and in other cases not at all. As in any relationship, adoptive parents can control only their part of it. Birth parents may live complicated lives, and some are not able to integrate their adopted children into their new lives.

When Natalie's older daughter's birth mother chose their family, they began corresponding and wrote for three months before the child was born. Then, Natalie and her husband flew to the state where the birth parents lived, and saw them every day for a week after her daughter's birth. They visited again six months later, when the adoption was finalized. However, that was the last time Natalie and her husband saw the birth parents, who split up soon afterward. The couple knew their break-up was coming, which was the main reason they placed their daughter for adoption.

Natalie said, "We kept in contact until my older daughter was four. But then, all our letters were returned, and the birth mother's phone was disconnected." A challenging aspect of this situation has been Natalie's attempt to explain it to her daughter. "She sent [my daughter] a wonderful letter when she was one year old about why she made the adoption plan," Natalie said. "But after the birth mother had another baby, our letters and cards to her were returned, too. We loved her birth father's grandparents and are still in contact with them. We're very grateful for that."

Many parents want an adoption that is open, or at least as open as possible, because they believe it's in the best interest of their child to have as few secrets as possible. At the same time, they realize that birth parents differ in the degree of openness that they want, and that some birth parents are not stable enough to continue a long-term relationship.

 ### THE BRAIN PART: WHAT YOU NEED TO KNOW

During the past fifteen years, adoption agencies have changed their practice of only approving confidential adoptions, and they now promote not only openness about adoption in the family, as in telling the child about his history, but also openness between adoptive and birth families. In confidential adoptions, agencies give only minimal information about the birth family to the adoptive family and the adopted child. The flow of information stops shortly after the adoption is finalized. The birth parents and the adoptive parents never meet. The official terms for different types of openness include *mediated* and *direct contact* or *fully disclosed*.

Mediated means that the agency gives non-identifying information to birth families and adoptive families, and the agency workers act as go-betweens or mediators. Families might exchange photos, letters, or gifts, and might meet occasionally. In fully disclosed adoptions, adoptive and birth families have direct communication and contact, and they receive identifying information about each other. All adoption professionals say that contacts and relationships between birth and adoptive families are "subject to change," as Natalie and her family discovered.

Each type of adoption has positive and negative aspects for families. These are summarized in Degrees of Openness in Adoption: Pros and Cons on page 58.

Very little research has been published on the correlation between different levels of openness in adoption and the different outcomes for children. The definitive study in this area found that adopted children's satisfaction with the level of openness in their adoption did not differ according to the degree of openness—children reported being satisfied with the degree of openness regardless of the level (Grotevant & McRoy, 1998). All children in the study showed similar curiosity about their birth families, regardless of the amount of information they had received. Likewise, children had similar sophistication in their understanding of adoption, regardless of the level of openness. All children in the study had self-worth scores in the positive range, indicating good self-esteem. Self-esteem did not vary by level of openness, how the child perceived the openness, or whether the child was included in contact with the birth parents. The study's most important finding was that children's social and emotional adjustment was not strongly related to the degree of openness in their adoption. A more recent study of 152 adopted adolescents by some of the same authors (2006) showed that 74 percent of teens who had contact with their birth mothers were satisfied with the contact, and those who were not satisfied wanted more contact. Among the teens who had no contact, about half wished they had contact and half did not.

A new study coauthored by Drs. McRoy and Grotevant with Lynn Von Korff (2006) found that adolescents who had more long-term contact with birth parents had lower levels of acting out, according to the adolescents themselves. Their parents' reports, though, showed no differences by level of contact. Because there were only ninety-two adolescents in the study

Degrees of Openness in Adoption: Pros and Cons

Degree of Openness	Advantages	Disadvantages
Confidential	1. The adoptive parents do not have to "share" their child	1. The adoptive family may be tempted to deny that their child is adopted, or to "pass" as a non-adoptive family
	2. The adoptive parents do not have to "compete" with birth parents and so may feel more entitled to their child	2. The lack of access to the child's medical and/or family history may contribute to the child's questions about his identity
Mediated	1. The adoptive parents have more control over the contact with birth parents	1. The adoptive parents have no real relationship with the birth mother
	2. The roles of the adoptive parents are more clearly defined	2. Children receive information only if the adoptive parents pass it along
	3. Children have access to more information about themselves and their birth family	
Fully Disclosed	1. Adoptive and birth families can have full and real relationships, reducing the impact of fantasies and myths	1. Adoptive and birth families can have difficulty setting boundaries
	2. The adoptive parents have less fear of the birth parents' desire to take back their child	2. Birth parents with severe emotional or physical problems can become dependent on the adoptive parents
	3. Children have direct access to their birth parents and a connection to their genetic and biological family history	3. Children can experience grief and loss if the birth parents sever contact after several years
	4. Children's familiarity with their birth family can reduce confusion and questioning about their identity	

and the findings were not conclusive, adoptive parents should not take this result as the final word. The main conclusion that adoptive parents should take from both studies is that choosing one degree of openness over another probably will not have a large impact on the adopted child's ultimate adjustment.

THE PRACTICAL CONSIDERATIONS

If you choose a private adoption, in which you advertise for a birth mother and meet her, you will have the maximum amount of contact—a fully disclosed adoption. The same degree of openness through meetings is also available from some agencies for U.S. adoptions, and many agencies offer mediated contact with birth parents. The amount of information about birth parents available in international adoption varies dramatically. In some areas of some countries, birth parents attend ceremonies at which adoptions arc finalized. In other places, birth parents abandon children and there is no information about them at all.

Your preference for the degree of openness will determine which type of agency you choose. Remember that, in the end, the level of openness probably will not have a large impact on your child. It will, however, make a difference in your daily life—so think through the best fit for yourself.

WAITING: THE LABOR OF ADOPTION

The snail's pace of adoption can be maddening. We live in a fast-paced world of ATMs, instant messaging, and drive-through pharmacies and burger joints, but there is no drive-through adoption, and we wouldn't really want it even if it were possible. If speed feels like the most important part of the process for you, try to determine what's driving your sense of urgency. Are you afraid that if it doesn't happen *now*, it never will? That time is running out?

Here are two bits of very blunt but crucial advice from parents who've been there:

Vent. And then: Get over it.

If you don't, you risk being influenced by unscrupulous "get a child now" pitches by telephone and over the Internet. One Sunday I met with a couple who had planned an adoption from the Ukraine, only to find that

---

their agency had closed that program. They switched agencies, and the new agency called with information about a toddler in Vietnam. The catch: the agency rep called on a Friday, telling them that they had to decide by Monday morning if they wanted to adopt the child, or the agency would refer the child to someone else. They were, understandably, so anxious that they were almost bouncing off my ceiling. Because they felt that speed was most important, the agency's unethical pressure fed into their fear that time was running out. They were being asked to make one of the most important decisions of their lives, with scant information, in only two days. Many people spend longer than that deciding on a refrigerator. In the end, they decided to adopt the child, and the family is doing well. Other families, though, have been pressured into sending off checks for thousands of dollars to "hold" a child in a high-pressure scenario like this one.

For many parents, the real consideration is whether they can wait months or years. Obviously, your age will play a part; if you have waited as long as most adoptive parents, you are over thirty-five when you start the process and are constantly doing the math (when she's ten, I'll be forty-five, or fifty-six, or whatever). You might not feel that you have the luxury to wait for a birth mother to choose you, in a domestic adoption.

Nearly every adoptive family has a story about waiting. Rita and her husband adopted their daughter from Guatemala. They received their referral when the little girl was four months old. After that, Rita said, "we were caught in the bureaucratic nightmare of immigration in our local office. This was shortly after 9/11, but we never really knew for sure what the holdup was. Our paperwork started expiring, so we had to re-do everything. I contacted our senators and congress people, anybody who could help, and one of our senators was really a lot of help. This whole time, our daughter was in foster care which we paid for, and I thought at one point I should go live there while we waited for the paperwork to clear so I could be with her. But my husband worked full-time and I was afraid if I left the U.S., no one could follow up the paperwork. We finally were able to travel to pick her up an entire year later. It was so frustrating!"

It helps to remember that you'll spend the rest of your life with your child. Even when she's off at college, he's married and the father of your grandchildren, or they're traveling in South America, they will still be your children. They will call you and e-mail you. They'll send you postcards and dirty laundry. They'll ask for advice, or for a loan. Thinking about the decades in the future that you will have with your child can transform your attitude about waiting for a few more months, or even a year, or two.

How else can an impatient prospective parent "get over it" without descending into resignation and despair? The rest of this book is full of suggestions about concrete actions that you can take to get ready for your child's arrival, without letting "busyness" take over your life.

When you have done all of the things on your list, and on mine, there might still be that dim hour in the middle of the night (let's say at 2:30 a.m., my favorite time for intrusive thoughts) when you're too tired or too fuzzy-brained to do one more chore. That's a signal to do even more self-care (especially emotional care), meditation, prayer, support, and faith—but don't limit your caring to 2:30 a.m.

Your decisions on the five major aspects of adoption will determine your next decisions: Will you adopt in the United States or in another country? If in another country, which one? Chapter 3 will help you to consider and make these choices.

Balancing Heart, Brain, and Practical Considerations

At some point in this process, you will probably go through at least one conflict between your heart's desire, your brain's knowledge, and what is possible in practical terms. You might need to abandon—or say a long goodbye to—one of your heart's desires in order to get the best for your child-to-come. Or, even harder, you might need to say farewell to a vision of yourself. This could be an idealized vision of yourself as a parent. It could be an unhealthy view of yourself as a victim of circumstances. On the positive side, it will be comforting to remember that your emotional work through this struggle will not be wasted. (Of course, though, few of us willingly take on such spiritual lessons!) You will learn from it, and it will make you a better parent, because throughout your life with your child, there will be conflicts between what you want for your child and what it is possible for you to give him. You can choose to embrace the decisions that you are making now about your child in the course of the adoption process. Your process of making these choices is an important part of creating your family and of making your family what it is meant to be.

Let go of: "It has to be this way . . ."

To arrive at: "This is how it is, and here is how I feel about it . . ."

So you can: Decide what you will do

If you can't seem to decide—and making these decisions is extremely hard—give yourself a little time. Maureen described the "see-saw" that she and her husband were on when they could not agree about decisions. "But then," she said, "he turned forty, and he went into a diabetic coma. When God hits you with a brick like that, things become clear. All of the stupid stuff goes away, all the stops, the barriers. He woke up from the coma, and after he said he wanted a cannoli, he said he wanted a kid." They began their parent training shortly after he came home from the hospital.

Sometimes the decisions are not hard and fast. Carol said that for her and her husband, "It wasn't a decision, it was an evolution. I had decided I was going to adopt, but 8 months later we did it completely differently." Their plans to adopt internationally changed radically and they adopted their daughter through their faith community.

Finally, remember that at the end of this process you will have a child in your home, and let yourself be open to that child. Senator Mary Landrieu said, "Adoption has been the most wonderful thing that could have happened to me or my husband." It will be for you, too.

1. Make contact with any adoptive families that you can. Attend adoptive family and waiting family support groups. Ask local adoption agencies and social workers whether they sponsor a group, or whether there is an independent local group.

2. Join online discussion groups related to the types of adoption that you are considering. Yahoo! Groups online lists many; and you can simply Google for groups related to everything from infertility support to adoption from China.

3. If you're considering transracial adoption, ask multiethnic families about their lives. Online chat groups and listservs are also excellent sources of information about over-all daily life in a multiethnic family. Here are some questions:

   ❏ What has it been like for your family to have a child of a different race from yours? Or, what has it been like to have a child who matches part of your ethnicity?

   ❏ How have the local schools reacted to your family? What reactions or comments have you received from children in your child's class and their parents?

   ❏ Do you know other multiracial families that we can talk to?

4. Take care of the basics: enough sleep, exercise, a good diet. Nurture yourself as if you were pregnant (just don't eat as much).

5. Begin to prepare for the baby or child:

   ❏ Think about your work schedule.
   ❏ Look for babysitters.
   ❏ Interview child care providers.
   ❏ Sign up for a day care space.
   ❏ Take a parenting class.

6. Continue your adoption journal from chapter 1.

7. Make sure that you either own or have access to all of the current tools of the adoptive parent's trade:

   ❏ computer
   ❏ Internet connection
   ❏ a little Internet knowledge
   ❏ a lot of skepticism
   ❏ willingness to put yourself on(the)line to get the information that you need.

8. Look at your family fantasy from chapter 1. What can you add to it now, after you have thought through all of the questions in this chapter? Or what would you like to change?

9. Check in with yourself on using the four basic coping strategies from chapter 1.

   ❏ **Hope**: Are you carrying your parent talisman? How has that felt?
   ❏ **Support**: Have you found one person with whom to talk about adoption? How was that? If it wasn't a positive experience for you, keep looking for Ms. Right or Mr. Right.

- ❏ **Faith**: What did the universe write to you about your adoption plans? Write another note and see what is in store.
- ❏ **Happiness**: What is *not* wrong today? Which one thing can you do to help yourself feel happy?

The next sections in this workbook will help you in your choices about specific parts of adoption.

YOUR CHILD'S AGE: QUESTIONS TO HELP YOU DECIDE

- ❏ Do you long to cuddle a small infant in your arms?
- ❏ If you adopted a toddler, would you grieve the loss of your child's babyhood so much that you couldn't delight in his toddler explorations?
- ❏ Do you already have children? If so, you have experienced the joys of 2 a.m. feedings, working with sleep deprivation, and endless diapers.
- ❏ How do you envision integrating an older child into your family?
- ❏ How will you handle language differences? If your child comes from abroad, can you learn enough of his native language to respond to your child's basic needs from the beginning? Or can you find a translator? Can you learn and teach simplified sign language?
- ❏ Can you learn enough about abused and neglected children's "miscues" resulting from their anger and distress to respond to your own child's actions appropriately?
- ❏ Can you get perspective on your toddler's transition problems, and not downplay them as a case of the "terrible twos" or as the result of a "flaw" in your child?
- ❏ How do you think your child will act?
- ❏ Who do you think your child will be?

YOUR CHILD'S RACE AND ETHNICITY: QUESTIONS TO HELP YOU DECIDE

If you think that you might want to adopt a child of another race, here are some questions to consider and answer. Remember that there are no wrong answers at this point, and you don't have to plan out your child's entire life today. You can explore your possibly unconscious prejudices at https://implicit.harvard.edu/implicit/demo/takeatest.html. This website has short, five-minute online tests based on ten years of social psychology research into implicit or unconscious bias. On the site, you can also register to access the database of research on this topic.

If you think that you are truly meant to adopt a child of a race different from your own, but you have negative answers to some of these questions, it doesn't mean that you should stop. It just means that you'll have extra work to do after your child comes home. If you can agree to do that, you'll be fine!

- ❏ How does your extended family feel about people of your child's race or ethnicity? If some or all of them have negative attitudes, how will you deal with that? Is it something that you can live with? How will you protect your child from their negativity?

❑ How many people of your child's race live in your neighborhood? If there are none, how do the neighbors feel in general about people of your child's race—for example, are they actively welcoming, or neutrally ignoring, or hostile?

❑ What will your child's experiences in your town be like? How diverse are your church or religious institution and local schools? How do you think children experience diversity in those settings?

❑ How would you describe an Asian person? An African-American person? A Latino person? A white person?

❑ How do you compare children who are Asian, African-American, Latino, white? How do you compare teenagers who are Asian, African-American, Latino, white?

❑ How will you deal with public attention, especially when your child is young and strangers feel more free to ask you questions about her background? For example, people might assume that you're in an interracial marriage because your child doesn't look like you. How would that feel to you?

❑ How much can you learn about your child's birth culture, language, and/or country?

❑ Will you travel back to your child's country later?

❑ How will you help support your child's development of racial or ethnic identity?

❑ Are you willing to spend money on culture camps, language lessons, and other activities?

❑ Can you move outside your own racial comfort zone to meet and spend time with people who are very different from you?

❑ Can you teach friends and family about your child's experiences, and help them to respect your child's race?

YOUR CHILD'S HEALTH: QUESTIONS TO HELP YOU DECIDE

❑ Have you and your family faced challenges in the past? What were they, and how did you deal with them? How can you use that experience in parenting a special-needs child?

❑ In general, how do you feel about taking risks? When you think about unknowns in your life, how do you feel? Some anxiety is normal; a lot of anxiety, which might come out in an extreme desire to control a situation immediately, can mean that your risk tolerance is low.

❑ How do you handle rejection? Emotionally handicapped children frequently reject everyone in their lives for a long time, before they begin to heal and to develop the ability to respond normally to love and affection.

❏ How do you think about success? Do you define success as achieving a certain goal? Or could you define it as making progress toward a goal? If your child is developmentally delayed, she might come close to reading at grade level with a lot of extra tutoring, but she might never make it to college. How would that feel to you? Social worker Karen Horridge counsels, "If it's really, really important that your child be able to go to Harvard, look into adopting a child without special needs."

❏ How flexible are your work schedules? Can you or your spouse or partner take time off for a child's doctor's appointments, counseling, school meetings, and therapy? How much time will you be able to take?

❏ Do you have high-quality medical, psychological, and other therapeutic services close to your home? Do you know how to evaluate and get a full spectrum of services for your child?

❏ Will you be able to support a special needs child financially? Do you need an adoption subsidy? How much? How will you handle the costs twenty years from now, if your child is unable to live independently?

❏ Do you have health insurance? What does it cover?

❏ How do you feel about therapy and counseling? Would you feel ashamed that your child needed it, or could you go to therapy with your child to learn ways to help her heal?

❏ How do you react to physically handicapped people? Do you feel repulsed, scared, embarrassed for them or for yourself?

❏ How does the rest of your family feel about this prospective adoption? Could they embrace a handicapped child?

❏ Are you prepared for a lifelong medical commitment? Is your family? Would they help you to raise a special-needs child?

❏ How comfortable are you asking for help?

❏ Could you accept the fact that your child had endured abuse or neglect, without blaming anyone or rejecting your child's biological family?

QUICK REFERENCE ADOPTION SUMMARY

Use the summary in Which Child and Adoption Attributes Mean the Most to Your Family? as a starting point for your exploration of different types of adoption. Rate each attribute on the scale. Use the numbers in the weighting system below, from 1 to 5. You can also mark an attribute as something you consider a Must. This would mean that this attribute, for you, is beyond important. Look at the attributes that come out as most important for your family.

Then turn to Where to Find the Child and Adoption Attributes That Are Right for Your Family to decide where to begin your search for your child. At this stage in your journey to parenthood, remember that your child is waiting for you. When he, or she, or they, arrive in your home, they might not fit the exact picture that you have in mind right now. However, you can be assured that he, or she, or they, will be exactly right for your family.

Which Child and Adoption Attributes Mean the Most to Your Family?

Child attribute and adoption type	Very Important 5	Somewhat Important 4	Important 3	A Little Important 2	Not Important 1	Must Have
Infant (0–12 months)						
Toddler (12–24 months)						
Older child (25 months or older)						
Boy						
Girl						
White						
African-American						
Mixed race or ethnicities						
Asian and other ethnicities						
Medical information complete						
Basically healthy						
"Special needs"						
Fully disclosed adoption ("open")						
Mediated adoption ("partly open")						
Confidential adoption ("closed")						
Low cost						
No wait time for placement						
Wait time usually in months						
Wait time in years						

Where to Find the Child and Adoption Attributes That Are Right for Your Family

Child attribute or adoption type	U.S. domestic, private	U.S. domestic, public	International
Infant (0–12 months)	♥	♥ sometimes	♥
Toddler (12–24 months)		♥	♥
Older child (25 months or older)		♥	♥
Boy	cannot choose	♥	♥ choice depends on country
Girl	cannot choose	♥	♥ choice depends on country
White	♥	♥	♥ depends on country
African-American	♥	♥	♥ (a few African countries allow adoption)
Mixed race or ethnicities	♥	♥	♥
Asian and other ethnicities	rarely	rarely	♥ sometimes
Medical information complete	♥	♥	♥ rarely
Basically healthy	♥	♥ sometimes	♥ sometimes
"Special needs"	♥	♥	♥
Fully disclosed adoption ("open")	♥	♥ sometimes	
Mediated adoption ("partly open")	♥	♥	♥ sometimes
Confidential adoption ("closed")		♥ sometimes	♥
Low cost	$10,000 and up	Usually no cost. Parents are sometimes given a subsidy for the child's care.	$9,000 to $31,000; average $20,000
No wait time for placement		♥	
Wait time usually in months		♥ sometimes	♥ sometimes*
Wait time in years	♥		♥ sometimes*

*Time varies by country, by agency, by season, and by unknowable and unpredictable forces. Check for current wait times when you research agencies.

References and Resources

Websites

- Child Welfare Information Gateway, on the website of the U.S. Department of Health and Human Services' Children's Bureau at www.childwelfare.gov. Their excellent section titled "Adoption Options" is a readable, user-friendly overview of adoption in the United States which you can download from www.childwelfare.gov/pubs/f_adoption.cfm. If you read it online, you can use the hot links within the booklet to access lists of adoption agencies, support groups for parents, information on transracial and international adoption, and more.

- North American Council on Adoptable Children (NACAC): www.nacac.org/howtoadopt.html. This online guide gives information about how to adopt from the U.S. foster care system. It also includes a list of publishers of adoption-related books, and a list of recommended books. Scroll down through the steps and you'll find hot links to searchable databases of adoption agencies and parent support groups, as well as questions to ask yourself about adoption.

- The National Council for Adoption (www.adoptioncouncil.org) is a nonprofit agency that often provides testimony to Congress on adoption. Their website has useful links to information and statistics. The organization is opposed to abortion and the site reflects that stance.

- The website of the U.S. Department of Health and Human Services provides statistics and research on foster care and adoption in the United States. A link to research is at http://www.acf.hhs.gov/programs/cb/stats_research/afcars/trends.htm#description. A link to statistics is at http://www.acf.hhs.gov/programs/cb/stats_research/afcars/tar/report11.htm.

- Yahoo! Groups includes groups for people interested in adoption in general, and for people interested in international adoption. The link for groups focusing on adoption in general is at http://dir.groups.yahoo.com/dir/Family_Home/Parenting/Adoption. The link for groups focusing on international adoption is at http://dir.groups.yahoo.com/dir/Family_Home/Parenting/Adoption/International_Adoptions.

- The Dave Thomas Foundation for Adoption (www.DaveThomas

FoundationforAdoption.org) is a foundation established by the creator of the fast food chain Wendy's. Look at the section titled "A Child Is Waiting: A Beginner's Guide to Adoption" for a good overview.

- The Evan B. Donaldson Institute (www.adoptioninstitute.org) is a private foundation with excellent publications. You can subscribe free to their e-newsletter and search archives for well written material on adoption.

Books

Adamec, C. (1998). *Is adoption for you? The information you need to make the right choice.* Hoboken, NJ: John Wiley & Sons. This book offers basic information to help you with your decisions.

Barr, T., & Carlisle, K. (2003). *Adoption for dummies.* Hoboken, NJ: John Wiley & Sons. This book includes very short treatments of nearly every issue in both domestic and international adoption.

Gilman, L. (1992). *The adoption resource book* (3rd ed.). New York: Harper-Perennial. This book is one of the first and best basic resource guides. It includes a list of questions to ask yourself to help you decide whether you are ready for adoption.

Salinger, W. (1980). *Folly river.* New York: Dutton.

ON CHILDREN'S AGE AT ADOPTION

Beckett, C., & O'Connor, T. (2006). Do the effects of early severe deprivation on cognition persist into early adolescence? Findings from the English and Romanian adoptees study. *Child Development, 77*(3), 696–711.

Hopkins-Best, Mary. (1998). *Toddler adoption: The weaver's craft.* Perspectives Press. Written by the mother of a boy adopted from Peru, this book is recommended by adoptive parents as the best one on adopting toddlers. It includes discussion of adjustment and attachment issues, but it has a bias toward worst-case scenarios.

Juffer, F., & Rosenboom, L. G. (1997). Infant-mother attachment of internationally adopted children in the Netherlands. *International Journal of Behavioral Development, 20*(1), 93–107.

O'Connor, T., Bredenkamp, D., Rutter, M., and the ERA study team. (1999). Attachment disturbances and disorders in children exposed to early severe deprivation. *Infant Mental Health Journal, 20,* 10–28.

O'Connor, T., Marvin, R., Rutter, M., Olrick, J., Britner, P., & the ERA study team. (2003). Child-parent attachment following early institutional deprivation. *Development and Psychopathology, 15*(1), 19–38.

O'Connor, T., Rutter, M., Beckett, C., Keaveney, L., Kreppner, J., & the ERA study team. (2000). The effects of global severe privation on cognitive competence: Extension and longitudinal follow-up. *Child Development, 71,* 376–90.

O'Connor, T., Rutter, M., & the ERA study team. (2000). Attachment disorder behavior following early severe deprivation: Extension and longitudinal follow-up. *Journal of the American Academy of Child and Adolescent Psychiatry, 39*(6), 703–12.

Rutter, M., & the ERA study team. (1998). Developmental catch-up, and deficit, following adoption after severe global early privation. *Journal of Child Psychology and Psychiatry, 39*(4), 465–76.

Simmel, C., Brooks, D., Barth, R. P., Hinshaw, S. P. (2001). Externalizing symptomatology among adoptive youth: Prevalence and pre-adoption risk factors. *Journal of Abnormal Child Psychology, 29*(11), 57–78.

ON TRANSRACIAL ADOPTION

Websites

- www.bridgecommunications.org/speak:html. This link leads to the website for the training group run by Toni Ayers, adoptee and adoptive mother, and her colleagues.
- PBS series on race and ethnicity, from 2003. Race: The power of an illusion. http://www.pbs.org/race/000_General/000_00-Home.htm.
- Ethical issues and adoption reform are discussed in a new parents' group: www.groups.yahoo.com/gropu/PAPPAC/.

Articles and Books

Fong, R., & Wang, A. (2001). Adoptive parents and identity development for Chinese children. *Journal of Human Behavior in the Social Environment, 3*(3/4), 9–33.

Register, C. (1991). *"Are those kids yours?" American families with children from other countries.* Free Press (Macmillan). This is an excellent compilation of different families' experiences with adopted children from various countries.

Trenka, J. J., Oparah, J. C., & Shin, S. Y. (2006). *Outsiders within: Writing on transracial adoption.* Cambridge, MA: South End Press. This book contains short essays and poems by adults who were transracially adopted as children. The majority see themselves as "outsiders," and most are angry about their adoption.

Whitten, K. L, & Wilson, M. W. (2000). *Parenthood in America: An Encyclopedia.* Interracial Families. New York: ABC-CLIO.

Yoon, D. P. (2001). Causal modeling predicting psychological adjustment of Korean-born adolescent adoptees. *Journal of Human Behavior in the Social Environment, 3/4,* 65–82.

ON THE HAGUE CONVENTION

- www.rainbowkids.com. This site, run by an adoptive mom, adoption advocate, and adoptee, has excellent articles on international and transracial adoption, as well as links to agencies and waiting children.
- www.travel.state.gov/family/adoption/convention/convention_2290.html.

ON OPEN ADOPTION

Websites

- http://www.openadoptioninsight.org/gift_of_a_child_in_open_adoption.htm. This website contains writings by birth mothers in open adoptions. It is maintained by Brenda Romanchik, a birth mother.
- http://www.adopting.org/Courtney.html. This website contains more writings by a birth mother. These are very honest and forthright. All adoptive parents should be familiar with the feelings that this birth mother relates.

Articles and Books

Berge, J., Mendenhall, T., Wrobel, G., Grotevant, H., & McRoy, R. (2006). Adolescents' feelings about openness in adoption: Implications for adoption agencies. *Child Welfare, 85*(6).

Grotevant, Harold G., & McRoy, Ruth G. (1998). *Openness in adoption: Exploring family connections.* Thousand Oaks, CA: Sage Publications.

Homes, A. M. (2007). *The mistress's daughter*. New York: Viking. This memoir by a critically acclaimed novelist and short story writer describes her experiences learning about her birth family, after her birth mother initiated contact with her. This book is not about open adoption, but rather about the experience of an adoption that became open after the author reached adulthood.

Korff, L. V., Grotevant, H., McRoy, R. (2006). Openness arrangements and psychological adjustment in adolescent adoptees. *Journal of Family Psychology, 20*(3).

ON ADOPTED CHILDREN'S HEALTH

Websites

- An excellent website for peer-reviewed medical information written for lay readers: www.nlm.nih.gov/medlineplus. Sponsored by the National Library of Medicine.
- University of Minnesota International Adoption Clinic (http://www.med.umn.edu/peds/iac/). Click on "Downloads" for articles on the health of international adoptees.
- American Academy of Pediatrics (http://www.aap.org). Enter "adoption" in the search box, and you will get a listing of adoption specialists by state.

Article

Albers, L., Johnson, D., Hostetter, M., Iverson, S., & Miller, L. (1997). Health of children adopted from the former Soviet Union and Eastern Europe: Comparison with preadoptive medical records. *Journal of the American Medical Association, 278*(11), 922–24.

3

Where Is Your Child and Who Will Help You Find Her?

Look Before You Leap . . . or Sign Anything

Fear not, for I am with you. I will bring your offspring from the east,
and from the west I will gather you.

Isaiah 43:5

When we boarded the plane for Vietnam on my forty-sixth birthday, my vision of the country was based on Dan Rather's broadcasts from Saigon thirty years earlier. I knew that *cha gio* were fried spring rolls. I knew that we would land at Tan Son Nhut airport, scene of the massive Babylift of 1975. I knew that there were rice paddies, and coconut palms, and in my ignorance the Rogers and Hammerstein tune floated in: "Coconut palms, and banyan trees, and coral sands, and . . . Tonkinese." How could I imagine that my daughter waited there? But she did, and once I was on the plane, I didn't have to imagine it any more. It was becoming real. And it was wonderful.

As Julie said, "I was in a total state of wonderment on the plane to China. If I'd seen a pig walk down the aisle in a dress, I wouldn't have been surprised."

Before Julie and I were looking for pigs in dresses, though, we went through another series of decisions and choices. It might seem that you've been there and done that, after the work in chapter 2. But you're not quite ready to get on a plane or to welcome your child home.

> *Your child is waiting for you somewhere.*
> *Your job is to find the people*
> *who'll help you find her, or him.*

First, keep that thought in front of you. You might want to write it out again (and again) with those colorful markers you bought for chapter 2. Post it over your desk, or in your kitchen, or anywhere you need a reminder.

This chapter will help you find the people who'll help you find your child. It covers decisions about U.S. and international adoption, and about adoption agencies. Look at your list from chapter 2 and the summary table to decide which sections in this chapter will help you the most. A particular challenge in these decisions is that they involve not just your heart and your head, but also a coldly rational business perspective. That business part is easy to forget. When you begin looking into agencies, you'll confront sentimental writing and advertisements for children as "little angels" along with idealized photos of perfect-looking babies.

But now that you've gone through the decision-making in chapter 2, you're learning to separate the heart, brain, and practical parts of adoption decision-making. You might decide ultimately to give more weight to your heart than to your brain and to the practicalities, but you will be able to make a conscious choice about it. This is the chapter that reinforces the rational decisions and helps you to look before you leap.

For European and Canadian readers, please check on the requirements for agencies in your country because there are significant differences from U.S. policies. In the United States, for example, families can specify the gender and age of the child whom they think would be right for their family. However, in both Denmark and Italy, national law specifies that families cannot choose gender or age. In the United States. there are many agencies of all types, and the licensing requirements for them are very vague. In Denmark, by contrast, only two agencies are licensed to perform international adoptions and domestic adoptions are very rare. Using Your Heart and Brain to Make Adoption Choices summarizes the four major types of adoption and gives you a preview of your work in this chapter.

U.S. Adoption through Private Agencies or Private Arrangements

U.S. private adoptions generally happen in two ways. Adoptive parents can make a private contract with a birth mother to adopt her child, or they can work with an agency that places U.S.-born children. There are many issues

Using Your Heart and Brain to Make Adoption Choices

Choice	Heart Part	Brain Part	Practical Considerations
U.S. adoption through private agency or private arrangement	• Birth parents choose who will adopt their babies • Adoptive parents must make their families more public to be chosen • Wait time can be long	• Few U.S.-born infants are placed for adoption by birth parents • Children's health varies, especially in long-term needs; but health information is reliable and easily known	• Wait time can run to years for an infant • Many of these adoptions are fully disclosed • Basic arrangements can be simpler than in international adoption, but sometimes an attorney's help is required
U.S adoption through public department of social services	• Love is not enough to successfully parent a child with special needs • "Parents have to understand that children carry their pain for many years" (—T. King, director of Tri-Area Foster Families) • Be clear about who you expect your child to become	• Places children from foster care • Most children are over five years old, have a medical or emotional disability, and are nonwhite • All children need therapeutic parenting • Be familiar with all issues in transracial adoption	• Sometimes foster parents can adopt children whom they have cared for, but there is no guarantee • Financial subsidies from states and agencies can help with costs • Children might have significant special needs, but there is help available
International adoption	• You adopt a culture when you adopt a child, so it is an opportunity for your family to embrace a new culture • Health status of your child may be unknown • Communities differ in how well they accept foreigners	• Most internationally adopted children do very well in the long term • International adoption pediatrics is a new medical specialty that can help • Countries vary in requirements for adoptive parents • Be familiar with all issues in transracial adoption	• Wait times vary greatly by country and by many other factors • Children's age and health varies by country • Countries can change their requirements or entire adoption programs suddenly
The adoption agency and a home study social worker	• You must feel very comfortable with the agency and the workers • Your agency should reflect, respect, and support your values • The agency will become an important part of your family's history • You must do your best to make sure you have an ethical in-country facilitator in international adoptions	• Adoption is part family-building, part business • Let your brain guide the business part, so you're not hooked by impatience for a child, adorable photos, or phrases • Your home study and adoption can be done by different agencies • Ask many adoptive parents for references • Check the facilitator's reputation carefully via the Internet	• Fees can vary significantly • Check on whether your preferred adoption agency will accept a home study by your preferred home study agency • Time required for meetings and education sessions can be a challenge • In-country support and requirements vary greatly in international adoption

related to the logistics of finding a birth mother and arranging legal contacts, but this book is not meant for legal advice. Instead, it covers the emotional aspects of decision-making about a domestic adoption that you should think about. The major questions are:

1. How do you feel about the birth mother's control over where she will place her child? Put another way, do you feel comfortable competing with other prospective adoptive parents for a birth mother?
2. How comfortable are you with an open adoption? This means working at a long-term relationship with birth parents.
3. How do you feel about being a public person? Prospective adoptive parents often post their photos and family information on the Internet in hopes of finding the birth mother, and child, of their dreams.
4. How long can you wait?

THE HEART PART

As we saw in chapter 2, open adoption is now the norm in the United States. In the ideal world of open adoption, the birth parents and the adoptive parents meet, choose each other, and work out a relationship in the best interest of their child. This relationship might be based primarily on visits, or be limited to exchanges of cards, letters, and photos. Sometimes extended family members, such as grandparents, are also involved.

Joan, the former labor and delivery nurse, said, "We first started a domestic adoption, so we'd have the birth parent connection. I thought that would be such a gift for the child, and I wanted a newborn. Also, I thought I'd know about the health of the birth mother and her pregnancy."

Those are some positive sides to openness. However, there are negatives, too, such as the ones that Natalie mentioned, including the risk that a birth parent might drop out of the picture after establishing a relationship with her child. It is a challenge for some adoptive parents to negotiate their relationship with the birth parent *before* the adoption is finalized. Toni Ayers said, "I became [the birth mother's] support for her adoption decision because she was very young, only sixteen. I didn't have other children, so we spent more time together than I think was appropriate. I had to set boundaries and tell her it wouldn't be healthy for me to have those conversations with her. I won't choose that involvement again, even if I choose open adoption."

There is little solid scientific evidence that open adoption leads to better psychological adjustment. So, while open adoption is a worthy goal, children have the same opportunity to grow up healthy and thriving regardless of the degree of openness.

In U.S. domestic adoption, birth mothers have an important role in choosing the people who will adopt their children. Adoptive parents, who are often in their thirties or forties, might resist the idea that their family's future rests on the possibly volatile decision of a pregnant teenager. If you choose U.S. adoption, then you will want assurances from your agency that any teen birth mothers they work with have enough support from social workers, psychologists, and their extended family to make a solid decision.

On the other hand, you might find that you can connect in a special way with a young birth mother. Carol and her husband had completed a home study for an international adoption when, to their amazement, she found out that she was pregnant. They put the adoption on hold, only to endure the tragedy of a miscarriage.

"We hadn't thought about adopting in the United States," she said, "but then we heard about Diane. The birth parents were in our faith community and wanted to place her with adoptive parents of the same faith. They had chosen other adoptive parents, who weren't able to adopt Diane at the last minute because of their own health problems. Diane was due to be born in two weeks, in another state. I put off calling the agency for a week, and when I did, the social worker said, 'We'd been waiting for you to call! Today we were going to give the birth parents a list of people outside your faith. If you want them to consider you, please send me your biography now.' I sent the bios, and that afternoon the social worker called to say the birth parents wanted to meet us."

Carol had many negative stereotypes about open adoption and about birth parents. "I'd heard that open adoptions would be terrible. I thought foreign adoption would be best because we wouldn't meet the birth parents. When I talked to the agency, they promoted meeting the birth parents so they could approve us. I was skeptical at first—I'd thought she'd be poor, a teenager who couldn't keep her baby . . . all the stereotypes. But then I talked to the birth mother on the phone. [The birth parents] sounded like me twenty years ago; they read a lot, they like music, they shared our faith. I thought, are we really that far apart?"

Adopting domestically sometimes means becoming a more public person or couple so that birth mothers can learn about you. Are you open to being a "featured family" on an adoption website that tries to convince pregnant women to place their children for adoption? Your photo will be on the Internet, along with your letter to the birth mother and perhaps a photo album of your family, from home to pets to vacations to cousins. Adopting through private arrangements brokered by attorneys will also involve being public. One lawyer's website promises that most couples will be chosen by birth mothers within four months of "being marketed." In addition to promoting themselves on the Internet, adoptive parents seeking birth mothers place ads in college newspapers, alternative weeklies, and other places. As with an agency, this part of the process means putting yourself, along with your hopes and dreams of parenthood, "out there."

Long wait times can also challenge parents adopting domestically, depending on their age and ethnicity. There are no statistics on how long parents might wait for a private arrangement to work out, but estimates range from two to seven years for a healthy white infant. *Work out* here means that the adoption is finalized. In a private adoption arrangement, adoptive parents often pay a birth mother's expenses during her pregnancy, and might also pay for medical costs and hospitalization. There is no guarantee that the birth mother will place her child with the adoptive parents, though, and she has a legal right to change her mind about placement. The amount of time birth parents have to change their minds varies by state. No matter how much adoptive parents pay in expenses, birth parents, of course, cannot be forced to relinquish their child.

Joan and her husband connected with one birth mother, whose pregnancy went to term. Joan said, "At the last minute she changed her mind about us, and said she wanted her baby to go to a 'real family'—one with a child already in it!" They were trying to adopt a healthy, white infant, so they also pursued adoptions with two other birth mothers. Unfortunately, neither of these worked out.

On the other hand, Toni Ayers said that she and her husband were open to any child. They had also been very involved in a lot of different cultural communities. Their agency contacted them about a young birth mother who was interested in placing her child with them. After the four nervewracking months that it took for their attorney to find the birth father, their adoption was finalized.

Many prospective adoptive parents also have a great fear that birth parents will challenge them for their children years after the children have been placed. While Carol didn't worry about this, her family did. "My mom and dad didn't want to see any photos of the birth parents, and my mother-in-law wasn't interested in knowing about them," she said. "They were afraid for my heart."

The fear that a birth parent will reclaim his or her child stems from media hype about a handful of dramatic cases. Fortunately, such cases are very rare.

THE BRAIN PART: WHAT YOU NEED TO KNOW

There are very few U.S.-born infants of any race placed for adoption. (In fact, white birth mothers are the most likely to make adoption plans.) The percentage of U.S. babies born out of wedlock who were placed for adoption dropped from 80 percent in 1970 to about 2 percent in 2005. A 1995 study of adoption trends in California found that birth mothers who placed their children independently were about seventeen to thirty years old and had no more than a high school education. Most were not related to the adoptive parents. Many of these birth mothers were involved in the selection of the adoptive parents. They had some contact with the adoptive family, but the study did not follow them over time, so it could not say for certain how long such contact lasted. Another study the same year, by Child Trends, a research organization in Washington, DC, found that very few pregnant U.S. teens chose to place their children for adoption. In 1995, 51 percent of teens who became pregnant gave birth, 35 percent had abortions, and 14 percent miscarried. Less than 1 percent chose to place their children for adoption. This portrait doesn't necessarily apply to teen girls and women placing children with all agencies in all states, though. For example, Minnesota's Children's Home Society and

Family Services notes that the birth mothers who place their child with this organization vary greatly.

Children adopted domestically through private agencies or private arrangements are almost always infants. Most are placed with the adoptive parents immediately, because the adoptive and birth parents have met ahead of time. Adoptive parents often take their babies home from the hospital and might be present at birth. They therefore have the maximum amount of time with the baby to help him become securely attached. Also, because the adoptions are open, the agency will have information about the birth mother's health and about her family's medical history. All of this information is available to adoptive parents.

The children are adopted as infants, so they have a good chance to grow up with healthy outcomes in their adoptive homes. As we talked about in chapter 2, children adopted early in life, especially as infants, tend to have the best adjustment later in life. There is risk, though, as in any kind of parenthood, that children adopted early might develop physical or emotional problems later.

For prospective adoptive parents, it is important to find out whether you are legally allowed to adopt in your state. If you are single, gay or lesbian, or living with a partner but unmarried, not all states or agencies will welcome you as an adoptive parent, despite excellent research showing very positive outcomes for children of gay and lesbian parents (Brodzinsky et al., 2002; Patterson, 2005, 2006; Patterson et al., 2002). As this book was going to press, New Hampshire and Michigan were considering bills that would permit unmarried and same-sex couples to adopt jointly. New Hampshire already permits children to be adopted by unmarried couples and single adults, including gay individuals, but the state has been inconsistent in applying the law to gay couples; the current bill would eliminate discrepancies among different counties. The Michigan bill would permit unmarried couples, including same-sex couples, to adopt jointly; currently, only single people and married couples can do so. Of course, you should check with local agencies or attorneys for requirements as you begin your process.

THE PRACTICAL CONSIDERATIONS

Sometimes adoptive families make contact with a birth mother or birth parents, and later decide to enlist an adoption agency to help them with the process. This approach combines private adoption with agency-facilitated domestic adoption. Some agencies will assist the families in what is called a *designated* adoption, in which the birth mother has already designated the adoptive family. Fees usually vary depending on the services provided.

Many people imagine that private domestic adoption is more expensive than international adoption. Sometimes it can cost as much as $40,000, but it could cost as little as $5,000. Families for Private Adoption, a volunteer group in Washington, DC, estimates that average costs range from $10,000 to $15,000. Toni Ayers said that her first adoption cost less than $10,000. There is a federal tax credit for actual adoption expenses in all types of adoption, for up to $10,160 for families who qualify.

In the United States, any individuals or companies can sell their services as adoption "facilitators." They require no credentials or state licensing, except in California, and some states ban them outright. There have been difficulties with some of these companies. For example, a for-profit company recently declared bankruptcy and is the target of a criminal investigation in Atlanta. The company worked with a long list of clients and adoption agencies, who lost money and time in the process. If you choose a reputable, established agency, you should not need a facilitator. (See the end of this chapter for a list of questions to ask agencies.)

Finally, parents will need to learn about advertising, and about "selling" themselves. If you're attempting a private adoption, learn about family contract law in your state. See the references and resources section at the end of this chapter for recommended books and websites. Most agencies recommend that you have an attorney to help with finalizing the adoption. Attorneys' fees will be in addition to adoption fees.

U.S. Adoption Through Public Departments of Social Services

Adoptions from foster care are considered "legal risk" adoptions, because of the possibility that the birth parents' parental rights will not be terminated and the child will be returned to one or both of them. For example, in 2004 there were more than five hundred thousand children in the foster care system. But 183,000 were waiting for adoption, and only 51,000 were actually adopted during that year, according to the Children's Bureau of the federal Administration for Children, Youth and Families. The wait time to adoption is decreasing—in 2004 it was just fifteen months for children in foster care.

The national Adoption and Safe Families Act (ASFA) of 1997 created a major reform of foster care and adoption in the United States. It requires states to begin steps to terminate parental rights for a child who has been in foster care for fifteen of the last twenty-two months. ASFA also provides incentive payments to states to increase the number of adoptions of waiting children, and the act allots new funding for states to promote and support adoptions. There is still a general preference for returning foster children to their biological families if possible, but the new law does encourage agencies to free more children for adoption, and to do so quickly if birth parents' rights are terminated.

Adoptions from foster care have increased by 57 percent since the passage of ASFA. In 1996, the year before ASFA, thirty-one thousand children were adopted from foster care, and by 2004, fifty-one thousand were adopted. Many states had started reforms to move children into permanent families even before the federal statute.

THE HEART PART

One of my first jobs was working in public relations for a state department of social services. Every month, a sympathetic reporter with the statewide newspaper wrote a feature for us on a "waiting child." The stories ran with a photo of the child, and the reporter's interview. This feature was called "A Child Is Hoping." Occasionally we'd get lucky and a local television or radio station would pick up a story. Every month, I'd get a lump in my throat, thinking about how long the children had waited, and were likely to wait, for their family. There's a part of me that longed to adopt each child—the heart part. But as a young single woman, I knew that I wasn't ready for motherhood.

Twenty years later, I worked with children from foster care, but as a developmental psychologist. Their life histories still can bring a lump to my throat. They are compelling, dramatic stories that can be worse than anything Charles Dickens ever imagined. While many children are resilient—able to withstand the harshest circumstances—others are not.

Unlike me, Maureen adopted her daughters from foster care because she knew that she and her husband could parent children with special needs. "We'd thought about adoption all along. When we first got married, we thought about being house parents in a group home. We knew we could work with special needs kids."

Veteran social worker Theresa King, who has worked to place African-American children for thirty years, says, "Parents considering adopting from foster care have to get real clear about why they want to do it. Do a real introspective review of who you are. What's happened to you in your life to make you who you are? How's this going to affect your parenting? You have to understand that love isn't enough. Sometimes parents think that if they just love this child, she's going to forget about her birth family and forget about their sorrows. They have to understand that's not the way this works. If you can at least begin to hear that message, you can be successful."

Theresa cautions, "I've had experience with so many families that just absolutely refuse to hear it. They just really believe that when we bring this kid into our middle-class home with our middle-class values, everything will be wonderful. I especially felt that when I worked with disadvantaged teenaged birth mothers placing children with middle- and upper-class African-American families. They wanted their child to become an ideal kid, because they have an image to uphold in their community. I've even had children returned because they were causing the parents embarrassment in the community. But parents have to understand that these children carry their pain for many years. You have to be honest with yourself and be willing to change yourself. You can't expect the child to adapt to you completely. You might have to change your beliefs and values to help your child attach to you."

Karen Horridge, an adoption social worker with a department of social services for many years, agreed with Theresa's advice to parents. She said, "I have a very upper-middle-class African-American couple who adopted two boys. They expect them to do well, and they're really focused on the boys' school success. Their two birth sons go to prestigious colleges. I think one [of the adopted sons] will do well, but the other one will struggle more."

Karen noted, "A good question for parents to ask themselves is: Who do you want your child to be? Do you want your child to go to M.I.T. or Harvard, and make great discoveries in physics or neurology? Or is it enough that your child can be a good citizen and support himself or herself, whether he goes to college or not?"

Parents who not only hear but also understand the message that love is not enough have the luckiest children—lucky because they were removed from an abusive home and placed with parents who are not only loving and warm, but also skillful and patient. These adoptive parents understand on the deepest level that parenting their child might not lead to a picture-perfect family of please-and-thank-you manners, cozy evenings roasting marshmallows by the fire, and a quiet little voice saying, "I love you, Mommy." At least, such an ideal situation will not be reached any time soon. These adoptive parents are prepared for months, if not years, of challenging behavior—and understand that the tantrums and "defiance and willfulness" are really the child's shorthand for pain and anger. These adoptive parents are also prepared to give unconditional love and acceptance *without getting it back immediately.*

 ### THE BRAIN PART: WHAT YOU NEED TO KNOW

In general, children on "waiting child" lists are over five years old, have a medical or psychological disability, are members of a sibling group, and are nonwhite. They are considered "special needs" children because of their prior experiences. Karen Horridge said, "When you read home studies you see that parents are willing to take physical special needs, and I think it'd be great if that's all we had to deal with. It's nothing compared to some of the emotional and behavioral needs our children have."

Almost all of these children need "therapeutic" parenting, which can be learned and put into practice very well. My research shows that most of these children can form a secure attachment to a parent, regardless of what kind of abuse they have suffered. Even children whose abuse was considered severe could still form secure attachments. But their behavior could try the patience of a saint. Parents who persevere, though, will know a rare kind of parenting satisfaction in seeing their children eventually heal and grow up to become the best people they can be.

Theresa King advises parents considering adopting through foster care to take part in pre-service training sessions for foster parents. Her agency offers a series of classes as part of the foster parent licensing process. This is part of a mutual assessment between parents and the agency to decide whether both want to proceed. Ms. King said that it's perfectly fine for people to get to the end of the training and then decide that foster-to-adopt parenting is not right for their family.

 THE PRACTICAL CONSIDERATIONS
Karen Horridge recommends that if you're considering this type of adoption, you become respite care parents for children in foster care. This means that you take care of children for a day or a weekend to give the foster parents a break. That way, you can see firsthand how children from foster care might fit into your family. Your local department of social services can tell you how to be certified to provide this service.

The Children's Bureau of the Department of Health and Human Services maintains the Adopt U.S. Kids website (AdoptUSKids.org), which includes photo listings of "waiting" children. These children have been in foster care and are now free for adoption—the social work definition of "waiting." According to the site, 6,979 children from Adopt U.S. Kids are now living with their adoptive or "forever" families. Most children can be adopted as soon as a home study is completed.

You can also opt for a "legal risk" adoption, and become licensed as both a foster and adoptive parent. You can be simultaneously approved as both a foster and adoptive parent. Sometimes a child is placed in foster care with a family who goes on to adopt him. There is generally no cost to adopt through the foster care system. For some children, federal or state subsidies are available to help families with the costs of their care.

International Adoption

The Four C's of International Adoption
Complicated
Complex
Convoluted
Caveat emptor (Latin for *Let the buyer beware*)

International adoption is a huge subject and involves at least eighty countries. This section is a guide to the types of decisions you will make if you decide that international adoption is for you. There are several books and many websites that can help you with specifics and logistics; the best ones are listed in the references and resources section at the end of this chapter.

 THE HEART PART

There are six main principles of the heart in international adoption: blind commitment; love of your child's home culture; community integration; child matching practices; agency ethics; and, frequently, transracial adoption.

Joan, mother of two girls from China, said, "With international adoption you usually know absolutely *nothing* about the baby's background, so you have a bigger commitment to make at the beginning, to the unknown." Parents do receive a medical report but, as we saw in chapter 2, this report is often unreliable. You should consider that if you adopt a child from abroad you will probably know very little about his or her health status. Pre-placement care can range from excellent foster care to a damaging experience at an orphanage. Children's ages range from a few months to years. Very few newborns are placed for adoption internationally. If you adopt internationally, your agency will ask you to fill out extensive information about the type of child you think would fit best in your family. But there are still more unknowns in international adoption than in domestic adoption. For most countries, parents are asked to commit to a child on the basis of little information and a great deal of faith. Chapter 4 describes the emotional aspects of this experience for adoptive parents, because it can be one of the most difficult parts of adoption.

Another important consideration of the heart is whether you can embrace your child's culture as easily as you embrace your child. Think about how willing you are to learn about your child's culture, have a relationship with the country and its people, cook new food, meet new people in your community from your child's country of origin, attend different religious services, travel to cultural events in different cities, attend culture camps in the summer as a family, learn a new language, and socialize with families who have children from your child's country. If you're open to all of these new adventures, international adoption is for you. If you prefer to keep to your routine and your current friends and culture, you might not be a good candidate for international adoption. As in the considerations about transracial adoption, throw the *should*'s out the window. Maybe you believe that you *should* feel open to international adventures, but truthfully you're most happy to stay at home. That's perfectly fine, and you can honor your own preferences and desires.

Some parents say that they felt "drawn" to a particular country. One mother planned to adopt from Guatemala, but the babies she kept envisioning were not Latino; they were Vietnamese and Chinese. She eventually decided that that was a strong message to make a move toward considering Asian adoption. She was tuning in to her own vision of her child—as I encourage everyone to do. Julie and her husband had a home study written for Russia, but as time came to send off their dossier, Julie became more and more anxious. She finally decided that it was because she was not convinced that Russia was the right country for them. She was right: they brought home their Chinese toddler in June 2006.

If your child is transracially adopted, you will adopt all of the issues involved in being a multiracial family. These include little annoyances, such as ignorant questions from strangers. The issues can also be larger and more hurtful, such as rejection of your child by children at his school, or by unenlightened adults in your community. You will be a visibly different family and as such you will challenge some people's preconceived ideas about what a family is—matching mom, dad, and kids—every time you walk out your door. Your extended family, community, schools, religious organizations, and other groups can have a large influence on your child's adjustment, as discussed in chapter 2.

In earlier sections of this chapter, we looked at how birth mothers choose adoptive parents of domestically adopted newborns. Different parents have different reactions to that method of "matching." In international adoption, parents and children are matched in different ways. For example, in China, decisions are made at the national level. In some Russian provinces, however, adoptive parents have been asked to choose a child from among several in an orphanage. As you consider various countries and agencies, be sure to ask about this issue. The idea that a "people's committee" assigns a child can seem terribly bureaucratic and arbitrary. On the other hand, having to choose a child yourself can be daunting. Think carefully ahead of time about each of these processes if you are considering several countries.

Finally, there is the question of country and agency ethics. As we discussed in chapter 2, ethical considerations are a major issue in transracial and international adoption. Some countries have a reputation for having very "clean" adoption processes, and others do not. Unfortunately, this very important aspect of international adoption can change from month to month. This means that you need to do your homework, including continuing to check the resources listed at this chapter's end.

What does this very large issue of ethics mean for your heart as an adoptive parent? Think of it this way. You are creating your child's adoption story—and life story—right now, with the decisions that you make. In the future, when your child asks detailed questions about her adoption, you will want to be able to tell her about the people at the adoption agency who helped you to find her. You'll want to have photos of the nice facilitators in country. Above all, you'll want to know that all of these people are as honest as you are and that they did their jobs with complete integrity. You'll want to be able to tell your child with absolute assurance that her agency never exploited poor birth parents, regardless of conditions in her country.

 THE BRAIN PART: WHAT YOU NEED TO KNOW

Adopting a child from another country can seem like a totally impossible endeavor if you've never done it. But for all of us who have adopted internationally, there's a first time, and it *is* possible. There are three major considerations to think about: first, how internationally adopted children fare in the long run; second, requirements for adoptive parents from the countries that you have chosen; and third, ways to get specialized consultation about children's health status before adoption.

Children's Outcomes

Most internationally adopted children do very well in the long term. As we discussed in chapter 2, even some children from the most deprived orphanages in Romania are doing well. The same general guidelines apply as with any adopted children. In most cases, the younger the children are at placement, the more easily they attach to their adoptive parents, the more physically healthy they are, and the fewer developmental delays they have. As is often the case in adoption, these norms do not always apply, and they should not be interpreted to mean that children adopted at older ages cannot attach, grow up healthy, and achieve on grade level. This rule also does not guarantee that children adopted at a very young age will *not* have later challenges.

In beginning your research, a crucial question is why children are placed for adoption in that country. The best sources of information will be other adoptive parents, reliable Internet sources, international adoption pediatricians, and experienced adoption agencies. Find out, first, why children are placed for adoption. In most cases, the answer will be that the birth parents cannot afford to feed them, much less send them to school. China is the well-known exception.

Second, ask about general health issues in the country. Dr. Mark Mendelsohn, director of the International Adoption Clinic at the University of Virginia, said that international adoption pediatricians have identified a small number of common problems in children from various countries. In China, there is higher lead exposure, rickets (caused by iodine deficiency), and hepatitis B. Russia and Eastern Europe have higher rates of alcoholism in adults, so children are at greater risk for fetal alcohol syndrome or fetal alcohol spectrum disorders. These include mental retardation, birth defects, abnormal facial features, growth problems, central nervous system problems, trouble remembering or learning, vision or hearing loss, and behavior problems. Belarus has the additional problem of exposure to radiation from the Chernobyl accident. Korean children might be at higher risk of hepatitis B, and in Guatemalan children parasites are a common problem. All of these countries have higher rates of tuberculosis than do Western countries, according to Dr. Mendelsohn.

"The good news is that, in general, HIV incidence is low," Dr. Mendelsohn said. "Children must be screened for this abroad and the tests are pretty accurate."

These systemic, country-wide problems were far too big for me to get my head around when we first began our international adoption process. I was clearly mired in a mindset derived from living in a privileged, Western, developed country. I remembered books about pregnancy (which I'd read during my fertility treatments) and those public health campaigns about being good to your baby before it's born. I knew about prenatal care, eating well and not smoking. Looking back, I can't believe how naive I was. I even asked our in-country facilitator about women's smoking habits in Vietnam. He laughed, and said, "They're too poor to buy cigarettes." Many are too poor to buy food, too, if their rice harvest fails or is washed away. On a visceral level, that's still hard for me to understand.

Requirements for Adoptive Parents

Different countries have different requirements for parents who want to adopt from them. For example, Korea, Thailand, and Ethiopia require parents to be at least twenty-five but no older than forty or forty-four or fifty, respectively China wants parents to have a net worth of at least $30,000 plus $10,000 for every child currently in the home. Some countries require couples to be married; others accept singles. Some have a maximum age difference between parents and children. All countries require parents to be "healthy." Korea and Thailand specify no obesity, while Russia and Kazakhstan consider depression to be a deal-breaker. China requires parents to have at least a high school education. These examples are just for illustration. Every source I used for this list included the caveat, "These requirements are subject to change."

When you are ready to begin your process, look at agency websites and, for U.S. citizens, the U.S. embassy sites for the countries that you're considering. For example, Vietnam's requirements are available at http://hanoi .usembassy.gov/adopting_procedures.html. The State Department also has very clearly written guidelines that include documents you must have to bring your child home, such as an orphan visa. The State Department's website is listed at the end of this chapter. It is updated frequently and includes current warnings about countries that have ethical—or legal— problems.

Specialized Medical Consultation

As described in chapter 2, international adoption pediatricians can help prospective and new parents evaluate information about their children. As you gather information about adopting from various countries, check on whether pediatricians whom you might use have any experience with children from those countries. The doctors will be able to give you up-to-the-minute information about any health issues in children from your chosen country.

Once you are in your child's birth country, you will also want access to a pediatrician, preferably one who speaks a language that you speak. You should ask whether you will be able to see a pediatrician in-country when you're interviewing agencies. It's incredibly reassuring to know that you will have a competent doctor to call—and communicate with—if your child is sick and you're half-way around the world from home.

THE PRACTICAL CONSIDERATIONS

There are four major practicalities that can influence your decision to choose international adoption. First, there is wide variation in wait times between countries and within the same country. Conditions in international adoption change so rapidly that your expected or projected wait time will almost certainly change during your adoption process. If you select a country or an agency based on a short wait, be aware that this time could change. Wait times quoted by agencies are, at best, estimates.

Second, as opportunities for international adoption have increased, so have the number of websites for international adoption agencies and for children waiting to be adopted from particular countries. There are also many chat groups organized by country, or even by province, and by stage of adoption. A list of relevant websites can be found at the end of this chapter.

Third, if you adopt internationally you will need to add the logistics of international travel *with a young child* to all the other adoption arrangements. For most countries, you will have to travel there in order to finalize your adoption. Most of these countries are developing, so you will need to take the usual precautions in travel. These include immunizations for diseases that are virtually unknown in the United States and Western Europe, such as typhoid. For some countries you'll need to take anti-malaria drugs while you're there. In country, you'll also need to avoid eating fresh fruits and vegetables unless you wash them yourself, to drink only bottled water, and to prepare your baby's formula with boiled or bottled water only. All of these precautions are very manageable, as those of us who have adopted internationally can tell you. If you hold on to your sense of adventure as you hold on to your child, the travel can even be fun.

Finally, conditions in international adoption change, sometimes rapidly. Countries can alter their requirements for parents, or entire adoption programs, suddenly. Unstable political conditions occasionally make travel dangerous to a previously "safe" country.

Many people know from news reports that China, Guatemala, and Russia have been the primary countries from which Americans adopt children. As I was writing this book, major changes occurred in the process of adoption in all three. In April 2007, Russian authorities announced that they had halted the work of all foreign adoption agencies for several months. Their action shut down the placement of children from one of the most important countries for U.S. families seeking to adopt. A short while earlier, the U.S. State Department had issued a warning that it could no longer recommend that U.S. families adopt from Guatemala. China, meanwhile, tightened its requirements for adoptive parents. That country now excludes, among others, prospective adoptive parents who are obese or who have taken antidepressants. The closing of these three countries to some or all adoptive parents has sent many to other countries, thus increasing wait times for most families—and for the children who are left behind, waiting for their countries to re-open.

Meanwhile, in late 2006 Madonna traveled to Malawi to adopt a young boy. Her trip turned the adoption spotlight to Africa, where there are twelve million children orphaned by HIV/AIDS alone, as well as others orphaned by war, famine, and other catastrophes. When I was writing this book, only Ethiopia, Sierra Leone, and Liberia had laws or policies that permitted international adoptions, but everything in international adoption is subject to change. Stay tuned.

Choosing the Adoption Agency

The choice of your agency is one of the most important decisions that you will ever make. It's like choosing your obstetrician, pediatrician, labor coach, best friend, travel agent, and priest—all in one package. The agency and its employees will be a very important part of your life for at least a year, and you will never forget the way you worked with them to bring your child home. So choose carefully. Before you even begin to get information from specific agencies, read as much as possible and talk to parents who have experienced and completed the kind of adoption you are planning to make, whether international or domestic.

Senator Mary Landrieu said, "We had a very easy process. A lot had to do with the quality of the agency. That's why I believe in licensing and making sure the professionals in the field are highly qualified. Just as biological parenting isn't for everyone, adoptive parenthood isn't either. You have to have people talking you through the risks and rewards, and making sure people are ready."

Some agencies provide social workers to write your home study. You might decide, though, that the perfect international agency for you is one that is located a thousand miles away. You can still use that agency, but you will need a local home study agency or social worker. You can locate one through local parents' groups or your local department of social services.

Your social worker and/or agency will also provide education and some training for you as an adoptive parent. While you're interviewing people and agencies, ask them to describe their general view of adopted children and adopted people. If the agency or person has a generally negative attitude, consider moving to another agency or worker. Your agency's negativity can color your expectations about your child and your experiences as a parent, and it can even discourage you from adopting. Read chapter 4, on myths about adopted children, before you interview agencies and workers. If you hear too many myths, consider another agency or worker. Also, if you become uncomfortable with your agency or with a worker during the process, fire that agency or worker and move on. Before you sign a contract, know what your liability would be if you had to withdraw from it.

 THE HEART PART
The choice of an agency has three major parts: business savvy, consumer awareness, and emotions. There is one area where your heart can guide you well, and two areas where your heart can lead you astray.

First, your heart—the emotional, intuitive side of you—must embrace the agency and your home study social worker. You will need to feel very comfortable with your home study social worker because you will establish a close relationship with her (this person is almost always a woman). As part of the home study, she will ask you extremely personal questions, about your childhood, your marriage, your parenting beliefs, and more. You wouldn't bare your soul to just anyone, and you shouldn't do so to a social worker with whom you're not completely, 100 percent comfortable.

Even then, the process might feel very intrusive. Pediatrician Mark Mendelsohn recalled, "I was taken aback at all the questions our social worker asked that had nothing to do with parenting, like a lot of specifics about my religion. I almost felt like I was supposed to bend the truth so we'd make it through the home study and be approved. I struggled with that."

The ideal home study will help you reflect on the ways your own childhood prepared you for parenting. It should also help you reaffirm your commitment to becoming a parent. Carol said, "Our home study was so fabulous! Our social worker took lots of time with us, and it was wonderful. I felt like it helped solidify my decision [to adopt]. The home study also made it more vivid to me, that this is what we wanted."

In addition to feeling comfortable with the social worker, you will also want to know that the agency's ethics and business practices align with your heart-felt values. Ensuring that you are comfortable with your agency's ethics will involve a lot of brain work and practical work, which will be discussed later.

There are two ways that your heart can lead you astray as you choose an agency. First, you can let your baby hunger rule. Second, you can be hooked by marketing phrases that remind you of language you hear in church or that are calculated to grab your most emotional—and vulnerable—side.

Your Brain on Baby Hunger

Remember those old public service ads aimed to convince kids not to do drugs? One showed a man saying, "This is your brain," as he held up an egg. Then he said, "This is your brain on drugs," as he cracked the egg into a pan and fried it. Similarly, when you're consumed with longing for a baby, the part of your brain that could make rational decisions goes into hiding. An MRI would probably show the big mushy areas as pale pink or pale blue—your brain on child hunger. Learn to recognize these moments. Do your best to follow your own reasoning as you experience these emotions, because your longing can lead you to rationalize that any child would fit right in and that he must come *right now or else*, no matter how the agency gets the child, no matter what the agency asks of you. If you act on these desperately urgent feelings, you might soon regret it.

Surfing with Salt

As you research adoption on the Internet, you'll see language that appeals to your longing for a child, and possibly to your religious affiliation, either in websites' descriptions of services, or in the name of the agency. You might even see vague statements warning you away from other sites. Here are some examples from website copy:

- "May God bless your journey to your child."
- "Not all christian [*sic*] adoption services are founded on a Biblically based lifestyle."
- "Discover a magical haven where miracles unfold and families are built each day."
- "Helping build families, one miracle at a time."

Adoptions—and our children—are indeed miracles. However, when you read agency web pages, remember that these are advertisements, even if they are from faith-based agencies. Keep in mind that some agency ad copy and website copy—not to mention those photos of adorable children—are designed to appeal to your heart, and to push your heart to overrule your brain and your practical side. Remember that a standard advertising practice is to use babies, kittens, or puppies to sell a product—think toilet tissue, fleece robes, or allergy medicine. The part of you that responds so well to such ads will respond to the baby photos on the web. However, you need to choose your adoption agency using all parts of your decision-making ability. And in an area that's as sensitive as this, you might need your adoption *doula*—or your attorney—to keep you grounded in facts. As my granny in South Carolina used to say, "Take it with a grain of salt." When you see marketing text and photos on agencies' websites, think of how you would react to them if they came to you in a direct mail solicitation, or were printed in your newspaper beside a vacuum cleaner ad. As you surf the web, keep that salt shaker nearby.

Facilitators in International Adoption

If you plan to adopt internationally, an important part of your research into the agency is to find out as much as you can about the agency facilitator. This important person works in the country where your child was born. The facilitator finds children for your agency to place. Sometimes the facilitator is part of the agency's staff and works directly for the agency. Agencies can also use independent consultants or contractors who are authorized to work in one or two provinces or states, or in several orphanages in a country. Facilitators might also work on aid projects funded through your agency.

Unfortunately, some very responsible and reputable agencies have worked with facilitators who, the agency later discovered, were working unethically. Such facilitators move from one agency to another. While agencies might not disclose information on their facilitators to prospective adoptive parents, families might be willing to pass it on. Adoptive parents' lists are the best way to get information about particular facilitators.

Learning about an agency's facilitators is not an optional moral nicety. The U.S. Citizenship and Immigration Services (CIS) offices at foreign consulates frequently ask adoptive parents who their facilitators were during their time in-country. Adoption agencies are charged with granting visas only to true orphans. Facilitators with questionable ethics are known to the U.S. government, and the use of them will be a red flag that your child might not be a true orphan and therefore not eligible for a visa. In other words, do your homework!

THE BRAIN PART AND THE PRACTICAL CONSIDERATIONS
There are three major aspects of the brain part and the practical considerations. The first is that adoption agencies are in business. Some are for-profit, some are nonprofit, but all—except for government-run agencies—are in business to provide a service for money. Second, like businesses in all sectors, some agencies are better than others, in terms of effectiveness, efficiency, and ethics. Finally, you can split your business between an adoption agency and a home study agency or private social worker.

The Business of Adoption

First, adoption agencies include a number of business models: from publicly funded organizations to private nonprofits to for-profit companies. Because there is a business side of adoption, adoptive parents become the "consumers" of adoption services. We ignore the business side at our peril, especially if we let our child hunger rule our heads. You need your brain—like you've never needed it before—as you choose an agency. If you have taken in the warning about web ads, you are well on the way to being an informed adoption "consumer."

It's hard to confront the business aspect of adoption. We might think that business is for banks and groceries—it has no business being a part of adoption, which we can romanticize in pastel soft-focus with words like "little angels" and "chosen children." But there *is* a business aspect to adoption, because large amounts of money are involved. (Re-read the ethics section in chapter 2 if this concept is still foreign to you.) Of course, baby-selling is illegal everywhere. But there is money, sometimes lots of money, involved in almost all adoption services—to find children, to match them with adoptive parents, to create home studies for parents, and to examine the families after the child is placed with them.

Harvard Business School professor Debora L. Spar (2006) writes that in adoption language orphans are not sold—they are "matched" to adoptive parents. She points out that we don't usually talk about adoption in terms of profit-making businesses. However, she argues that there is in fact a "market" for babies, a market in which parents choose traits, clinics woo clients, and specialized providers earn millions of dollars each year. In this market, commerce often operates without many rules, or with inconsistent rules.

Spar writes, "My husband and I were . . . in the process of thinking about possibly adopting a third child (we already had two through old-fashioned means). And as I was doing personal research into adoption, it struck me one day that adoption was really just the flip side of reproductive technology: Both had become ways for acquiring children through what were essentially market means." She advocates more government oversight of the baby business, and notes that people in the adoption market are obviously engaging in a hugely personal, hugely emotional transaction. They don't want to see their family life as the stuff of markets, but they need to be aware that the business of adoption does operate that way.

According to Spar, adoption is regulated more thoroughly than is high-tech reproduction. Still, some adoption advocates argue for even more regulation and oversight. Spar recommends more generous tax credits to substantially reduce the cost of adopting available children, and to make adoption more feasible for lower-income families. She also advocates open discussions about cost and easier access to information about adoption.

What is a good way to find information about adoption? Word of mouth is the best way. Because the adoption community in any city is small, most adoptive parents turn to the Internet for virtual community. A four-year-old discussion group on Yahoo! called Adoption Agency Research has sponsored very frank discussions about international adoption agencies. This group is open *only* to parents, or consumers; the list moderators are vigilant about not offering membership to agency workers or representatives. (You can visit this discussion group at http://groups.yahoo .com/group/Adoption_Agency_Research).

On-line lists are the best place to research agency facilitators, too. One implication of the history of ethical problems with facilitators is that prospective adoptive parents need to do their own research. You might feel that you shouldn't question your agency about their ethical practices, or look as if you are micromanaging their choices of people to work with in-country. However, your agency will play an important role in your family's formation, and you want them to be as ethical as you are. The task of evaluating your agency's ethics might seem incredibly daunting, but it is in fact doable with Internet access and a little organization.

Some Adoption Agency Businesses Are Better Than Others

Adoption agencies are in business to provide a service, which is to match parents and children, and to make sure that the child ends up with the right parents. As a consumer, you must do your homework to find the agencies that are best at placing the children who are right for your family. You should hold faith based agencies to the same high standard as others; don't leave your brain on the altar. Just remember that your definition of a "better" agency might be different from someone else's. For example, if your most important consideration is speed of placement, you will judge your agency mainly on that criterion. The agency might do everything else well, but that will be less important to you. The services should be effective, efficient, and ethical. In international adoption, all aspects of the agency's work must meet these three criteria, including the work of all contractors, subcontractors, and in-country facilitators.

These warnings shouldn't scare you away from adoption. As Mary Landrieu points out, "Most agencies run beautifully. And most adoptions go off without a hitch. It's just a handful of cases that cause the headlines. But those few can deter birth mothers from placing for adoption and adoptive parents from adopting."

What should you expect from an adoption agency? Here is a short list adapted from the Adoption Agency Research Group's website. Every agency should

1. Respond to your inquiries in a timely manner.
2. Provide a transparent process, including names of staff and facilitators.
3. Follow ethical business practices.
4. Respect all local and foreign laws, including holding appropriate licenses.
5. Take responsibility for the actions of everyone involved in your adoption (both in your home country and abroad).
6. Offer a clear and easy process for resolving disputes.
7. Provide a complete itemization with receipts of all monies involved.

What are some hallmarks of a clean adoption process?

1. There have been no reports or even whispers about the coercion of birth mothers to place their babies, for money or for any other reason or "consideration."
2. There are no requests for large amounts of cash to be brought into a country. You should need cash for incidental travel expenses only, not for payments to the orphanage or to government officials.

3. International agencies encourage parents to talk to other parents, and to newly returned families.
4. Agencies are accredited by the Council on Accreditation (www.coanet.org).

Finally, think about what is most important to your family. As you evaluate information from other parents, here is some advice about how to judge what you learn. Some parents might complain that it took longer to get a referral or placement than the agency had promised. Remember that no agency can make guarantees about time, and that your wait might be much shorter. Also, unfortunately, promises of very young babies being referred or placed very quickly raises a red flag: how is the agency finding all those babies? In international adoption, a parent might complain that the agency promised a healthy toddler but their child had scabies or intestinal parasites. Both of these ailments are fairly common in orphanages in developing countries, and they are easily treatable, so such a story should not disqualify the agency. However, suppose that a family tells you that their agency would not send them a photo or medical information, and insisted that they accept the referral. Or a family might tell you that they accepted the referral of a child, but when they arrived in the country, they realized that the child they were given was different—the classic "bait and switch" technique. In either case, be very cautious about using such an agency. Sometimes adoptions do fail to go through for really valid, and ethical, reasons. (See the discussion in chapter 5 on the failed adoptions that some families experienced). However, if a referred child disappears and the adoptive parents are not able to adopt her for mysterious reasons, it could mean that the agency was presenting prospective adoptive parents with information on an "ideal" but unavailable child, who might have been adopted long ago.

Which Fees Are Reasonable?

My husband likes to tell the eye-rolling story of an instance when, new-car shopping, he questioned a $150.00 line item on the sticker price called *ADM*. Turns out *ADM* stands for *Additional Dealer Markup*. If we think that *all* of the people involved in adoption work in that field only for love of God's little angels, we could be led down the primrose path. Adoptions are expensive enough without paying an "additional markup."

Note whether you are required to pay a fee to receive an application packet. One agency charges a whopping $195 for their packet. Their website states, "We strongly encourage all families considering adoption to first order our information packet and speak with our staff before starting the application process. It is important to become comfortable with our staff and programs prior to joining the [agency] family." Note the last phrase, which plays on your desire for family: "joining the . . . family." Real families don't charge a fee to join.

Most other major agencies provide information and their packets free. Most do charge a registration fee, which is about $45 to $50, and an application fee of $200 to $500. You should also expect processing fees. These vary widely depending on the agency, the type of adoption, and the services you request. If I had included detailed information about processing fees in this book, it would have been out of date by now, when you're reading it.

When should you pay a fee? As my granny used to say, "Never buy a pig in a poke." (For city folks, a *poke* is a burlap sack which you can't see through.) But sometimes adoptive parents are asked to send in a fee, possibly a hefty one, *before* they see a contract from their agency. Paying such a fee is the same as buying a pig in a poke, or a diamond sealed up in a box. There is a new database at the Adoption Agency Research Group's site on Yahoo! where adoptive parents have submitted blank contracts from various agencies, so future adoptive parents can know what they are getting into before they apply to an agency. You should know ahead of time what you agree to do with your agency, and what your agency agrees to do for you. It is a waste of an application fee if the terms of the contract are not acceptable. Contract review prior to application makes more sense, but not all agencies work that way. Of course, you are free to choose one that does.

Split Your Business Between an Adoption Agency and a Home Study Agency

You can use one agency for the adoption and another for your home study and post-placement follow-up visits. In fact, unless you live in a major metropolitan area, this kind of arrangement will likely work better for you.

The only drawback is that you will have to research and interview two agencies. In some areas, you might decide to use an independent or freelance social worker to prepare your home study. In either case, apply the same criteria used in your choice of an adoption agency to choose the home study social worker or agency.

• • •

*If an adoption deal seems too good to be true, it almost certainly is—
even if the website promises miracles.*

• • •

Troubleshooting

WHAT HAPPENS IF YOU HAVE TO CHANGE COUNTRIES?

This happens to many parents. We assumed that we would go to China, like many of our friends who had adopted infant girls. We had our home study written for China, and our State Department papers were approved for China. However, just as the document arrived, our agency warned us that Beijing was about to change its requirements for parents. Meanwhile, they anticipated a moratorium on adoptions. The thought of more delays made me want to tear my hair out.

Our agency suggested that we move to its Vietnam program, then very new, with only a few children placed. We said *no* immediately. We were afraid of being guinea pigs. But as we considered Vietnam, we realized that we still felt a connection to that country because of the Vietnam War. As strange as it seems, we felt drawn to this country that we had seen only on the nightly news during the war, when we were teenagers. Then, we decided that we could be not guinea pigs but pioneers. This is just one of the amazing ways that accepting the process of adoption has changed us, changed our minds, changed our lives.

In the past, some people have changed countries because the country closed its borders to international adoption, as did Romania and Cambodia. Just stay tuned to the news from your agency or via the Internet to keep up with current events. The best advice? Be ready with plan B, or even plan C. Don't be surprised and, especially, don't be devastated, if you have to implement an alternative plan. To make a possible geographic change easier, choose an agency with programs in more than one area or country.

Have a second-choice agency in mind in case things don't work out with the first one. Changing to a different agency will seem almost like a divorce if you are well into the process, but sometimes the need does arise. There could be a personality clash with your social worker. There could be a contract dispute about your home study. Your agency might change policies to one which would exclude you and your partner from adopting. The country where your agency is most active could close.

• • •

It's impossible to plan for all events or outcomes. This chapter has covered some of the major tasks and challenges that other adoptive parents have faced. Above all, keep your eyes on the prize: You will have a child at the end of this arduous process.

GETTING STARTED

1. To help you decide on a country:

- ❏ Get a special box. If you want to, color and decorate it.
- ❏ Inside, place the adoption fantasy narrative that you wrote after chapter 1. That writing shows your idea of your child.
- ❏ Sit with it in your lap. Imagine that your child, represented by the writing in the box, looks like a child from the United States—or from Vietnam, or Guatemala, or China, or Kazakhstan.
- ❏ Imagine what it feels like to hold that child.
- ❏ Then, put down the box, walk out of the room, and close the door.
- ❏ How does it feel to close the door on that country? If you feel sad, that's your cue that the country might be right for you. If you feel neutral, you can walk away and it'll be okay.

2. Create a plan for researching agencies. Divide the work with your spouse or partner. Make up a spreadsheet with tasks, deadline dates, and who is responsible.

QUESTIONS FOR AND ISSUES TO EXPLORE WITH
ADOPTION AGENCIES

General Agency Information

1. Start by looking at agencies' websites for general information. At this stage, look at the following:

- ❏ Types of adoption offered: facilitated, matching of birth mother and adoptive parents, or international
- ❏ Requirements for parents: age, marital status, health status, others
- ❏ Costs
- ❏ Services, including which countries are covered and which in-country services are provided
- ❏ Availability of open adoption; or, for adoptions that are not open, how the agency deals with information about birth parents, details of the child's relinquishment, and placement
- ❏ Availability of post-adoption support, both short-term and long-term. Agencies with adolescent and teen support programs tend to have a better sense of the lifelong journey of adoption.
- ❏ Number of adoptions per year

2. If you are adopting internationally, use the U.S. government websites to stay up to date on the relevant rules, regulations, and situations in countries you are considering.

3. Also, if you are adopting internationally, ask the international adoption agencies which in-country facilitator(s) they use. Use the same criteria to evaluate the facilitator as you do to evaluate the agency.

4. Choose at least five agencies, which match your criteria for children, country, and requirements of adoptive parents, to investigate further.

5. For these five agencies, do the following:

   ❑ Obtain references from adoptive parents at different stages in their adoption process, and from adoptive parents who completed adoptions at different times. Ask the parents whether they experienced any problems. The existence of problems should not necessarily disqualify an agency, because adoption is complex. Instead, ask how the agency responded to and helped solve problems.

   ❑ Network as much as possible. Don't rely solely on the references from parents that the agency gives you. Join local and Internet-based adoptive parent support groups. Internet chat groups specifically for adoptive parents are extremely important and valuable resources.

   ❑ Check on adoption professionals and agencies with the licensing authority in their home state. Ask whether there have been any complaints. The authority is usually the state's department of social services or department of health and human services. If neither of those departments is the licensing authority, the adoption unit at the state department of social services can tell you whom to contact.

   ❑ Check on nonprofit agencies at www.charitynavigator.org and www.give.org.

   ❑ Also check with the state's attorney general's office regarding all agencies and professionals you are considering using. Ask whether there have been any criminal actions or complaints. Some people advise checking with the Better Business Bureau, but this is generally not effective for adoption agencies because the Better Business Bureau is run and supported by businesses. You can also Google names of companies and individuals to see whether there is any negative publicity or legal action recorded.

   ❑ Look for complaints at www.theadoptionguide.com. This award-winning site is a valuable resource to help you avoid adoption fraud.

Research Specific to International Adoption

❏ Contact the foreign country's U.S. embassy or consulate. They may be aware of any problems with the agency or facilitator you are considering. Also, you can e-mail the U.S. consulate in the foreign country. The officer responsible for issuing orphan visas will know which adoption agencies, facilitators, and attorneys have had a history of solid ethical practices.

❏ Ask about the qualifications of in-country staff. Get copies of professional credentials. There have been unfortunate instances in which people such as taxi drivers, furniture refinishers, and local hustlers have been given the responsibility to "procure" children for certain agencies.

❏ Ask how often the agency staff travel to the country you are interested in. Do they speak the language, or are they totally dependent on local translators and go-betweens? How much do they know about the culture?

❏ Ask how in-country staff are paid. Are they salaried, or do they earn money based on how many children they place? Workers paid on contingency have an incentive for placing a lot of children quickly. Service may suffer under this kind of plan.

❏ Check the agency contract to make sure that it states that the agency is responsible for the actions and work of the in-country facilitators.

❏ Ask the agency to describe a typical experience in the country for adoptive families. Then ask adoptive parents who have used the agency about their in-country experience to make sure that the accounts are similar.

❏ Find out how, and whether, your agency will prepare you for your trip. Will they advise you about possible attachment problems, medical conditions, and communication problems (especially with older children)? Do they offer a special training package?

❏ Ask how the agency supports you in teaching your child about her birth culture. Do they offer special help for transracial adoptions?

❏ Find out whether the agency encourages you to talk to other families, and to join Internet lists.

❏ Ask for an itemized list of agency fees.

❏ Ask the parents you talk with how much money they spent, especially in the foreign country.

❏ Be certain to ask whether they were required to take large amounts of cash into the country. If so, that raises a red flag for possible bribery and corruption, and reinforces the idea that international adoption is a black-market bazaar for babies.

❏ Ask how the agency determines that children are eligible for adoption, and therefore eligible for orphan visas to the United States or to your country. As

mentioned earlier, there have been cases of children with fraudulent paperwork, and of outright baby-selling.

❑ Ask about the agency's long-term goals in the country. Will they be working
there in ten or twenty years, in case your child wants to search for his birth
family? If not, are there plans in place to facilitate such searches?

❑ Ask the agency whether there is a refund policy for failed adoptions. What con-
stitutes a failed adoption, according to the agency? This definition could include relinquishment to the foster care system, failure to thrive, undisclosed
medical conditions, or inability to bring a child home.

❑ Ask the agency to describe the health of children whom they place for adoption.

❑ Ask the agency why children are placed for adoption in the orphanages they
work with.

❑ Ask the agency which processes they use to screen children for HIV, hepatitis
B, hepatitis C, and other diseases.

Caution Signals

Any one of the following *might* indicate that an agency is being less than completely honest,
open, and ethical:

1. You are offered a referral before you have a completed and approved home study.
2. Your agency discourages you from talking to other adoptive parents or families, and
from joining Internet groups.
3. Children adopted from your agency were later relinquished to your country's foster care
system. This shows that the agency failed to give accurate medical information to the
adoptive parents, did not prepare adoptive parents, or did not match them with a child
they could parent.
4. You are given only a couple of days to make a decision about a referral. You should
have at least a week to decide, especially if you want to review medical information.
5. An agency tells you something that does not match the regulations or laws in the
country you are interested in.
6. An agency tells you that you must sign a waiver stating that you will not sue the
agency or report them to your state licensing authority in case of problems. This is illegal intimidation.

FINAL ADVICE

If you're having trouble detaching from the emotional pull of a child's photo or if you suspect
that your baby hunger is ruling your head, consider hiring or consulting an experienced and
reputable local adoption attorney. This dispassionate professional can help protect your emo-

tional and financial interests. Ask your attorney to review all documents. This is an additional expense, but spending a few thousand dollars here can sometimes save you from losing tens of thousands in adoption fraud.

References and Resources

ON ADOPTION IN GENERAL

- The Child Welfare Information Gateway is located on the website of the U.S. Department of Health and Human Services' Children's Bureau at www.childwelfare.gov/adoption. Their excellent "Adoption Options" is a readable, user-friendly overview of adoption in the United States which you can download free. If you read it online, you can use the hot links within the booklet to access lists of adoption agencies, support groups for parents, information on transracial and international adoption, and more. See especially the overview of adoption types at www.childwelfare .gov/pubs/f_adoptionoptionglance.htm.

ON LESBIAN AND GAY PARENTING

Brodzinsky, D., Patterson, C., & Vaziri, M. (2002). Adoption agency perspectives on lesbian and gay prospective parents: A national study. *Adoption Quarterly, 5*, 5–23.

Patterson, C. (2005). *Lesbian and Gay Parents and Their Children: Summary of Research Findings*. Washington, DC: American Psychological Association. Available via the Internet: www.apa.org/pi/lgbc/publications/ lgparenthome.html.

———. (2006). Children of lesbian and gay parents. *Current Directions in Psychological Science, 15*, 241–44.

Patterson, C., Fulcher, M., & Wainright, J. (2002). Children of lesbian and gay parents: Research, law, and policy. In B. Bottoms, M. Kovera, and B. McAuliff (Eds.), *Children, Social Science and the Law* (pp. 176–99). New York: Cambridge University Press.

ON PRIVATE ADOPTION

Websites

- Information on the Wednesday's Child adoption program for waiting U.S. children, run by the Freddie Mac Foundation, can be found at

http://www.freddiemacfoundation.org/ourwork/adopt_res.html. This site also has a rich list of links to other reputable, well researched sites.
- The Adoption Institute's policy brief on gay and lesbian adoption can be found at http://www.adoptioninstitute.org.
- Families for Private Adoption (www.ffpa.org). This volunteer organization promotes private adoption and provides information for families.
- Yahoo groups: 2adopt, adoptionscams, waitingtoadopt.
- American Academy of Adoption Attorneys (www.adoptionattorneys .org). The AAAA is a national group of attorneys who practice adoption law and who subscribe to the academy's code of ethics. The academy promotes adoption law reform and puts out information on ethical adoption practice.

Books

Burns, S. (2003). *Fast track adoption: The faster, safer way to privately adopt a baby.* New York: St. Martin's Press. The author has a Psy.D. degree and is an adoptive mother. The book describes her family's use of advertising for a U.S. birth mother to find their second baby more quickly than their first.

Hicks, R. B. (1999). *Adopting in America: How to adopt within one year.* San Diego, CA: Wordslinger Press. The author is an adoption attorney. This book is useful for legal issues in domestic, U.S. adoption.

ON U.S. ADOPTION THROUGH A PUBLIC AGENCY

- The Child Welfare Information Gateway provides a directory of resources on thirteen adoption topics, such as kinship adoption, open adoption, adoption assistance, and post-placement assistance. Go to www.childwelfare.gov/pubs/f_adoption.cfm.
- Foster care and adoption: The following two government sites provide statistics and research on foster care and adoption in the United States.
  www.acf.hhs.gov/programs/cb/stats_research/afcars/trends.htm# description
  www.acf.hhs.gov/programs/cb/stats_research/afcars/tar/report11.htm
- The North American Council on Adoptable Children (NACAC): www.nacac.org/howtoadopt.html. This online guide gives information about how to adopt from the U.S. foster care system. It also includes a

list of publishers of adoption-related books, and a list of recommended books. Scroll down through the steps and you'll find hot links to searchable databases of adoption agencies and parent support groups, as well as questions to ask yourself about adoption.

- Casey Family Programs for foster families and researchers at the University of Tennessee have developed tools to assess, prepare, and support foster families. Take a look at www.fosterfamilyassessment.org.
- The National Child Traumatic Stress Network is an organization devoted to diagnosing, treating, and preventing traumatic stress. Read their white paper report, *Complex Trauma in Children and Adolescents*, at www.nctsnet.org.
- Adopt US Kids, a program to promote adoption of waiting children in the United States, keeps a national photo listing of children at www.AdoptUSKids.org.
- Kidsave (www.kidsave.org) promotes adoption of waiting U.S. children, and sponsors visits of older children from orphanages in Eastern Europe and the former Soviet republics to the United States.

ON INTERNATIONAL ADOPTION

Websites and Related Media

- www.orphandoctor.com. This site is run by Jane Aronson, M.D., director of International Children's Health Services in New York City. The "Medical Resources" tab is especially helpful.
- www.Pediatrix.com, website of a company in Florida that provides a metabolic screening kit. Ask your adoption pediatrician whether this kit would be right for your child. If you are adopting internationally, ask whether you should consider taking the kit overseas with you, or sending it ahead before the adoption is finalized.
- The U.S. Department of State provides recorded information on international adoption for several countries on a twenty-four hour basis through recorded telephone messages at 1-888-407-4747.
- The State Department also has an excellent booklet online at www.travel.state.gov/family/adoption/notices/notices_473.html. It covers all U.S. federal laws related to international adoption and is written in easy-to-understand language. It also has sections on different coun-

tries; click on a country, and within the country booklet, click on the embassy website.

- For specific country information, go to the U.S. embassy website for the country. For example, you can review all agencies licensed in Vietnam, see the provinces they work in, and stay abreast of updates and changes to Vietnam's adoption laws at www.hanoi.usembassy.gov/orphan_visas.html.

Books

Bascom, B. B. (1997). *The complete guide to foreign adoption: What to expect and how to prepare for your new child*. Simon & Schuster. A book on practical logistics.

Davenport, D. (2006). *The complete book of international adoption*. New York: Broadway Books. This book is a very thorough guide to the subject, containing useful charts with information organized by country. If there is no updated edition, verify the specific requirements with another source.

Erichsen, J., & Erichsen, H. (2003). *How to adopt internationally: A guide for agency directed and independent adoption*. Mesa House Publishing. The authors are founders of Los Ninos International Adoption Center in Texas. The chapter titled "Choosing the Right Agency" includes an excellent discussion on choosing a reliable, ethical, and reputable adoption agency.

ON CHOOSING AN AGENCY

Websites

- The National Adoption Directory. The Children's Bureau of the U.S. Department of Health and Human Services maintains this list, but warns that the listing does not mean that the Bureau endorses or has investigated every agency. There are also links to your state's adoption licensing officials. Visit www.childwelfare.gov/nad/index.cfm.
- The Council on Accreditation (COA) standards. The latest Council on Accreditation standards for both public agencies and private organizations are available on the organization's website. The U.S. Department of State has designated COA as the sole national independent organization to accredit agencies providing inter-country adoption services in the

United States that work with sending countries that have ratified the Hague Treaty. Visit www.coastandards.org/.

- "Ten things your adoption agency won't tell you," an article from *Smart Money* magazine, offers a succinct list of ten items to consider when you are looking for an agency.
- "Why adoptive parents should care about ethics and fraud." An excellent position paper by Ethica, "An Independent Voice for Ethical Adoption." www.ethicanet.org.
- "How to complete an ethical adoption from Vietnam," on the website of Mam Non, a nonprofit organization "Sharing Vietnamese Culture with the Adoption Community." The site owner, Linh Song, is a Vietnamese-American social worker with experience in adoption, and currently the director of Ethica. The guidelines are excellent for anyone investigating adoption agencies. Visit www.mamnon.org.
- A checklist for evaluating international adoption agencies, and links to archived reports on agencies: www.adoptionagencychecklist.com. The site owner and author—and his family—were victims of adoption fraud. The tone of his site reflects that.
- The business of adoption: www.theadoptionguide.com.
- The adoption tax credit: www.irs.gov/taxtopics/tc607.html.

Book

Spar, D. (2006). *The baby business: How money, science and politics drive the commerce of conception*. Boston: Harvard Business School Press.

4

Fire-setters, Egg-suckers, and Oreos
Scary Myths and Reassuring Realities
about Adopted Children

I t was a warm May evening in Virginia, so I swept the porch and arranged some plants in what I hoped was a maternal way. Our social worker was coming over for our "education session" as part of our home study. I wanted to impress her with my homemaking and my snack layout on a pretty plate. (I didn't know then that few people "fail" a home study.) I put some colorful cushions on the porch chairs, and helped her set up her prepared chart. She flipped through pages of basic information on stages of child development, with theories by Jean Piaget and Erik Erikson, whose work I had read so carefully in graduate school. Then, she flipped to the little shop of horrors: we should prepare for everything from developmental delays to fire-setting. She described her experiences in public schools with adopted children. She told us flatly, "Your child *will* have a learning disability because she's adopted."

My husband and I sat silently. I began to sweat a little, as I tried to remember what I had learned about the causes of learning disabilities.

The social worker then said, "How does that make you feel?"

I answered, "Skeptical." I knew that some learning disabilities—a very general term—have genetic causes and that others have environmental causes. Genetic predispositions to learning difficulties can be worsened by poor environments, or improved with good parenting and rich educational resources.

I could also have answered, "Scared," because I was being "taught" something that wasn't supported by my knowledge of developmental psychology. I set out to learn more about the facts. Along the way, I ran into a thicket of myths intertwined with scientifically demonstrated facts. I decided then that research in adoption would be my academic focus. Through it all, the myths about adopted children and adoptive families have been as omnipresent as Muzak.

To understand and appreciate the myths, here's a little history: When the ancient Babylonians, the first writers, started taking notes, they recorded adoptions on clay tablets. Everyone was doing it: married couples, single women, and even single men (Stone & Owen, 1991). They had good reason—they were adopting children so that they would have someone to inherit their money and property.

In Greece, the tragedy of Oedipus and his family supplied names for later Freudian pseudo-diagnosis. Oedipus, you might remember from high school literature, was a king of Thebes who ruled well and long, until problems arose in his city. In the play by Sophocles, people believed he was at fault, so his old advisor set out to uncover the problem. Oedipus, it turned out, had been born to the king and queen but, because of a prophecy that he would kill his father and marry his mother, he was left to die on a mountaintop. (This practice seems barbaric, and it was, but it wasn't uncommon.) But a kind shepherd saved baby Oedipus and gave him to King Polybos and Queen Merope in Corinth. His fate was right on his heels, though, and Oedipus learned about the prophecy. Unfortunately, because he thought the prophecy meant that he would kill Polybos and marry Merope, he fled to . . . Thebes. On the way, he fought with a group of men on the road. Of course, the one he killed was his father. In Thebes, he met and fell in love with Queen Jocasta, who was, alas, his birth mother. When Oedipus learned the truth about all of his family relationships, he blinded himself and went into exile (Sophocles, 1949/1976).

There are lots of ways to read this story. First, there's the traditional literary view that the ancient Greeks believed that Fate was stronger than free will, so there was no escape for Oedipus from the gods' prophecies. Second, an adoption-related view from the mid-twentieth century has an even nastier take on the story: Oedipus killed his father and married his mother *because he was adopted*. That notion is enshrined in the subtitle of a chapter in a book for adoption professionals: "Oedipus Was Adopted" (Brinich, 1990, p. 48). It reinforces many facets of prejudice against adopted children and adopted people. It is based on decades of bias, and on biased research. This chapter is devoted to blasting those biased views.

Third, there's this much more enlightened view: the Oedipus story has little to do with adoption, except as a plot device in a metaphorical construction. Fourth, the tale could be seen as an argument against secrecy—a warning to us to tell children early and often that they're adopted. The story could even be read as an argument for open adoption—after all, a boy in an open adoption could not marry his biological mother by mistake, because he would know who she was.

The way in which the Oedipus story has been used by mental health professionals is an unfortunate example of general anti-adoption bias. Other media sources love adoption, too—when it goes wrong. We have all seen sensational news stories about contested adoptions, in which birth fathers appear suddenly from abroad to rip toddlers from their loving adoptive parents' arms.

An example of anti-adoption bias that is more mundane, but equally damaging for adopted children, comes from, of all places, Carlton Cards. One Valentine's Day card meant for a sister was supposed to be funny, ironic, and "edgy." Instead, it comes across as prejudiced and lame. Here is the text (Wegar, 2000):

> Sis, even if you were adopted,
> I'd still love you . . . not that you are,
> of course. At least, I don't think so.
> But, come to think of it, you don't really look like
> Mom and Dad. Gee, maybe you should get a DNA test
> or something. Oh well, don't worry about it.
> We all love you, even if your real parents don't.
> Happy Valentine's Day.

The sensationalism and bias surrounding adoption are direct descendants of the secrecy surrounding sex in the 1950s. The shame associated with out-of-wedlock sex, pregnancy, and birth was reflected in language: children were called *illegitimate*. Their mothers were considered mentally ill because they had had sex outside of marriage. The myth prevailed that "illegitimate" babies and their "immoral" mothers were almost exclusively lower-class, rural Southern whites, or inner-city African-Americans. The sexual revolution of the 1960s made sex before marriage socially acceptable. More unmarried women, and girls, chose to raise their children as single mothers. This trend altered the definition of a "problem" pregnancy, at the same time that higher divorce rates made it more difficult to distinguish never-married mothers from divorced mothers (Baran & Pannor, 1990).

Supported by laws protecting birth parents' privacy, social work practice in the 1950s through the 1970s emphasized secrecy. Agencies tried to match children to adoptive parents so that they could "pass" as a biological family, and some children did not learn about their adoption until adolescence or adulthood (Watkins & Fisher, 1993). The secrecy surrounding infertility might have affected parents' attitudes toward adoption and thus their children's adjustment, although the nature and extent of that effect was not scientifically studied. Now, such secrecy has all but disappeared. Today, some adoptive parents post photos of their children and adoption stories on their personal websites. The Internet has also created a worldwide community of adoptive families, where adoptive parents and adopted adults regularly discuss everything from strollers and formula to racism and adoption fraud.

The previous era of secrecy surrounding adoption and some biased research into adopted children's adjustment have contributed to national prejudice against adopted children. Sociologist Katarina Wegar (2006) says that images of adoption in the media and popular culture contribute to negative attitudes about adoption. As mentioned earlier, a survey by the Evan B. Donaldson Adoption Institute found that although the majority of adults in the U.S. sample said that adoption serves a useful purpose in society, one-third of them questioned the mental health of adopted children. Dr. Wegar wrote in the journal *Family Relations* (Wegar, 2000) that adoptive families are seen as "abnormal, pathogenic, and unworkable." The prejudice against adoptive families contributed to the secrecy surrounding adoption in the past, and it continues to support biased attitudes in the present (Wegar, 2000, 2006). According to Adam Pertman, executive director of the Evan B. Donaldson Adoption Institute, "The corrosive combination of secrecy, stigma, and shame that has enveloped adoption for generations has led a clear majority of people to assume—to varying degrees to be sure—that it is a problematical, 'second-best' alternative to biological family formation" (Pertman, 2006, p. 60).

How does this prejudice and bias affect adoptive families? There are three aspects of life in which it is important. First, you will encounter bias somewhere, some time. Maybe you have seen it already during your adoption process. As discussed in chapter 1, there is no single unifying myth of how adoptive parenthood is supposed to be. We have only bits and pieces of ideals, so moving forward feels like trying to create a play with only a few pages of script and a whole lot of improvisation. You might also hear myths after your child comes home.

Second, bias can creep into teachers' reports of child behaviors. If researchers use teachers' reports and nothing else, they might reach incorrect conclusions (Freundlich, 2002). Wierzbicki's (1993) analysis of a large group of adoption studies found that differences between adopted and non-adopted children were larger when the rating systems were more subjective, and when ratings were made by someone other than the adopted child or adolescent. He attributed this effect to anti-adoption bias. In this chapter, we will cautiously interpret any studies that are based solely on parent or teacher reports. The more aware you are that your child's community members and even educators may harbor anti-adoption bias, the less likely you are to be blindsided by a disparaging comment from a stranger or, worse, from a school counselor or other professional who could have a profoundly influential role in your child's life.

Third, and most important: parental expectations have a significant effect on how children act and ultimately on who they become. If we adoptive parents expect that our children will become delinquents, that expectation increases the chance that they will. The figure on the next page shows how this cycle works. If social workers guarantee that our adopted children will have learning disabilities, and we're foolish enough to believe it, then we might assume that our kids cannot learn as well as others and, as a result, hold them to lower standards for their school work. If our children's teachers believe these myths, they're likely to see a link between our children's problems, whatever they may be, and adoption. We might agree with them, and with the myth, and fail to educate those teachers and school officials. If we believe that our children are more likely to be men-

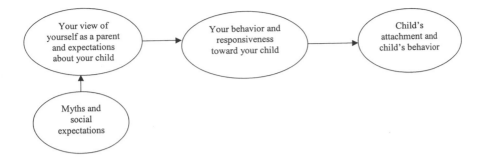

tally ill, we risk interpreting every four-year-old snit or six-year-old melt-down as a "symptom."

This chapter gives you reality checks for five myths about adopted children. The myths are like little grenades of prejudice. You are bound to hear some of them go off—out of someone's mouth, or in your own mind. When you do, you will be ready with your summary of findings from forty years of studies in psychology to put out the fire and to help heal the hurts that your children might feel. You'll also be reassured that your children have a good chance of growing up healthy and whole. And you'll be reassured that adoption is not abnormal or pathogenic, as some of the old papers called it. You can be a pioneer in showing the benefits of adoption for children—benefits that are priceless and innumerable. This chapter concludes with five scientifically tested ways to evaluate information about adopted children (or about anything else).

The Fire-setter and the Egg-sucker

Myth: Adopted children are more likely than non-adopted children to be socially maladjusted and to engage in delinquent behavior.

This myth is as old as the Oedipus story and as modern as the *Omen* film series. Here's another relevant cultural snapshot, from a classic novel for young adults, *Anne of Green Gables*. In the opening of this well-known work, author L. M. Montgomery has Mrs. Rachel speak for legions of people in the United States and Europe. In the passage below, Marilla has just announced that she and her brother intend to adopt an orphan from an orphanage in nearby Nova Scotia.

Mrs. Rachel prided herself on always speaking her mind; she proceeded to speak it now, having adjusted her mental attitude to this amazing piece of news.

"Well, Marilla, I'll just tell you plain that I think you're doing a mighty foolish thing—a risky thing, that's what. You don't know what you're getting. You're bringing a strange child into your house and home and you don't know a single thing about him nor what his disposition is like nor what sort of parents he had nor how he's likely to turn out. Why it was only last week I read in the paper how a man and his wife up west of the Island took a boy out of an orphan asylum and he set fire to the house at night—set it *on purpose*, Marilla—and nearly burnt them to a crisp in their beds. And I know another case where an adopted boy used to suck the eggs—they couldn't break him of it. If you had asked my advice in the matter—which you didn't do, Marilla—I'd have said for mercy's sake not to think of such a thing, that's what."

This Job's comforting seemed neither to offend nor alarm Marilla. She knitted steadily on.

"I don't deny there's something in what you say, Rachel. I've had some qualms myself . . . as for risk, there's risks in pretty near everything a body does in this world. There's risks in people's having children of their own if it comes to that—they don't always turn out well. And then Nova Scotia is right close to the Island. It isn't as if we were getting him from England or the States. He can't be much different from ourselves."

(From *Anne of Green Gables*, by L. M. Montgomery, first published in 1908; quote from the illustrated edition, Tundra Books, McClelland & Stewart Young Readers, Toronto, 2000, p. 7).

This book became a movie in 1934, which was remade in 1985; then it became a Disney television series and a sequel film in 2000. Mrs. Rachel's infamous attitudes have been repeated in various forms for nearly one hundred years.

However, what does scientific research say? Taken all together, the studies say that the myth is just that: a myth. Remember, too, that the studies are designed by researchers who live in a world prejudiced against adoption and colored by a bias toward uncovering pathology (Wegar, 2006).

The majority of studies have either found no differences between adopted and non-adopted children or have found that adopted children were better adjusted on some measures.

Seven studies since 1990 have found that adopted children and adolescents generally score similarly or even better on social competence than non-adopted peers. This means that they are able to make and keep friends, behave in an appropriate way at school and in the community, and have empathy for others. My own research with over seventeen thousand U.S. families found no difference between adopted and non-adopted adolescents in delinquency or illegal drug use (Whitten, 2002). This conclusion was supported by three studies that reached the same results (Borders et al., 1998; Lipman et al., 1992; Sharma et al., 1996, 1998).

An interesting—and frustrating—example of anti-adoption bias mixing with adolescent pranks came from an unlikely source, a study in the prestigious journal *Child Development*. A study based on surveys completed by 90,118 adolescents had found that adopted adolescents were more likely to report substance use and less likely to report good grades (Miller et al., 2000). The differences were greater for adopted boys than for adopted girls, and were greater for adolescents at ages 10–13. When the scientists looked harder at the data, they found that some students had lied about being adopted, and those who lied also reported very high levels of drug use, so the findings were not reliable.

ACTING OUT, DEPRESSION, AND PROBLEM BEHAVIORS

The scientific results are mixed on the differences between adopted and non-adopted teens in acting out, depression, and problem behaviors. My own research found no differences in this area, and four other studies also failed to find differences. One study from New Zealand showed that adopted children had higher rates of behavior problems (Ferguson et al., 1995), but the overall differences due to adopted status were small.

Finally, there is no clear pattern of risk for various aspects of social maladjustment across these between-group studies, most of which do not control for the effects of age at placement or pre placement care. Effect sizes for adoption status were small to moderate, and were lowest for children placed in infancy with two-parent families.

While we are talking about the myth that adopted children are good candidates for psychopathology case studies, we should also touch on the stereotype of the adopted child as a perfect, ideal child. Although this view pops up rarely in the popular imagination, several stories and movies portray adopted children in this way. You've probably encountered this view at least once, and your child might run into it, too. The musical *Annie*, based on the *Little Orphan Annie* comic strip, idealizes the little girl who steals the heart of Daddy Warbucks. It also shows her as the answer to his problems—the "happy adoptee as solution for adult loneliness," as Christine Gaily calls it (2006, p. 74). This view also characterizes *Pollyanna*, a Disney film from 1960 starring Haley Mills, and a 2004 PBS special from the BBC. This stereotype is evident, too, in *Oliver!*—a perky 1969 musical remake of Dickens's *Oliver Twist*, with its horrific orphanage, inner city exploiters of children, and a psychologically improbable hero. Oliver shows no psychic scars from his lifetime of trauma—he is not only perfect but also perfectly resilient, with none of the behavioral challenges that many real children experience after similar ordeals. In short, Oliver is an "ideal" boy from the adult point of view. This stereotype of the ideal adopted child is just as mythical as negative stereotypes of adopted children. Both extreme stereotypes deny children the chance to become fully, imperfectly human.

The Young Murderer or "Bad Seed"

Myth: Adopted children are more likely than non-adopted children to have a mental illness.

The notion of the "bad seed" has been with us forever. This idea holds that adopted children come from flawed genetic backgrounds; read: poor and dumb, at best, or drug-addicted and criminal, at worst. This notion was publicized in 1956 in a movie titled *The Bad Seed*, starring Nora Kelly and Patty McCormack. The film is the story of sweet, eight-year-old Rhoda, the daughter of a military officer and his wife. The little girl is the picture of a 1950s middle-class ideal: blonde, white, and adorable. However, she has an evil secret: she is gradually revealed as a liar and a murderer. As her mother investigates, she learns that she herself was adopted as an infant. Her birth mother was infamous, acquitted of murder three times although she was almost certainly guilty. The mother confronts Rhoda, who admits that she murdered two people. After a third murder, the mother tries to commit suicide. Message: you can't escape your genetic background. This inspiring view of adoption was remade in 1985 for television.

Few movies had a more negative effect on people's attitudes about adoption, according to Christine Gailey (2006). She interviewed adoptive parents about films with adoption themes, and she found that many had seen *The Bad Seed* as children. However, their memories of the plot were incorrect. They remembered the murdering child, not the distressed mother, as the adoptee.

The theme of the bad seed continued in the series of *Omen* movies that began in 1976. The more modern twist in this series, reflecting current trends in international adoption, is that the children are adopted from other countries or have a foreign birth parent.

Support for the myth of the "bad seed" comes from fifty years of psychoanalysis. According to Freudians and the psychoanalytic school, adopted children cannot work out their Oedipal conflicts because they do not live with their biological parents. A very brief version of the Oedipal theory goes like this: Children feel sexual desire for and want to marry their opposite-gender parent. To make this happen, they imagine that they have to kill the same-gender parent. A major task of childhood is to resolve conflicting feelings of love, desire, and hate toward parents. According to this logic, adopted children avoid this crucial developmental task, especially if they know that they are adopted. This view, widely accepted among mental health professionals during the first half of the twentieth century, contributed to the practice of secrecy about adoption and to the recommendation that parents *not* tell their children that they were adopted.

What's wrong with these vintage clinical studies? First, studying only in-patients can skew the sample group. Second, current scientific thinking says that comparing children based on their membership in any group, such as "adopted" or "African-American," leads to faulty conclusions. (Unfortunately, such faulty correlational work is appealing to some researchers because group membership is a variable that is relatively easy to measure.) Third, adoption has changed radically over forty years, adopted children are a very diverse group, and the experience of adoption does not affect all adopted children similarly. The changing nature of adoption over time means that studies of its effects probably did not measure the same construct in 1960 as they do today. However, scientific research builds current studies on the foundation of past findings, so the older studies are often quoted in papers published today. In this way, contradictory results based on faulty methods have been repeated for nearly fifty years.

Prejudice against adopted children and their families has supported secrecy associated with adoption. Biased attitudes about adopted children and their biological families are evident from the 1960s (e.g., Simon & Senturia, 1966) to the present (Wegar, 2000), particularly in language used about adoptive families (e.g., van den Akker, 2001). When adopted children were found to be overrepresented in mental health facilities, some authors used the mythology of gender roles to explain this situation. For example, "The anxiety around the childless state is of particular importance in those individuals whose sexual identities seem precariously balanced and where the need for a child serves to reinforce their biologic-sexual-social role, demonstrating their femininity or masculinity to both themselves and society. In cases we have seen there has always been one partner, usually the wife, much more anxious to adopt than the other" (Simon & Senturia, 1966, p. 863). Another paper offered a psychodynamic explanation: "The hostility between the parents for their childless state is projected onto the adopted child; the adopted child may act out the unconscious hostile and sexual impulses of one of the parents" (Offord et al.,1969, p. 114).

More recent, and more sophisticated, comparisons of large groups of adopted and non-adopted children have found no differences in general mental health (Brodzinsky et al., 1987; Brodzinsky et al., 1984; Cederblad, Hook, Irhammar, & Mercke, 1999; Miller et al., 2000). My own research with more than seventeen thousand U.S. families found no differences in depression, anxiety, or delinquency, although adopted adolescents had higher rates of suicide attempts than did non-adopted young people (7.6 percent vs. 3.1 percent), even when the two groups had the same levels of depression and aggression. The good news is that a lot of family time together and good communication helped to protect adolescents from making suicide attempts. One study came to different conclusions: it found higher levels of attention-deficit hyperactivity disorder and oppositional defiant disorder among domestically adopted children than among non-adopted youth (Simmel et al., 2001). The children with clinical ADHD and ODD were more likely to have been adopted after age two, to have had multiple foster home placements, and to have experienced abuse or neglect, than adopted children with mild symptoms.

Two new theoretical papers propose that adoption does not constitute a fundamental risk for negative outcomes because the experience of adoption is determined by culture, society, and communities, as much as by families (Leon, 2002; Smith, 2001). Recent work also highlights the potential confounding effect of anti-adoption bias and stigma (Johnson, 2002; Leon, 2002; Wegar, 2000). Four theories guide adoption research. First, the stress and coping model of adoption adjustment notes the changing nature of adoption since 1970 and considers biological influences or environmental factors, which could be cultural or interpersonal (Brodzinsky, 1990). However, this model assumes that "adopted children are at increased risk for various psychological and academic problems" (p. 3). The theory proposes that children's cognitive appraisals and coping mechanisms influence adjustment, and that these develop with age. By elementary school, children understand that in order to be adopted, their birth parents had to relinquish them. Children may mourn the loss of their birth parents, and possibly other losses, such as that of their birth culture and language (Brodzinsky et al., 1984). Cultural and interpersonal factors receive little attention in this model, however. As Leon (2002) points out, a child's increasing exposure in elementary school to the Western emphasis on biological families as "real" and adoptive families as "deviant" could explain this shift in adopted children's reactions to adoption, as much as the development in cognition during this period. Researchers need to take an expanded perspective on adoption that includes not only family-level factors but also cultural biases.

Why should you care about theories or scientific history? This background matters because the early studies have had a long-term influence on adoption research. They are still cited as "scientific" truth. Unfortunately, they are sometimes still quoted uncritically in references for adoption professionals, pediatricians, and parents. For example, a recent child development manual for pediatricians echoes psychodynamic rationalizations from the 1960s: "Adopted children feel unwanted, and adoptive parents may have feelings of hostility because of their inability to have children of their own" (Gupta, 1999, p. 186). These manuals are the scaffolding that holds up conclusions your social workers will use to make recommendations about your child. Be ready to question authorities—social workers and other adoption professionals—when it looks like they are falling into the trap of bogus science.

The Poor Student

Myth: Adopted children have low IQs, have learning disabilities, and do poorly in school.

As described earlier, some school counselors and social workers believe this myth and pass it on to clients, colleagues, and children. This section will show you the facts.

Early studies in behavioral genetics asked whether IQ was inherited, and used adoption studies to answer the question. This theory is a variation on the idea of the "bad seed"—both suggest that genes can determine your life. The answer, though, was complicated. There is a strong relationship between children's IQ and their biological parents' IQ. But at the same time, adopted children had average IQs about ten points higher than those of their biological parents (DeFries et al., 1994; Scarr & Weinberg, 1976; Schiff et al., 1982). There were no differences in IQ between internationally and domestically adopted children. A long-term U.S. study found that adopted children had average or above-average scores on the subtests that would show whether they were learning-disabled (Rhea & Corley, 1994). All children in this data set were adopted domestically as infants (Wadsworth et al., 1993). Later studies on the IQs of internationally adopted children are summarized below.

Studies of the correlation between adoption and placement in special education classes have yielded mixed results. Two Dutch psychologists compared the cognitive development and school performance of a group of adopted children, their non-adopted siblings, and children still in institutions (for example, orphanages). The IQs of adopted children were, on average, twenty points higher than the average for the children still in institutions, and roughly the same as those of non-adopted siblings. However, adopted children were twice as likely as non-adopted siblings to be in special education classes. A group of U.S. scientists followed adopted children from birth and found that at age twelve they were no different from non-adopted children in IQ, school achievement, or placement in special education. The Americans speculated that studies suggesting a higher prevalence of learning problems in adopted children are based on indirect evidence and are subject to biases and other methodological problems.

The title of the Dutch psychologists' paper sums up the facts: "Adoption Is a Successful Natural Intervention Enhancing Adopted Children's IQ and School Performance" (van IJzendoorn & Juffer, 2005). If a child has a genetic tendency toward low IQ, adoption can raise it somewhat. Can adoption turn that child into the next Nobel Prize winner? Probably not. On the other hand, does an adopted child automatically face placement in special education? Again, probably not. IQ, learning disabilities, and school performance are as variable in adopted children as they are in non-adopted children.

The Oreo and the Banana

Myth: Adopted children have problems with maladjustment and identity, especially if they are adopted transracially.

As described earlier, this myth was reinforced in the 1970s by the National Association of Black Social Workers, who actively lobbied against transracial placement. Today, federal law forbids consideration of race in adoptive placement. However, some social workers, both white and African-American, still believe that nonwhite children, especially African-Americans, should not be placed with white parents. (There is less opposition to placing white or Asian children with black parents.) Those opposed to placing African-American children with white parents say that this practice results in children who are *Oreos*—black on the outside but white on the inside. Some people similarly oppose the placement of Asian children with white parents. They argue that this practice creates children who are *bananas*—yellow on the outside but white on the inside. As more mixed-race couples adopt, these issues will cease to be "problems."

Overall, research shows that the majority of transracially adopted children in the United States and Europe are well adjusted in school achievement, relationships with friends, and behavior. The families studied include different ethnic combinations of children and parents. In addition to African-American and white children placed with white parents, there are now more Asian and South American Native children recently adopted by white parents in the United States, Canada, Israel, and Western Europe. Studies have come to contradictory conclusions, but they have generally found that when parents support their children's ethnic socialization, the children have better relationships with the parents and have more ethnic pride.

For psychologists, though, the concept of racial or ethnic identity has been poorly defined. Scientists are only now defining this concept in such a way that it can be studied, particularly for African-Americans. Further, the link between ethnic identity and psychological health has rarely been empirically tested. Study results do not point to firm conclusions about the effect of transracial adoption on ethnic identity formation.

Early studies of Caucasian/African-American, African/British, or Asian/Scandinavian families assumed that children's ethnic identity was adequate because they had normal school achievement and peer relationships (Andressen, 1992; Barth & Berry, 1988; Bagley & Young, 1979; Silverman & Feigelman, 1990; Simon & Altstein, 1977, 1981, 1987). A long-term study in the United States found that racial socialization within the family alone did not affect transracially adopted adolescents' later psychological adjustment, but it did affect the extent to which they identified with people of the same ethnicity (in this case, African-Americans) (DeBerry, Scarr & Weinberg, 1996). A strong identification with other African-Americans and with Caucasian-Americans promoted healthy adjustment directly. However, when they were tested during later adolescence at the end of the study, 50 percent of the transracial adoptees were rated maladjusted, compared with 36 percent of adolescents adopted by parents of the same ethnicity. Five factors appeared to improve adjustment for transracially adopted children: the quality of their adoption experience, perceived adoption stress, perceived racial stress, belonging, and racial appearance (that is, looking more white than black) (DeBerry et al., 1996).

The role of family in the construction of racial identity was examined in a U.S. study notable for its use of very sophisticated statistical models (Yoon, 2001). Korean-born teens adopted by Caucasian-Americans had better mental health if they had positive feelings about their ethnic origins and if they felt that their parents supported their ethnic socialization. Parents' support played a significant role in connecting positive parent-child relationships to ethnic pride.

Two Swedish studies have found no effect of transracial adoption on the self-report of social competencies. The authors speculated that Sweden's openness to young people of different races contributed to their well-being (Cederblad et al., 1999). On the other hand, a Dutch study found that Thai-born adopted adolescents had less secure gender identities and poorer body image, possibly because they compared themselves negatively with their taller, paler Dutch peers (Hoksbergen, 1997). In another Dutch study, teachers rated adopted girls higher on social competence and more popular with their peers. The scientists thought that adoptive parents might work harder to foster social competence in their daughters as a remedy for racial discrimination (Stams et al., 2000). It is not clear, though, whether the results of these studies apply to families in other countries or to adopted children of all ethnicities.

Two European studies using a well-tested method found no effect of transracial international placement, but others have found that parents of transracially and internationally adopted girls rated their daughters significantly higher on depression, compared with parents of non-adopted girls (Hoksbergen, 1997; Stams et al., 2000). On a positive note, one study found that the family's interactions contributed most to children's depression and acting out. This finding is positive because it means that good parenting can be a protective factor for children (Cederblad et al., 1999).

Is Open Adoption for Everyone?

Myth: Adopted children must have contact with their biological parents to be healthy.

In the early 1900s in the United States, all states sealed adoption records, but this practice began to change in the 1970s. The Child Welfare League of America endorsed open adoption in 1986 and recommended that the level of openness be based on a consensus of all members of the adoption triad. As discussed in chapter 2, open adoption comes in many forms, and beginning an adoption with openness does not guarantee that the level of openness will continue unchanged. The degree of openness also varies greatly between domestic and international adoptions.

Open adoption is based on the theory that adopted children's "psychological problems are directly related to the secrecy or anonymity of the closed, traditional system of adoption" (Baran & Pannor, 1990, p. 318). That assertion assumes that all adopted children have psychological problems, and that those problems have a single cause. Such statements lead us astray into the forest of myth. It is entertaining to imagine Oedipus in an open adoption with Laius, Jocasta, Merope, and Polybus . . . perhaps with meetings facilitated by the old shepherd, or by the blind prophet Tiresius.

As mentioned in chapter 2, the definitive study in this area found no relationship between the degree of openness and adopted children's social and emotional adjustment (Grotevant & McRoy, 1998). The authors of that study did find that adoptive parents were generally satisfied with the level of contact with birth parents, while dissatisfied parents wanted more contact. Adoptive parents who had direct contact with birth parents were less afraid that the birth mother would try to reclaim the child. Adoptive parents who had direct contact with birth parents also felt a greater sense of entitlement to their child.

There is little question that adopted children need to know as much as possible about their birth families and cultures. However, the bottom line on open adoption is that the scientific studies still have not shown whether it helps or hurts adopted children.

The majority of adoption studies reviewed in this chapter, as well as most public policies dealing with family issues, reflect Western prejudice against adoptive families. Leon's (2002) insightful and creative essay points out the Western bias that only biological parents can be "real." He proposes that a major source of adopted children's stress is the conflict between their experience of their adoptive parents as their "real" parents and the cultural definition of their unknown biological progenitors as their "real" parents. He notes that cross-cultural studies highlight the difference between Western and Asian-Pacific views of adoptive and biological kinship, which serves to remind us that these views are cultural constructs.

Summing Up

The final word: you'll hear many myths about who or what your adopted children will be. Fire-setters. Egg-suckers. Murderers. Bad seeds. Perfect angels. Dumb. Learning disabled. Oreos. Bananas. All of these labels are extremes; as such, they can lead to entertaining stories. But they also contribute to bad science. All evidence-based research on adoptive families shows us that adopted children are like any other group of children. They have good days and bad days. Their bad days are mostly like other people's, although occasionally they have an "adoption-related" bad day. Some adopted children are better behaved than others, just as some non-adopted children are better behaved than others. In short, adoptees are a basically normal group. Research on families does not support the idea that adoption by itself causes children's problems. Adopted children are not fire-setters, egg-suckers, murderers, Oreos, or bananas. They are, simply, children.

Do-It-Yourself Reality Check

As you set out on your adoption journey, you'll run into prejudice, myth, and misinformation. Here are six scientifically tested ways to evaluate information about adoptive families. They come from basic scientific methods which are taught to all social scientists.

1. Studies should be based on a relatively large group, at least sixty children. If the sample is smaller than that, it probably does not adequately represent the population from which it is drawn. Beware of case studies that generalize from only one person's experience and try to apply it to all adopted children. No single adult adoptee or mental health professional's practice can represent all adult adoptees or practices. A particularly damaging use of this kind of anecdotal information comes from social workers and/or adult adoptees who assume that if an adopted person does not fit a certain preconceived idea, she is "in denial" about adoption issues or "repressed" in her feelings.
2. Studies of adopted children should take into account two very important influences: (a) the children's ages when they were adopted, and (b) how they were treated before adoption. Children adopted as infants have more positive long-range outcomes than do those adopted after toddlerhood. If the two groups of children are mixed together in the same study, it will be hard to say anything for certain about either group.
3. All adopted children are not the same. Do not believe any

source that suggests that they are. Red flags include blanket statements such as "Adopted children have developmental delays." Studies—and the social workers using them—should be careful with language to indicate which groups might be represented by their findings and which groups are not.

4. Children in the study should not be recruited only from mental health clinics. As described earlier in this chapter, the fad in adoption studies from about 1960 to 1980 was to compare the percentage of adopted children in clinics with the percentage in the population. This is not sound scientific methodology. Only by studying children from schools, churches, and community groups can we learn what normal development is like for all children, both adopted and non-adopted.

5. The study should be recent, from the last fifteen years. Adoption has been studied since 1960 in the United States and Europe. However, the experience of adoption for children and families has changed radically since then. A study result from the 1970s or 1980s will probably not apply to children today. Many excellent U.S. and European studies have been published since 1990 and cover children adopted transracially, in open adoptions, and from foster care.

6. Studies of changes in children's adjustment as they get older, or changes in their understanding of adoption as they mature, should follow the same group of children and interview them periodically over time. Some studies have tried to do this with different groups of children at different ages. However, if you compare a group of five-year-olds to a different group of ten-year-olds, you don't know for sure what the five-year-olds are going to be like five years later. The differences could be due to many things other than the age difference, such as different experiences the older group had before they were adopted.

1. Make a list of at least five negative messages you've heard about adopted children. Next to each one, write down where you heard it. Can you pinpoint a specific source? How many of the negatives are something "everybody knows"?

2. Compare those messages to the information in this chapter, and write down the evidence-based reality beside the negative message.

3. Look back at your lists from chapter 1, and see whether any negative messages or myths slithered in. If they did, write down the evidence-based reality beside that message.

4. With the myths and the corresponding scientific realities in mind, make a list of five attributes that you think your adopted child will have.

5. Check in with yourself on using the four basic coping strategies from chapter 1.
   - ❏ HOPE: Are you carrying your parent talisman? How has that felt?
   - ❏ SUPPORT: Have you found one person with whom to talk about adoption? How has that felt? If this strategy has not yet worked for you, keep looking for Ms. Right or Mr. Right.
   - ❏ FAITH: What did the universe write to you about your adoption plans? Write another note and see what is in store.
   - ❏ HAPPINESS: What is not wrong today? Which one thing can you do to help yourself feel happy?

References and Resources

Andressen, I.-L. K. (1992). Behavioural and school adjustment of 12- to 13-year-old internationally adopted children in Norway: A research note. *Journal of Child Psychology and Psychiatry, 33*(2), 427–39.

Bagley, C., & Young, L. (1979). The identity, adjustment and achievement of transracially adopted children: A review and empirical report. In G. K. Verma & C. Bagley (Eds.), *Race, education and identity*. London: MacMillan.

Baran, A., & Pannor, R. (1990). Open adoption. In D. M. Brodzinsky & M. D. Schechter (Eds.), *The psychology of adoption* (pp. 316–31). New York: Oxford Press.

Barth, R., & Berry, M. (1988). *Adoption and disruption: Rates, risks and responses.* New York: Aldine de Gruyter.

Borders, L. D., Black, L. K., & Pasley, B. K. (1998). Are adopted children and their parents at greater risk for negative outcomes? *Family Relations, 47,* 237–41.

Brinich, P. (1990). Adoption from the inside out. In D. M. Brodzinsky & M. D. Schechter (Eds.), *The psychology of adoption* (pp. 42–61). New York: Oxford University Press.

Brodzinsky, D. M. (1990). A stress and coping model of adoption adjustment. In D. M. Brodzinsky & M. D. Schechter (Eds.), *The psychology of adoption* (pp. 3–24). New York: Oxford University Press.

Brodzinsky, D. M., Schechter, M. D., Braff, A. M., & Singer, L. M. (1984). Psychological and academic adjustment in adopted children. *Journal of Consulting and Clinical Psychology, 52,* 582–90.

Brodzinsky, D. M., Singer, L. M., & Braff, A. M. (1984). Children's understanding of adoption. *Child Development, 55,* 869–78.

Brodzinsky, D. M., Radice, C., Huffman, L., & Merkler, K. (1987). Prevalence of clinically significant symptomatology in a non-clinical sample of adopted and non-adopted children. *Journal of Clinical Child Psychology, 16,* 350–56.

Cederblad, M., Hook, B., Irhammar, M., & Mercke, A.-M. (1999). Mental health in international adoptees as teenagers and young adults: An epidemiological study. *Journal of Child Psychology and Psychiatry, 40*(8), 1239–48.

DeBerry, K. M., Scarr, S., & Weinberg, R. (1996). Family racial socialization and ecological competence: Longitudinal assessments of African-American transracial adoptees. *Child Development, 67,* 2375–99.

DeFries, J. C., Plomin, R., & Fulker, D. W. (Eds.). *Nature and nurture during middle childhood.* Cambridge, MA: Blackwell.

Ferguson, D. M., Lynskey, M., & Horwood, L. J. (1995). The adolescent outcomes of adoption: A 16-year longitudinal study. *Journal of Child Psychology and Psychiatry, 36,* 597–615.

Freundlich, M. (2002). Adoption research: An assessment of empirical contributions to the advancement of adoption practice. *Journal of Social Distress and the Homeless, 11*(2), 143–66.

Gailey, C. W. (2006). Urchins, orphans, monsters, and victims: Images of adoptive families in U.S. commercial films, 1950–2000. In K. Wegar (Ed.), *Adoptive families in a diverse society* (pp. 60–70). New Brunswick, NJ: Rutgers University Press.

Grotevant, H. D., & McRoy, R. G. (1997). The Minnesota/Texas adoption research project: Implications of openness in adoption for development and relationships. *Applied Developmental Science, 1*(4), 168–86.

———. (1998). *Openness in adoption: Exploring family connections.* Thousand Oaks, CA: Sage Publications.

Gupta, V. B. (1999). *Manual of developmental and behavioral problems in children.* New York: Marcel Dekker.

Hjern, A., Lindblad, F., & Vinnerljung, B. (2002). *The Lancet, 360* (9331), 443–48.

Hoksbergen, R. (1997). Turmoil for adoptees during their adolescence? *International Journal of Behavioral Development, 20*(1), 33–46.

Johnson, D. (2002). Adoption and the effect on children's development. *Early Human Development, 68,* 39–54.

Leon, I. G. (2002). Adoption losses: Naturally occurring or socially constructed? *Child Development, 73*(2), 652–63.

Lipman, E. L., Offord, D. R., Racine, Y. A., & Boyle, M. H. (1992). Psychiatric disorders in adopted children: A profile from the Ontario Child Health Study. *Canadian Journal of Psychiatry, 37,* 627–33.

Miller, B. C., Fan, X., Christensen, M., Grotevant, H. D., & Van Dulmen, M. (2000). Comparisons of adopted and non-adopted adolescents in a large, nationally representative sample. *Child Development, 71*(5), 1458–73.

Miller, B. C., Fan, X., Grotevant, H. D., Christensen, M., Coyl, D., & Van Dulmen, M. (2000). Adopted adolescents' over-representation in mental health counseling: Adoptees' problems or parents' lower threshold for referral? *Journal of the American Academy of Child and Adolescent Psychiatry, 39*(12), 1504–11.

Offord, D. R., Aponte, J. F., & Cross, L. A. (1969). Presenting symptomatology of adopted children. *Archives of General Psychiatry, 20,* 110–16.

Pertman, A. (2006) Adoption in the media: In need of editing. In K. Wegar (Ed.), *Adoptive families in a diverse society* (pp. 60–70). New Brunswick, NJ: Rutgers University Press.

Rhea, S. A., & Corley, R. P. (1994). Applied issues. In J. C. DeFries, R. Plomin & D. W. Fulker (Eds.), *Nature and nurture during middle childhood* (pp.

295–309). Cambridge, MA: Blackwell.

Scarr, S., & Weinberg, R. A. (1976). IQ test performance of black children adopted by white families. *American Psychologist, 31*, 726–39.

Schechter, M. (1960). Observations on adopted children. *Archives of General Psychiatry, 3*, 21–32.

Schiff, M., Duyme, M., Dumaret, A., & Tomkiewicz. (1982). How much could we boost scholastic achievement and IQ scores? An answer from a French adoption study. *Cognition, 12*, 155–96.

Sharma, A. R., McGue, M. K., & Benson, P. L. (1996). The emotional and behavioral adjustment of U.S. adopted adolescents: Part 1—An overview. *Children and Youth Services Review, 18*(1–2), 83–100.

———. (1996). The emotional and behavioral adjustment of U.S. adopted adolescents: Part 2—Age at adoption. *Children and Youth Services Review, 18*(1–2), 83–100.

———. (1998). The psychological adjustment of United States adopted adolescents and their nonadopted siblings. *Child Development, 69*(3), 791–802.

Silverman, A. R., & Feigelman, W. (1990). Adjustment in interracial adoptees: An overview. In L. M. Brodzinsky & M. D. Schechter (Eds.), *Psychology of adoption*. Oxford: Oxford University Press.

Simmel, C., Brooks, D., Barth, R. P., Hinshaw, S. P. (2001). Externalizing symptomatology among adoptive youth: Prevalence and pre-adoption risk factors. *Journal of Abnormal Child Psychology, 29*(11), 57–78.

Simon, N. M., & Senturia, A. G. (1966). Adoption and psychiatric illness. *American Journal of Psychiatry, 122*, 858–68.

Simon, R. J., & Altstein, H. (1977). *Transracial adoption*. New York: John Wiley.

———. (1981). *Transracial adoption: A follow-up*. Lexington, MA: Lexington Books.

———. (1987). *Transracial adoptees and their families: A study of identity and commitment*. New York: Praeger.

Smith, J. (2001). The adopted child syndrome: A methodological perspective. *Families in Society: The Journal of Contemporary Human Services, 82*(5), 491–500.

Sophocles. (1949/1976). Tr. Dudley Fitts and Robert Fitzgerald. *Oedipus Rex*. San Diego: Harcourt Brace & Co.

Stams, G.-J. J. M., Juffer, F., Rispens, J., & Hoksbergen, R. A. C. (2000). The development and adjustment of 7-year-old children adopted in infancy. *Journal of Child Psychology and Psychiatry, 41*(8), 1025–37.

Stone, E. C., & Owen, D. I. (1991). *Adoption in Old Babylonian Nippur and the Archive of Mannum-mesu-lissur*. Winona Lake, IN: Eisenbrauns.

van den Akker, O. B. A. (2001). Adoption in the age of reproductive technology. *Journal of Reproductive and Infant Psychology, 19*(2), 147–59.

van IJzendoorn, M., & Juffer, F. (2005). Adoption is a successful natural intervention enhancing adopted children's IQ and school performance. *Current Directions in Psychological Science, 14*(6), 326–30.

Wadsworth, S. J., DeFries, J. C., & Fulker, D. W. (1993). Cognitive abilities of children at 7 and 12 years of age in the Colorado Adoption Project. *Journal of Learning Disabilities, 25*(9), 611–15.

Watkins, Mary, and Fisher, Susan. (1993). *Talking to young children about adoption*. New Haven: Yale University Press.

Wegar, K. (2000). Adoption, family ideology, and social stigma: Bias in community attitudes, adoption research, and practice. *Family Relations, 49*, 363–70.

Wegar, K. (Ed.). (2006). *Adoptive families in a diverse society*. New Brunswick, NJ: Rutgers University Press.

Weiss, A. (1985). Symptomatology of adopted and non-adopted adolescents in a psychiatric hospital. *Adolescence, 20*, 763–74.

Whitten, K. (2002). *Healthy development of adopted adolescents: The role of family, school and community*. Doctoral dissertation, University of Virginia.

Whitten, K. L, & Wilson, M. W. (2000). Interracial families. In *Parenthood in America: An Encyclopedia*. New York: ABC-CLIO.

Wierzbicki, M. (1993). Psychological adjustment of adoptees: A meta-analysis. *Journal of Clinical Child Psychology, 22*(4), 447–54.

Yoon, D. P. (2001). Causal modeling predicting psychological adjustment of Korean-born adolescent adoptees. *Journal of Human Behavior in the Social Environment, 3/4*, 65–82.

5

The Commitment
Will You Love This Child Forever and Ever and Always?

OEDIPUS: Why did he call me "son"?
MESSENGER: I will tell you. Long ago he had you from my
 hands, as a gift.
OEDIPUS: Then how could he love me so, if I was not his?
MESSENGER: He had no children, and his heart turned to you.
 SOPHOCLES, *Oedipus Rex,* tr. Dudley Fitts and Robert
 Fitzgerald, New York: Harcourt Brace & Co., 1976

This is the moment that you've been waiting for, waiting for months, years, maybe all your life: The Call. The momentous call from the adoption agency, telling you that your child has been born, or that the birth mother has chosen you, or that your child is waiting and ready for you to bring him home—the child to whom your heart will turn. It's a call adoptive parents never forget. It comes after you've made decisions about what kind of child you think you can parent, after you've chosen an agency, done enough paperwork for two dissertations, submitted your dossier, and waited. And waited some more. Finally, The Call.

In adoption jargon, this is called *a referral.* Not *a child,* or *a baby,* or *a possible child* or *possible baby.* Using the term *referral* is a convenient way for everyone involved—from the agency to you—to distance themselves from the emotional side of this momentous decision and think about it with a little objectivity. The agency will then ask you to decide whether to adopt *this particular child.* This decision feels very different from the ones discussed in chapters 2 and 3, because a real child is involved, maybe the child you've been waiting for all your life.

. . .

The Rules

1. You can never have enough information to make a decision about whether to parent a particular child.
2. You can never be completely sure about a decision with so many unknowns.

. . .

For some parents, there is no decision at this point in the process. Carol described her and her husband's experience of learning about their daughter's imminent birth in the United States: "The moment I decided, I never thought about who she was. It was as identifiable as a fetus, but I knew nothing about this baby. There was no decision; we wanted a baby, planned on adopting, and wouldn't this be nice if this was a continuation of the process we started. There was no more decision than [the decision about] getting pregnant."

It happened so fast, she said, "It was too much for me to believe. We were headed out of town [to her daughter's birth in another state] and we had to stop at K-Mart for diapers, a car seat, and baby clothes. I had bought nothing!"

For other parents, though, this decision feels excruciating. Maybe that is the big reason that the universe gave us strong hormones so we would want to have sex, get carried away by passion, and make babies without thinking. We're not supposed to think about it. But that's exactly what adoption requires us to do. We have to think about this particular child whom the agency or the attorney or the birth mother or the People's Committee for the Protection of Children "refers" to us. We have to decide consciously whether to take that child into our family. Then, we have to commit to this child, and enter into a contract to bring this child home. That's another reason that this decision can be so heart-wrenchingly hard. Even parents adopting their second or third child might go through this.

If this sounds like a description of you, that's fine—there's no one right way to go through such an important life transition. This just means that you need a thorough review of all the information you have in order to feel comfortable with your decision. There are some steps that you can take to help you with the decision. As in all adoption decisions, these steps have a

Using Your Brain and Heart to Decide Whether to Adopt a Particular Child

Considerations for Your Brain	Considerations for Your Heart
Information about this child—narrative, photos, videos, doctors' reports	Does this child <u>feel</u> like the right one?
Information about your future with this child—how will you deal with developmental delays, health conditions, or language barriers in this child?	Do you still want to be a parent enough to step into the wide unknown future with this child?

brain part and a heart part. The summary in Using Your Brain and Heart To Decide Whether To Adopt a Particular Child shows how you can divide them.

Get Information That You Can Trust

This is where your hard work in researching and interviewing agencies pays off. You've chosen a reputable agency or attorney, so you know that your adoption and your referral are ethical. You trust your agency to give you factual information. You know that the child referred to you is the child that you will actually meet, not part of a "bait and switch" scheme. You trust the information that your agency gives you.

There are different kinds of information available in domestic and international adoption, of course. Many people choose domestic adoption because they want to be sure that they have information on their child's medical history and family background that is as complete as possible. Only rarely in international adoption is much information available about the child's medical or family history. In domestic adoption, though, a crucial bit of information is the name and address of the birth father, because he must relinquish his parental rights to the child in order for the adoption to be finalized. Adoptive parents also need to know whether their child is a member of a Native American tribe. According to the Indian Child Welfare Act, Native American birth parents might have to sign before a judge that there was no coercion or pressure involved in the child's relinquishment.

Information about a referred child should include at least a photo and a written report with medical information, and you have a right to insist on at least that much. No ethical agency will insist that you accept a referral without these documents.

Pediatrician Mark Mendelsohn noted, "It's very rare to get full information on a referral. Pre-referrals are really hard."

Dr. Mendelsohn, director of the International Adoption Clinic at the University of Virginia School of Medicine, said that information varies by country. He described a current pre-referral case from China. "The little girl has one really stiff leg, which might indicate cerebral palsy," he said. "We've asked for more information, but the Chinese officials won't give it. Sometimes the same thing happens in Eastern Europe." According to Dr. Mendelsohn, Ukraine used to give no information, while Russia used to send videos, but those were rare in the days before Russia closed to U.S. adoptions.

He noted that monthly reports with height and weight and head circumference often come from Guatemala. "But sometimes," he said, "the measures aren't accurate. That makes the reports hard to read and interpret. We tell the family every possible interpretation, and then, it's a leap of faith. They'll just decide to take a chance on the child, or not."

When we adopted our daughter, her first medical report gave weight, height, and head circumference at birth and at three months. Then, there were two words, *Healthy child*. Many reports will be just as scanty and hard to interpret, so it's worth asking your agency to get more information if possible. Because it can be very time-consuming and expensive for agency staff to travel to an orphanage to obtain information, it's a good idea to target your questions carefully.

In the United States, parents are required to review information and make a decision on their own, with whatever resources they can collect. In Denmark, though, adoption agencies send children's medical reports to a pediatrician *before* the referral is sent to parents. The pediatricians are specially authorized to conduct these reviews. According to Hanne, parents wait a week or two while the pediatrician reviews the file. The doctor certifies that the child has no special needs, or that the child does, or that she isn't sure. The family can have their home study changed to approve them if the child's health status doesn't match the one for which they were approved.

Hanne's two children had very different types of information. The referral for her daughter from Vietnam came with a birth certificate and some medical information. Photos arrived some weeks later. There was not much medical information—just a brief note that the child was normal and healthy. Her birth certificate included information on her birth family, with names and ages. There was also a lengthy explanation of why she had been placed for adoption and the family situation. The papers were in Vietnamese and in an English translation. Hanne says, "Needless to say, we accepted her referral and returned the necessary 'we accept the referral' forms right away."

The referral for her daughter from China came with even less information. "Susan was found as an infant and brought to the orphanage when she was about nine days old," Hanne said. "The papers had an extensive medical examination and a developmental report. Some people say that there are sometimes problems with regard to the accuracy of the referral papers people get from China, but in our case we have found nothing that did not seem to fit. As with Katrine, we also had to wait for the pediatrician to review the papers before we got them. It only took about a week—which certainly was a long week! But what a reward when the papers finally came!"

Dr. Mendelsohn said, "When parents have a referral, I work with them on a personal list of additional information to try to get for their particular child. For example, if a child has been in an orphanage for a year or two, he might be developmentally delayed. So we wouldn't expect him to reach normal developmental milestones for that age. We have to adjust, taking orphanage time into account."

Your international adoption pediatrician should give you his or her prognosis not only for the physical health of your child but also for any cognitive and emotional issues to expect. These can include developmental delays, speech problems, or attachment barriers. If your pediatrician is not willing to talk with you about these issues, contact a psychologist with adoption experience to help you interpret the information that you do have.

Some adoptive parents have been successful in having medical exams conducted at city-based, Westernized hospitals abroad. Depending on the agency and the country, this might be done at the parents' expense. Internet-based parents' groups are good sources for these hospitals and for physicians trained in Western medicine. See the references and resources list at the end of this chapter for other sources of medical information in international adoption.

Sometimes, parents choose to travel without a referral and, of course, if there is no referral, there is no medical information and sometimes very little background information. Dr. Mendelsohn said, "I just had a call from a woman who's in Kazakhstan to adopt a child, but she had no referral when she left. She's single, on her own with an interpreter. She was shown five children. Then they asked her to pick one. I can't imagine doing that!"

You can also get a second, or third, opinion from medical experts in international adoption. Your agency should give you a list of pediatricians in your area. You can also have an evaluation of the report conducted by university-affiliated international adoption clinics. The first one to offer this service was the University of Minnesota's International Adoption Clinic (www.med.umn.edu/peds/iac). There is no set fee, but the "suggested donation" is $250 per child or sibling group and $125 for each unrelated child the clinic reviews in the future. The staff have many years of experience in international adoption, and they have published widely in this area. A similar service is offered at Tufts–New England Medical Center (http://www.nemc.org/adoption/), for a donation of $200 for children from China and $250 for those adopted from other countries. The reviewing physicians include Dr. Laurie Miller, author of *Handbook for International Adoption Medicine* (Oxford University Press, 2004). A third well-regarded site is orphandoctor.com, run by Dr. Jane Aronson, a pioneering international adoption pediatrician and adoptive mother. Dr. Mendelsohn recommends this site for its solid medical information on international adoption.

As demand for this service has grown, other groups of physicians have stepped in to offer it in a more traditional fee-for-service arrangement. A for-profit group of adoption physicians and professionals advertises its services on the web at adoptiondoctors.com. Current prices as of this writing are $300 for review of medical records from a domestic adoption, and up to $500 for an international one. The fees include written reports and in-country consultation by phone or the Internet.

As with other international adoption services, use your contacts with adoptive parents to choose the best one for your family.

INFORMATION IN DOMESTIC ADOPTION

In an adoption within the United States from foster care, you might receive a full file of information from the case worker, with reports dating back to the child's birth. In a private U.S. adoption, adoptive parents can ask their agency to help obtain information on family history. In addition to receiving medical information, you can have a local clinical psychologist help you to evaluate your child's development and any attachment issues that might be present. The person or agency who has custody of the child must first consent to this evaluation, though.

With an identified placement, there are three vital pieces of information. First, how did the birth mother make her decision to place her baby for adoption? When you know, you will be assured that she was not pressured in any way, and that she does really plan to proceed with the adoption. Meeting the birth parents can help to reassure you about this point. Second, who is the birth father, where can he be found, and does he agree to the placement?

"My first line of advice would be to get incredibly clear about the birth father," said Toni Ayers. She also advises having an attorney who can contact the birth father and help obtain relinquishment or terminate parental rights.

Third, you need to know whether the child is a member of any Native American tribe. The federal Indian Child Welfare Act (ICWA) gives Native American children unique status as members of sovereign tribal governments. It recognizes that Indian elders' teachings, values, languages, unique practices, and traditions are passed on and preserved through children. The Act establishes "minimum federal standards for the removal of Indian children from their families and placement in foster or adoptive homes which will reflect the unique values of Indian culture." Because ICWA is a federal law, it supersedes state law, and applies to all child custody proceedings related to "Indian children" in state courts. These include foster care placements, termination of parental rights, pre-adoptive placements, and adoptive placements. A person may define his or her identity as Indian, but in order for ICWA to apply, the child must be either (a) a member of an Indian tribe or (b) eligible for membership in an Indian tribe and the biological child of a member of an Indian tribe. If an Indian child is referred for adoptive placement to a non-Indian family, the tribe will be notified as a legal party, because from an Indian perspective, a child is a sacred and precious resource that belongs to the entire tribe. More information is available from the National Indian Child Welfare Association at www.nicwa.org/Indian_Child_Welfare_Act.

Remember that, regardless of how many evaluations or how much information you get, you will have concerns about whether your child is okay. Your concerns are like those of birth parents—they stem from fear of the unknown and, ultimately, the unknowable. Biological parents fear that their child waiting to be born is somehow not okay, despite ultrasound and high-tech prenatal care. For adoptive families, the child is already born and therefore all conditions are—at least in theory—knowable. Adoptive parents therefore want assurance from their adoption agency, in-country facilitator, social worker, physician, and God, that everything they can know about the child has been passed on to them. However, no one can—or should—make any long-term guarantees about a child. Also, there might be unforeseen issues, which your agency didn't know about and which you didn't prepare for. In committing to a particular child, then, we are swinging out on a trapeze and letting go, with only faith that another swing will meet us.

PETITIONING FOR A PARTICULAR CHILD

For some programs and countries, prospective adoptive parents petition for a particular "waiting child." In this case, the child's photo and medical information are posted on the Internet, or in a photo listing such as AdoptUSKids. The prospective adoptive parents can therefore evaluate known information about children and decide which one is most likely to fit their family. This process is similar to getting several referrals and then choosing one, based on what you know about the child and, as important, about yourself.

Julie, who wanted to adopt a special needs child, petitioned for three girls waiting for adoption in China. Once she and her husband decided to adopt a girl with special needs, and specified which needs they could take care of, they started with medical reports.

Julie said, "I tried not to get too attached. I looked only at their medical reports, not at their photos or names. My husband did, though, and fell in love with one little girl. We heard that seventy families petitioned for seventeen kids. We got the approval just before Christmas for Mary, the little girl my husband was so attached to. Our dossier went to China on February 6; we traveled June 14 and brought our daughter home June 29."

Compare Information on Children with Your Hopes and Dreams

Comparing children whom you learn about with your hopes and dreams might involve a couple of steps for you, depending on your family. If you have a clear vision of the child or children whom you think you can parent, compare that with what you learn about the child in your "referral." Try to fit that information about a particular child into your dream picture of parenthood that you started in chapter 1 and embellished in later work.

Meanwhile, be ready to individualize this process for your family. Some parents do not have a clear vision of their child, or of how their family will be. Maureen and her husband Henry, for example, said, "It was so clear to us that we weren't waiting for that perfect child or a child who met some preconceived idea we had. We had faith that whatever would happen, would be right. Just like we had faith that if we had a biological child—you never know. One of my sister's biological children has cerebral palsy and mental retardation."

When Maureen and Henry became foster parents, they provided respite care for three children. The boys were seven and nine; the girl had just turned five. They adopted the little girl, knowing all of her medical information. Maureen said, "We knew she came with a lot of high-end diagnoses. First it was 'global developmental delay.' She was eighteen months delayed in all areas, morbidly obese with high cholesterol. She weighed ninety-six pounds at age four. She had to have her teeth removed because they were rotten. As soon as she started kindergarten, she was an academic sponge, she gained ground in reading, lost weight, her cholesterol came down."

Go On to the Emotional Part of the Decision

This heart part of the decision on whether to adopt a particular child has two sections: Does this child *feel* like the right one, right now? Do you still want to be a parent enough to step into the wide unknown future with this child?

THE RIGHT CHILD, RIGHT NOW

Once you've thought through all of the information that you have, if you're still unsure, think about what you're afraid of. Accept your fears and uncertainties about your child, about the unknown, and about yourself as a parent, especially if this is your first child.

Then try this exercise. Go into a room with two chairs. Place one on each side of the room. Label one chair *[child's name]'s mom* or *[child's name]'s dad*. Label the other chair **not** *[child's name]'s mom* or **not** *[child's name]'s dad*. Bring in a notepad and a pencil or pen. Turn off all televisions, radios, and music, and let the room be silent. Set a timer for three minutes. Go to the mom or dad chair and sit in it with your referred child's report and photo. Close your eyes, breathe deeply, and visualize yourself with this child, as her parent. Give yourself three minutes in silence to see this picture. After the timer goes off, quickly write down your feelings and thoughts on the pad without editing or judging them. Forget how you "should" feel, or what people say you ought to feel or think.

Now, leave the photo in the parent chair. Set the timer for three more minutes. Go sit in the **not** *mom* or **not** *dad* chair. Close your eyes, breathe deeply, and visualize not parenting this child, leaving that to someone else, leaving this child to another family. When the timer sounds, quickly write down your feelings and thoughts on the pad without editing or judging them.

Compare the two lists. Did you feel warm and parental in the parent chair, and maybe sad and having a sense of loss in the **not** chair? This tells you that you are already feeling parental toward this child, and you should consider the chair exercise a clear message. On the other hand, you might have felt very anxious in the parent chair, and then relieved in the **not** chair—relieved that someone else would be parenting this child. This is an obvious message, too. But maybe your feelings aren't clear—you might have felt just a little (normal) anxiety in the parent chair, and some sadness but not too much in the **not** chair. If your feelings are not clear after this exercise, don't worry. There's another one in the next section!

RECONNECT WITH YOUR ORIGINAL GOAL: DO YOU STILL WANT TO BE A PARENT?

If your feelings were ambivalent in the chair exercise, your uncertainty could come from two basic sources. You might be feeling that the referred child is not right for your family. Or, you could be concerned about parenthood itself. That's not only okay, it's also a sign of maturity and wisdom.

Only a starry-eyed, brainless optimist would walk fearlessly into parenthood with no qualms at all. And only you can decide what your concern means: whether it is a true sense that the referred child is not right for your family, or a true feeling that you are not ready for parenthood yet. If you decide that you are not ready, again, that's not just okay, it's absolutely vital for your family.

In adoption, unlike in biological parenthood, you must make the decision to adopt over and over, sometimes for years. You are free to stop the process at any point, or to change major aspects of it. When Julie planned to adopt from Russia, her sleepless nights and anxiety told her that something wasn't right about the plan for a Russian adoption. Her family changed course to China. Along the way, she and her husband remained committed to their original goal—to adopt a child.

After months of waiting, Lorie's agency called her with good news— two brothers in Russia were waiting for adoption, and she was approved for them. "I hadn't considered international adoption, and I knew I wouldn't get to meet them." she said. "Also, financially, I wasn't ready to take on two."

Like Julie, she experienced great stress about the decision. "It was a heart-wrenching three weeks—no eating, high stress, trying to figure out if I should do that or not," she said. "In the end, I couldn't. So when Kyle came along [through the Kidsave Program], we got along well, had the same interests, and it just felt right. It could not have gone more smoothly." It had been two years since she started the process of adoption.

All of these adoptive parents were able to keep making that commitment over time. At first, they chose to take the next right steps in the process of adoption, as part of the decision to become a parent. In the end, their choices evolved into a commitment to be the parent of their child. That commitment is similar to the one that long-married people make, over and over, year after year, to stay married.

If you are a prospective adoptive parent who has a spouse or partner, you will be working on all of the decisions in adoption together. You will jointly choose whether to accept a particular referral, and whether you want to be parents. Just remember that both of you might not arrive at the same decision at exactly the same time or in the same way.

Differences between the Commitment Process in International and Domestic Adoption

In international adoption, the match between you and your child is made by your agency and an in-country group. Depending on the country, the in-country partner could be a government official or a committee in a province or city , with or without the contribution of an orphanage director. In most countries, you will be asked to commit to the "referral" before you travel, and you will be very strongly discouraged from changing your mind when you are in the country of adoption. Your adoption will become final in your child's country, so you will become your child's parent before you leave the country. In this process, there are rarely any birth parents asking to have the child returned.

In domestic adoption in the United States, the situation is almost the opposite, but that doesn't mean that it's anxiety-free. When a birth mother chooses adoptive parents, they are often involved with her during the pregnancy. Adoptive parents can be present during the birth and bring their child home from the hospital. As Toni Ayers described it, "I was at the birth [of my son]. I'd like to say it was beautiful, wonderful. But it was nerve-wracking. There was an underlying feeling of fear. . . . I didn't know which way the birth mother would decide. I was afraid to let go and just completely commit to him."

For Toni's son, it was four months from his birth to the time when his birth parents' parental rights were legally terminated, paving the way for his adoption. Toni said, "We actually had a lot of fun in those early months, even though I was nervous about the birth mother's decision."

Carol described a similar process. "I was keeping about 25 percent of my heart guarded," she said. "The birth parents signed an entrustment and then the legal relinquishment was three months later. It was always in the back of my mind that they could change theirs. My commitment to [my daughter] slowly solidified. Even if I had to give her back, she had a place in my heart already, just as my miscarried baby did. I knew I'd love her, this idea of God, and if her birth parents wanted her back, it was right and fair. She belonged to them until she was legally mine."

The birth parents did not change their minds, though. Carol said, "Maybe I was rationalizing that whoever she lived with would be the right parents. But I'm the lucky one who's here to guide her."

Not knowing whether a birth mother, and father, will allow an adoption to proceed can try the most serene adoptive family. This part of the process requires a special type of commitment, to the child and to the unfolding of the birth parents' decisions.

The Adoptions That Don't Happen

There are three general ways that possible adoptions fail to happen. First, adoptive parents might decide not to adopt a child because he isn't right for their family. Second, a birth parent might decide not to proceed with adoption after a child has been placed with a potential adoptive family. Finally, a family might lose a referral through problems with their agency or, in international adoption, with the orphanage or sending country.

THE CHILD NOT TAKEN

If deciding to accept a child is hard, deciding *not* to accept one can feel like tearing off a finger. It's a loss, no matter how you look at it, no matter how you phrase it. The clinical language *not accepting a referral* really means, on an emotional level, rejecting a child—that child in the photo, or even the baby in the orphanage.

Sometimes, parents decide not to adopt a child they have met or, even more wrenching, a child who has lived with them. Maureen recalls, "We had a Solomon's decision to make the summer we adopted our older daughter."

She and her husband had taken care of their daughter and two of her older brothers. Maureen said, "Here I was, the head of the behavior management committee at [a university-based child rehabilitation center] and I could not manage those three children in my home for a weekend. I couldn't do it. I was exhausted. I'd report what I did, and the social worker said, 'You can't keep that up.' I immediately started thinking how I could. But they told me, 'Maureen, you can't.'"

The social work team decided that each child was so demanding that they needed to be separated to make an adoption successful. As Maureen explained, the children were part of a group of seven siblings, who had been abandoned by their birth parents and had foraged for food for a while.

"They didn't have typical sibling behavior," she said. "It was more like animal pack behavior. They just clawed at each other and grunted, and their verbal skills regressed to this animal level."

That left Maureen and her husband with three photos on their kitchen table, and a social worker who told them, "Pick one."

"Who makes that decision?" Maureen asks me, and the universe. "Well, we did, but can you train for that? How do you get coached for who takes whom?"

Maureen asks the question and it floats in the air between us. Unanswerable.

"What child do you raise? What child do you bring into your home?"

That summer day at the kitchen table, Maureen and Henry made a list of pros and cons about each child, as her mother had often encouraged her to do for difficult decisions. Finally, they agreed to just say a name at exactly the same time, so they wouldn't influence each other's choice. They did—but the names were different. So they talked some more. Maureen recalled that the journals she kept at the time helped to clarify her thinking, and helped her to be clear about her values.

She said, "The nine-year-old really got into my heart, and the seven-year-old? I loved him to pieces. But when I looked at him with my clinical eye, I didn't think I could cope. He tore down the drapes—it was a house rule I forgot to talk about, no tearing down drapes! But we finally settled on our daughter. She truly was our choice."

THE FAILED ADOPTION

Toni Ayers and her husband were ready to adopt a second child and had just made up their minds to go with the next call they got about a healthy baby. They took a baby girl home from the hospital, ready to adopt her. However, it turned out that the birth mother had given inaccurate information about the birth father, and that a counselor had pressured her into agreeing to make an adoption plan.

Toni said, "We were more like foster parents who took care of her for three weeks and then turned her over to the birth father. I was really a basket case for about six months. I think it deterred me from adopting as quickly again because I'm afraid of the emotional upheaval."

Domestic failed adoptions like this one are not uncommon, and birth parents have a legally supported amount of time to change their minds about adoption after a child has been placed in a potential adoptive home.

THE LOST REFERRAL

Hanne and some others who have adopted internationally have experienced the grief of a lost referral. "Losing Anja was the worst experience I have ever had in my life," she said. "At the time, to me, she might as well have died. She had been exactly what I had dreamed about and she had been ours on paper, if not in person, for about five months. There had been problems during the wait—there were some signs that she might not have been well—we discovered she had a twin sister who remained with the biological family—and some other strange things. Perhaps I should have foreseen the outcome, but I was blindly in love with the girl I thought was my daughter—from the very first day of the referral when I only saw her Vietnamese name on a photocopy and nothing else."

According to Hanne, her family was not able to find out from their agency what had really happened. They never learned why the adoption was withdrawn, or what would happen to Anja. "Was she healthy?" Hanne asks. "Would she return to her biological family or would she stay at the orphanage? To this day, we still don't know."

GRIEVING THE LOST CHILDREN

After the losses that bring many people into adoption, you will not want to think that more might be involved. However, if you "decline a referral" or if an adoption fails to go through, it will feel like a loss.

Maureen said, of choosing to adopt only one of three siblings, "Once we'd made the decision, there was the grief and loss part. We didn't know we needed to grieve that we were not having a sibling group. We just were doing it by commiserating with the foster parents who had the boys after they left us."

Her experience underscores how important it is to have support from people who've walked the walk. As Maureen put it, "There aren't a lot of people who understand the kind of life choices we were making. Even my family just felt bad for me. My pop asked, 'Am I going to have three new grandchildren?' I said, 'No, Pop, you'll have one, but I don't know which one yet. Just send money!'"

Hanne described her grief this way: "When we lost Anja, I cried like I have never cried. Part of the problem was that I was feeling so sorry for myself. It felt so unfair; why did it happen to us? All these futile questions . . ."

In her healing process, she said, "The only little thing that helped me when I was feeling most down was that someone reminded me of the old saying 'rather loved and lost than not loved at all.' Strangely enough, I was able to take some comfort from that. I suppose it told me that my love for this little girl was good for something. And that it was okay that I would continue to love her."

Make Your Decision and Commitment to a Particular Child Concrete

The noted family psychologist Eleanor Maccoby writes that the best parents "assume a deep and lasting obligation to behave so as to promote the best interests of the child, even when this means setting aside certain self-interests" (p. 1013). She says that to maintain the difficult and demanding roles of good parenting requires "considerable effort and skill, and these in their turn must rest on parents having accepted an almost unlimited long-term commitment to promoting the child's welfare" (p. 1015).

The home study tries to determine how prospective adoptive parents will put that type of commitment into practice. The home study can both educate parents and challenge them to reflect on their degree of commitment to parenting. This stage of your commitment is public, since it involves the social worker. Your commitment to a particular child, though, is different. While parents do inform their agency, their commitment to a particular child is a private, personal, family decision.

My husband and I spent a weekend discussing our "referral," who miraculously morphed into our daughter. When we have an important decision to make, we like to discuss it under the open sky. That way, our ideas, worries, concerns, hopes, and dreams all go directly out of us and into the world, to God, to the wide universe. When we discussed our "referral," we hiked up to a mountain just off the Appalachian Trail. The summit is open to the broad sky, with a 360-degree view. As fate would have it, on that day there was a family picnicking when we arrived. The parents and children flew a kite and played chase through the September sun, the smells of peanut butter and mountain conifers and sweat swirling around. We felt the full-force fist of our envy of their family life. While the family laughed behind us, we talked about our "referral" not as the "referral" any more, but as the little baby girl in the picture. We wanted her there with us on that mountain. We knew then, simply, that we wanted to be her parents. We felt deeply peaceful about our decision, and also exhilarated.

To commemorate the decision, we picked up a piece of shale from the mountaintop. I cradled it in my arms, then we took turns carrying it down the mountain. A year later, we took our daughter to the mountain in a backpack carrier. We picked up another piece of shale, a very small one. Again, as fate would have it, the small rock fits perfectly into a hollow in the larger rock. Both have sat on our hearth for ten years.

I highly recommend that parents consider how to make their commitment concrete. You certainly don't have to haul a rock to be committed to a child. But think about something that would symbolize your resolve to be the best parent possible to this particular child.

Almost all adoptive parents have some kind of adoption ceremony with the child. In a domestic adoption, this might be an entrustment service, or the finalization of the adoption in family court. These ceremonies can reinforce parents' commitment to and responsibilities for the child, as a marriage ceremony reinforces partners' commitment to each other. Natalie, the mother of two girls in open adoptions, recalls the entrustment ceremony for her older daughter. "We flew to the state where she was born, and met her birth parents. Then, we had the ceremony in the hospital chapel. They wrote up their part, and we wrote ours. We all lit a candle to signify coming together to take care of our child."

In an international adoption, the ritual might be a "giving and receiving ceremony," or a court appearance. Our giving and receiving ceremony, which I described in chapter 1, was our public commitment ceremony. As strange as it seemed at the time, it is now an important part of our family lore. Every Adoption Day, we watch at least some of the two-hour videotape of the ceremony. Our daughter usually asks, "Where am I?" She also remembers that I was so happy I cried. Sometimes we fast-forward to my husband's speech. We also point out the family from Minnesota as if they were our family; indeed, now they are.

This chapter is about commitment, which is a process. Only the myths—and the liars—say that commitment is instant and unchanging. If it were, there would be no room for growth and development, for deepening love or maturing marriages. Try to be aware of where you are in the process, and of how firm you feel in your commitment to your child. You might feel as though you are in a cheesy mattress ad—*Extra firm? Or pillow soft?*—but give yourself permission to be wherever you are on that firmness scale, because just experiencing the work toward commitment will strengthen your devotion and will ultimately deepen your bond with your child.

1. When you are making the decision of whether to accept a referral, talk to other adoptive or foster parents. If you are adopting part of a sibling group, talk to the parents of the other siblings.

2. Keep a journal about your ideal child, or children, and use your journal to help yourself understand how you feel about the child or children who are referred to you.

   ❏ Write a page in your journal about what commitment means to you.

   ❏ Write the names of at least three people who are your models for committed parenthood.

   ❏ If your parents are not your models for commited parenthood, here is your spiritual homework: Go through all stages of grief about this loss, if you haven't already. Make a decision to give up blame and hostility toward your parents about this issue. Then, forgive them.

   ❏ List five ways that your model parents have shown their commitment to their children in daily life.

   ❏ List five ways that you will show that you are committed to your child. Use your list to start a scrapbook for your child about her life.

3. Have a commitment ceremony. Involve your religion if you have one.

4. Choose two concrete objects, one large and one small, that represent your commitment to your child.

   ❏ Place the large one in an important spot in your home.

   ❏ Carry the small one with you, in a pocket or your bag, as a daily reminder that you will soon be the parent of this child.

5. If you have to turn down a referral, give yourself time to mourn the loss of that child or those children.

6. Check in with yourself on using the four basic coping strategies from chapter 1.

   ❏ HOPE: Add your object that represents concrete commitment to your parent talisman. How does that feel?

   ❏ SUPPORT: How is your support system of adoptive or foster parents working for you during this time of crucial decision-making? Do you need more support? Where can you look for it?

❏ FAITH: Do you feel that your referral is the one whom the universe or God or your higher power intended for you? Write yet another note and see what is in store.

❏ HAPPINESS: What is not wrong today? Which one thing can you do to help yourself feel happy?

Reference and Resource

Maccoby, E. (1992). The role of parents in the socialization of children: A historical overview. *Developmental Psychology,* 28, 1006–1017.

6

Daddy Warbucks, Madonna, and Real People
Myths about Adoptive Parenthood

Just as there are myths about adopted children—for example, the stories of Little Orphan Annie, Anne of Green Gables, and the axe murderers—there are popular myths and misconceptions about adoptive parents and adoptive parenthood. Are we all rich, like cigar-chomping Daddy Warbucks, who saved Little Orphan Annie? Are we rich *and* glamorous, like the singer Madonna, whose adoption of a boy from Malawi generated a great deal of press coverage in 2006? Are we adopting a child to work on our farm, like the parents of Anne of Green Gables? Well, no—we're regular people, most of us, doing the best we can to have a family.

Many of us are creating our families differently from the way that we imagined we would. And our families will be different from the images that Hollywood and Madison Avenue use to sell us everything from mops to minivans. You know, the vision of Mom, Dad, Susie, and Johnny living in a two-story colonial with an SUV out front. In reality, that vision morphed into many different ones while we weren't looking—into the picture of a single mom with kids. Or that of mom and mom, with kids born to one mom who conceived through artificial insemination. Or the picture of dad and dad with adopted sons. Or . . . the list goes on, to the point that one-third of American children do not live with two married parents (U.S. Census 2000).

But most people still imagine that the nuclear biological family is the norm. So we'll confront myths and misconceptions about our adoptive families, and about ourselves as adoptive parents. We've probably heard most of these myths and misconceptions already, and they are brought to the foreground as we progress toward adoption. Israeli psychologist Rachel

Levy-Shiff writes, "The process of the procurement of a child is extremely tedious and anxiety-arousing, inducing self-defensive attitudes" (1997, p. 131). That's one response to the myths, and to the stress of the paper chase and waiting. We'll hear these myths not only during our adoption process, but after we bring our child home.

This chapter debunks six myths about adoptive parenthood, describes what they might mean for you, and explores ways to talk back to the myths. As you read about these mistaken ideas, you might feel that some apply to you more than others. Take note of the misconceptions that evoke the strongest reaction in you. Those are the ones that you'll want to spend more time with in the workbook section, because they're the ones that have slithered into your vision of your own parenthood.

Parental Love at First Sight

Myth: You will fall in love with the "referral"—the baby in the picture, or on the video.

At our first Christmas party after our daughter came home, our elderly neighbor asked, "Well, didn't you just totally fall in love with her as soon as you got her picture?" I knew that my neighbor was waiting for me to agree with her, to give everyone the socially correct answer. That is—"Sure, I loved her from the first second."

But the true answer was, and is, "No. My maternal love for her is much more complicated than that." I don't believe in love at first sight for parents, any more than I do for romantic partners. "Some Enchanted Evening" is a great song, but it's intended for entertainment. On the other hand, I *do* believe that I, like most adoptive parents, was *committed to* my child even before I knew that she existed, as odd as that might sound.

Carol said she could not commit to her daughter when she first learned about her. "I needed to absorb it," she said. "I'm not going to make commitments beyond my capability."

Some adoptive parents are able to say that it was love at first sight. However, they might be referring to commitment at first sight—a decision to love the child in the picture or in the video or on the computer screen. Such an instantaneous feeling of connection is definitely not true for other adoptive parents, who say that they feel like they are babysitting their children at first, until the attachment knits mother or father to child. Like bio-logical parents, adoptive parents might feel guilty if they don't feel an im-mediate rush of warmth toward their child. Also, they might feel like bad parents, or inadequate mothers or fathers. At this point the echoes of the experience of infertility and the long struggle to become parents can hum in our ears like bees, amplifying the voices telling us we're inadequate. It is important to understand that some people want and need more time to develop their love for their child. In reality, so do parents who claim an in-stant bond. The way that these quick-to-bond parents love their child after a year together is different—and, ideally, deeper and truer—from the way that they loved the child when they first met.

Parents who have had failed adoptions or who have lost referrals, or who have just had a long struggle with infertility, might be slower to allow themselves to let go. Toni Ayers, who lost a little girl whom she had cared for because of a problem with the birth father, said that the experience kept her from adopting again as quickly as she might have. Jody and her hus-band also lost two referrals from Vietnam. When they finally met their son and daughter at the orphanage, Jody recalled, "We didn't let ourselves bond immediately. I had to hold all the kids, not just the two referred to us. And my husband said we had to prepare ourselves if something went wrong."

This is a completely normal, self-protective reaction. Unfortunately, this kind of reaction is not discussed very often. And you will never see it in a movie. But if it's a true reaction for you and your family, give yourself permission to take as much time as you need to develop your love for your child.

Instant Parenthood

Myth: You will bond immediately when your child is placed in your arms, or on your lap, or in your home.

Like love at first sight, instant "bonding" is true for some parents. Carol said, "I thought I had to be ready for a mechanically created motherhood, and that I'd have to build my emotions for my child. I didn't want it to be that way, but I thought, 'She's not a baby from my womb, she's someone else's.' I had to be open to letting myself fall in love with this baby over time. But it didn't feel that way at all. Whenever I see an infant, it feels like glands in my throat are shooting something into me. With my daughter, it was very visceral, I wanted her snot and not another baby's, her poop, all of it. My body and my heart were her mother already. Intellectually, I was trying to pull back the reins until the adoption was finalized."

Senator Mary Landrieu had a similar experience. She said that the question of whether she would really be able to love her child did cross her mind, but only briefly. "I had strong confidence that I could, that my love would be there," she said.

My experience was more complex or restrained. When I first saw my daughter across a conference table in the city hall in Vinh Long, Vietnam, I longed to hold her so much that I cried. I cried about nearly everything during that ceremony, though, so it is hard to separate out the reasons. When her nanny from the orphanage finally handed her to me, I was thinking, "Finally, I can hold her." Did I "bond" with her? Not then.

Like Rita, though, I was completely committed with my heart and soul to be my child's mother. As Rita said, "As soon as they put Mary in my arms, I would have died for her. The love was overwhelming."

Mary Landrieu used similar language. She said, "If someone had walked up to the car and said, 'Your life or his,' I'd have said, 'Take mine.' I've not had biological children, so I don't know how biological mothers feel, but they say it's the same feeling. I felt that way within the first hours."

All solid relationships should be expected to take time to develop, just as mine did with my child, and as yours will with your child as you get to know each other better. Sometimes people use the words *bond* and *attachment* to mean the same thing. To psychologists, though, these are two different things. *Bond* is a general term for lay people, while *attachment* denotes a very specific relationship between parents and children. Chapter 7 describes different types of attachment and how they affect child development. For now, though, as we discuss myths, the main thing to remember is that a relationship or attachment develops one day at a time, one interaction at a time. The sum of these interactions makes up the style of relationship or the type of attachment between parent and child. So it's just not possible to have an *attachment* formed in an instant.

Some psychologists and psychiatrists have said that the potentially longer bonding period in adoption is a problem. They note that the paper chase of adoption differs from the prenatal opportunities to bond, or attach, that a pregnant woman might experience. But my study of foster families found that even foster children could be securely attached to their foster mothers. In foster care, children are often placed in emergencies, with no more warning to the foster mom than a quick telephone call. These parents' only opportunities to bond were *after* placement.

Of course, we might dream about a strong, immediate attachment. After having waited years for a child, we are especially vulnerable to thinking that we should experience such instant attachment, that we deserve it. But wishing and hoping don't make it so. And expecting quick attachment can set us up for serious disappointment. We can be especially disappointed if we were expecting some kind of cuddly behavior from our child. In fact, attachment studies tell us that we should expect the opposite of cuddles from any child older than six months.

The cuddles don't come immediately but, in most cases, they do come. Our daughter was ill when we first adopted her, and it took four days for her to trust me enough to let go and get really close. The moment is engraved in my memory: A warm December wind blew off the South China Sea as we stood on our hotel roof. My daughter nestled her face into the hollow of my shoulder. I felt a flood tide of feeling, like rushing water and iron-rich blood: Motherhood, in my body.

Saintly Parenthood

Myth: Adoptive parents are selfless saints who are "saving" children.

As I mentioned in chapter 1, one of my favorite cousins nominated my husband and me for sainthood because I was "saving a child from ignorance and poverty." It is undeniable that our daughter has more opportunities and resources in the United States than she would have had in the Mekong Delta. However, while giving our daughter these opportunities is part of our job as parents, it was not our motive for adopting her: We wanted to have a child, and Fate brought us to her.

Jody, a teacher, hears the same line about her three children. "My husband is French Canadian and I'm Caucasian," she said. "Our Asian children are obviously adopted. People say all the time, 'Oh, they're so lucky.' We always say, 'No, we're the lucky ones.' It's part of having a multiracial family."

For Toni Ayers, the myth of "saving" children relates to the ethics and the social class that surround adoption. "I've had these discussions with other families, wondering if a lot of adoption is about economic inequities," she said. "If you contemplate that long enough, a lot of emotions come up. What support is there for having those discussions? And the kids hear these messages, too—people saying they were saved from the ghetto, or ignorance, or whatever."

This myth is tacked on to societal expectations of the "good mother"— that impossible ideal who lurks in every woman's psyche as the goal that we always (of course) will miss. There is a fuzzier myth for fathers, and parenthood generally is not considered to be as central to a man's identity (March & Miall, 2006). For adoptive parents, the myth of saintly parenthood is at war with the myth of toxic parenthood, and we sometimes feel caught in the crossfire.

Do children fare better in healthy adoptive homes than in institutions? Unquestionably, the answer is *yes*. But that does not mean that adoptive parents are saints. The danger of the myth of saintly parenthood is that if we parents believe it, we might end up thinking that we are somehow better than the children we adopt, whom we carry away from neediness or ignorance or whatever we call their negative state before they reached us. Even worse, we might have certain expectations of our children as our reward for saving them—such as eternal gratitude, or eternal good behavior. In reality, the best reward that our children can give us is simply to be children in all their glorious, imperfect humanity.

Toxic Parenthood

Myth: Adoptive family relationships cause adopted children to turn out badly.

This myth is the flip side—for those of you who remember vinyl records, the B side—of the myth of saintly parenthood. As we saw in chapter 4's discussion of myths about adopted children, there is a long history of stories about adoptive families. A few cast parents in positive roles, but most describe us as maladjusted or worse. My favorite quote from this vintage genre asserts that in women in particular, "sexual identities seem precariously balanced and . . . the need for a child serves to reinforce their biologic-sexual-social role, demonstrating their femininity . . . to both themselves and society" (Simon & Senturia, 1966, p. 863). These views are rooted in the work of psychoanalysts, who thought that infertile adoptive mothers could not be good parents because their infertility was originally caused by an unconscious rejection of motherhood.

As mentioned earlier, authors of older studies also thought that adoptive families had to be dysfunctional because children could not work out their complexes with unrelated adults. The same authors thought that adoptive parents' problems caused problems for their child from the day that they brought their child home, even though this idea had not been tested scientifically. Another common idea about adoptive families is that they are based on loss.

We know from many studies that family relationships have an important effect on children's development (Bronfenbrenner, 1979; Collins, Maccoby et al., 2000; Maccoby, 1992). Generally, the empirical studies find that adoptive families have many strengths that help their children to do well. These positive factors include family integration or cohesion. One study found that U.S. parents with children from the former Soviet Union rated their families higher than the norm on family cohesion and expressiveness. The same group rated their families lower on conflict (McGuiness & Pallansch, 2000). My own research with more than seventeen thousand U.S. families found no difference between adopted and non-adopted teens in their belief that their families cared about them (Whitten, 2002).

Several studies on the quality of family relationships have found that, in comparison with non-adopted adolescents, internationally adopted adolescents generally had better relationships with their parents, fewer communication problems with both parents, more openness in communication with their fathers, and similar levels of parental support (Rosnati & Marta, 1997; Whitten, 2002). My research found that adoptive mothers were more comfortable discussing sex with their teenaged children than were non-adoptive mothers (Whitten, 2002).

An innovative Canadian study of the strengths of adoptive families found that, compared with non-adoptive mothers, adoptive mothers were closer to their extended families, had more social support, and had less adversity in their families of origin (Cohen et al., 1993). Adoptive fathers were closer to their in-laws and had more contact with their friends than non-adoptive fathers. Adoptive families had more psychosocial resources than non-adoptive families. In addition, adoptive parents had closer relationships with their spouses, and less conflict with them, than their counterparts in non-adoptive families (Cohen et al., 1993). In my U.S. sample, adopted teens shared significantly more activities with their father and with their mother than non-adopted adolescents (Whitten, 2002).

Even though not all psychologists have found ideal relationships between adoptive parents and children, the gains that children make in adoptive families certainly show the positive aspects of adoptive parenthood. This model is dramatically different from current emphases on pathological risk. Also, it is miles away from a pseudoscientific theory of an "adopted child syndrome."

Are Adoptive Parents "Real"?

Myth: Adoptive parents cannot be "real" parents.

The myth of unreal parenthood is enshrined in common language about adoption. You've almost certainly heard birth parents referred to as *real parents.* Remember the silly Valentine in chapter 4—"Sis, even if you were adopted. . . . We all love you, even if your real parents don't."

Many adoptive parents feel an electric mini-shock when we hear that we are not real. This idea is tiring and annoying and, for some of us, it can erode our confidence that we're really entitled to be our children's parents. Most of us manage to fight the myth, though, and that's good news for parents and children.

The myth of unreality lingers in the general view that adoptive parents can't love adopted children as much as they would love children born to them. Some adoptive parents struggle with seeing this attitude reflected from fellow parents as well as from society as a whole (March & Miall, 2006). Unfortunately, this idea is widespread. The Evan B. Donaldson Adoption Institute's survey of American attitudes about adoption found that 30 percent of people in the United States believed that adoptive parents and their children did not love each other as much as biologically related families did (Pertman, 2006). The authors suspect that the real percentage is higher, because some people may have given what they saw as the "correct" answer, even though they believed differently (Pertman, 2006).

While it's easy for me to just pinch myself and know that I'm real, adoptive families do challenge cultural views of what is "normal," "natural," and "real" simply by existing. When I became a mother, I didn't realize that I was becoming an advocate, too. As adoptive mothers and authors J. L. Surrey, B. Smith, and M. Watkins (2006) write, "Adoptive motherhood offers unique challenges, opportunities for growth, and experiences of risk and adventure in the embracing of diversity and the creation of family relationships, typically without personal or familial models" (p. 149).

Mary Landrieu agrees. "Our children are so emotionally, psychologically, and spiritually ours. Their features are a little different, but their mannerisms and their outlook on life are like mine. It just tickles me to no end. As an adoptive mom, it's an exciting part of parenting. I never wanted children who looked like me, I just wanted children who were healthy and happy. You understand the impact of nurture over nature with adopted children."

Happily Ever After . . .

Myth: As soon as your child comes home, everything will be wonderful.

Most adoptive parents are reasonably happy and content with their parenting once they settle into their relationship with a new child. Dr. Levy-Shiff et al. (1997) says that adoptive parents expected to have more positive experiences as parents than biological parents—so they proceeded to do just that. She says that our high expectations might come from our intentions and our hopes, which we often manage to turn into reality. They can also come from a long period of wanting and waiting for our child to come home. As we saw in chapter 1, hope and optimism, even if they are not completely rational, can help people to have better outcomes, even in something as supposedly divorced from feelings as living longer with AIDS. So it makes perfect sense that expecting the best can sometimes help us to get it.

The trap, though, is that when we have longed for a child for years, it can seem that once there is a child at home, everything *should* be wonderful. The reality check is that it will take time to get to know your child at home, even if you have had some time with her abroad. You have to know your child to respond to her needs. This will be a trial-and-error process, especially if you're a first-time parent. You might be learning the basic signals of a baby or toddler's hunger and need for sleep. Or you might be getting to know an older child who speaks a different language. Different types of adoption can present different challenges.

Toni Ayers had firsthand experience with the myth of happily ever after. She said, "Everybody thinks after you bring the baby home, it's all perfect and wonderful. But I was in such a state, with sleepless nights, wondering what the birth mother was going to decide."

Planning for some practicalities ahead of time will help. Arrange for you and your spouse to have as much time as possible with your child after homecoming—as hard as this can be with demanding work schedules. Also, make appointments to have your child examined by a pediatrician and developmental psychologist as soon as possible after homecoming, to alert you to underlying problems that you need to know about right away. Many health issues can be addressed with early diagnosis. If you are adopting an older child from foster care, see the professionals who have already established relationships with your child.

As you are planning for help for your child, plan for your own social life, too. As discussed in chapter 1, social support is an important coping mechanism. It will be very important in helping you to feel better about how you are adjusting to parenthood. It might be even more important for adoptive parents than for biological parents. Other adoptive parents can be especially valuable in this process because they've walked the walk, and might be less likely to repeat a myth to you.

If your rosy view of parenthood doesn't materialize, remember that post-adoption depression affects some people. It is similar to the postpartum depression that affects 10 to 15 percent of women from a month to a year after childbirth. Women experiencing postpartum depression feel restless, anxious, or sad. They have feelings of guilt, less energy than usual, and a sense of worthlessness. They often have trouble sleeping, and lose or gain a lot of weight. Some mothers worry about hurting themselves or their baby. Doctors aren't sure what causes postpartum depression, but many think that the shifts in hormone levels during pregnancy and birth cause chemical changes in the brain which trigger the condition. Of course, these hormones are absent from the adoption experience. But it's important to remember that becoming an adoptive mother is also a major life change that can bring significant stress and can contribute to depression.

The good news is that this kind of depression is an illness that can be successfully treated with medicine and therapy. Women treated with anti-depressant medicines and talk therapy usually show marked improvement. Don't hesitate to get help. First, tell another adoptive parent about your experience, and talk to your social worker during the post-placement visit. If talking to these people doesn't help to lift the gray clouds, ask your social worker for a referral to a psychologist or psychiatrist. Your child needs and deserves a functional, happy parent.

Finally, there is plenty of scientific evidence that the transition to parenthood is a very happy period for most parents, in spite of the many stresses that it brings. Parenthood can bring a couple together, and it can help single parents to strengthen their ties to their partner and to the community. Parenthood offers the realization of a longed-for family. It's not exaggerating to say that having an adopted child is a dream come true.

1. **Talk back to the myths.** In ancient Greek dramas there was a chorus, which offered comments about the action, and sometimes gave judgments about the characters. The chorus functioned as the voice of society. In our process, the myths about adoptive parenthood are like a Greek chorus, sometimes giving us a soundtrack of negativity. Here's how to talk back:

   - ❑ Write down each myth, and customize it to fit your family.
   - ❑ Do you have an example of a direct quote related to each myth from a distant family member, social worker, or other source?
   - ❑ Now, write a sentence or two to counter the myth, based on the information in this chapter.
   - ❑ Finally, write out a specific bit of dialogue or text that you can offer to the person conveying the myth. This text can be a proposed line of conversation with someone in your family or with a professional, or a letter to the editor.

2. **Work with your spouse or partner on activity #1.** This will help you both to deepen your understanding of the kind of family that you are in the process of becoming, and it will strengthen your intimate bond. Ultimately, a stronger couple means a stronger family for your child.

3. **Practice telling your own family's adoption story.** This narrative of how your child came to be in your family is part of your child's adoption story.

   - ❑ First, jot it down in a journal.
   - ❑ Then, work with it in a couple of ways. You can write it out more fully and illustrate it for your adopted child to come.
   - ❑ You can also record it on tape or on a DVD. Tell your story as a reporter, not as a mom or dad. Review your story and your performance when alone.
   - ❑ Then request help from a child—for example, your child-to-come's older sibling, a cousin, or the child of a close friend. This child can help you to tell your story in a way that relates well with a kid.

4. **If you are in a couple, give yourselves time to be a couple, not just co-parents.** Take time together to have fun, and focus on your favorite things that don't include parenting—enjoy dinner out, a movie, a play, a hike, a canoe trip, hang-gliding, or other interests. (Outings together to home study appointments or to the state capitol to have documents authenticated do not count!)

5. **Check in with yourself on how you are using the four basic coping strategies from chapter 1.**

❏ HOPE: Are you still carrying your parent and commitment talismans? How has that felt?

❏ SUPPORT: Are your support people helping you through? If not, where else can you look for support or who else can you contact?

❏ FAITH: Are you taking time to feel in contact with the universe, or God, or your higher power? How does that feel?

❏ HAPPINESS: What is not wrong today? Which one thing can you do to help yourself feel happy?

References and Resources

Bronfenbrenner, U. (1979). *The ecology of human development.* Cambridge, MA: Harvard University Press.

Cohen, N. J., Coyne, J., & Duvall, J. (1993). Adopted and biological children in the clinic: Family parental and child characteristics. *Journal of Child Psychology and Psychiatry, 34*(4), 545–62.

———. (1996). Parents' sense of entitlement in adoptive and non-adoptive families. *Family Process, 34*(4), 441–56.

Collins, W. A., Maccoby, E. E., Steinberg, L., Hetherington, E. M., & Bornstein, M. H. (2000). Contemporary research on parenting: The case for nature and nurture. *American Psychologist, 55*(2), 218–32.

Leon, I. (2002). Adoption losses: Naturally occurring or socially constructed? *Child Development, 73*(2), 652–63.

Levy-Shiff, R., Zoran, N., & Shulman, S. (1997). International and domestic adoption: Child, parents, and family adjustment. *International Journal of Behavioral Development, 20*(1), 109–29.

Maccoby, E. (1992). The role of parents in the socialization of children: A historical overview. *Developmental Psychology, 28*, 1006–17.

March, C. E., & Miall, K. (2006). Adoption and public opinion: Implications for social policy and practice in adoption. In K. Wegar (Ed.), *Adoptive families in a diverse society*, pp. 43–59. New Brunswick, NJ: Rutgers University Press.

McGuinness, T., & Pallansch, L. (2000). Competence of children adopted from the former Soviet Union. *Family Relations, 49*, 457–64.

Pertman, A. (2006). Adoption in the media: In need of editing. In K. Wegar (Ed.), *Adoptive families in a diverse society*, pp. 60–70. New Brunswick, NJ: Rutgers University Press.

Rosnati, R., & Marta, E. (1997). Parent-child relationships as a protective factor in preventing adolescents' psychosocial risk in inter-racial adoptive and non-adoptive families. *Journal of Adolescence, 20*, 617–31.

Simon, N. M., & Senturia, A. G. (1966). Adoption and psychiatric illness. *American Journal of Psychiatry, 122*, 858–68.

Surrey, J. L., Smith, B., Watkins, M. (2006). "Real" mothers: Adoptive mothers resisting marginalization and re-creating motherhood. In K. Wegar (Ed.), *Adoptive families in a diverse society*, pp. 146–61. New Brunswick, NJ: Rutgers University Press.

U.S. Census 2000. www.census.gov.

van Den Akker, O. B. A. (2001). Adoption in the age of reproductive technology. *Journal of Reproductive and Infant Psychology, 19*(2), 147–59.

Whitten, K. L. (2002). *The healthy development of adopted adolescents: The role of family, school and community*. Unpublished doctoral dissertation, University of Virginia.

7

Laboring through the Wait and the Harry Potter Effect
Knitting the Tendrils of Love Around Your Child

Most adoptions involve a wait—waiting for birth certificates to arrive, for social workers to make appointments, for a parenting class to start, for a birth mother to choose you, for a country to reopen, for U.S. government agencies to find your lost paperwork. It's easy to get caught up in fretting about all the administrative details, such as re-authenticating your birth certificate or getting plane reservations for a trip abroad. The wait time can also be discouraging, frustrating, and anger-provoking.

You'll feel better about the wait if you give yourself plenty of ways to keep busy—especially if they are related to making a nest for your child, physically and emotionally. Carol said, "I think it depends on your perspective whether you see the labor of adoption as a disease process—you don't have to wait passively. You can be proactive. You can have a life and carry it on."

This chapter includes stories and advice about waiting, the labor of adoption, from parents whose children have come home. It suggests two important, related areas to work on: building a relationship with your child to come; and practicing answers to the questions that your child will have about adoption. And, when you're ready for a break from emotional work, there's a list of adoption-related movies to enjoy.

Making the Nest

My nesting and waiting were symbolized by a baby sweater. I had put away my knitting needles when I started graduate school, and my nights were spent in reading or lab work, not needlework. But just after we completed our home study, I needed a concrete way to feel that I was connecting to my child to come. So I unpacked the needles, bought a pattern, and selected yarn. It had to be washable, and soft, and non-allergenic. It had to be warm enough for China, but not too warm for Virginia. It had to be the right weight for the pattern. Of course, the colors had to be right, too. Pink alone would be too sentimental, so I chose a color block pattern with one side pink, one side navy blue, and white binding.

On vacation that summer, I cast on the first stitches and started the pink side. I felt very happy as I knitted, imagining my baby daughter wearing the sweater. The bright colors would look lovely with her black hair and brown eyes, the soft yarn would feel good on her skin, and the sweater would keep her warm. I felt optimistic as I knitted.

But that September we learned that China was closing and we were advised to switch countries. I felt sad all over again, and I stashed the sweater. I turned my attention to a home study revision, changing our visa application, renewing our paper chase. Our dossier went to Vietnam the next January, and I started knitting again, slowly, a row or two at a time. We expected a referral by May—or we were hoping for one, anyway. We didn't get it, so I stopped knitting. We kept thinking (and hoping) that we'd get a referral any day, so we didn't plan a vacation. Since the referral didn't come, I didn't knit, either.

At the end of August, still without a referral, we scheduled a long weekend at the beach. The car was packed, and my husband was waiting, when I ran back to check one more time that the answering machine and fax were on, just in case we got The Call. And we did—at that moment. The agency's Vietnam coordinator said that there was a baby girl waiting for us. We were dumbfounded, and amazed, and ecstatic, and scared, and happy beyond words. So I took the sweater-to-be to the beach, and I began knitting and purling like a madwoman. Now our child was real, and the sweater had to become real, too. It did, and I first put it on my daughter in O'Hare Airport in Chicago, after our twenty-hour flight from the tropical warmth of Bangkok.

• • •

Other adoptive parents have experienced similar long waits and detours. Lorie, mother of Kyle from Kazakhstan, spent a year hoping for a child. "It was really discouraging," she said. "I had about given up." Then she learned about the Kidsave program, which connected her with her son. She had to wait for four months to bring him home, not long in the world of adoption. "I was still doing paperwork and I decided during that time that I would do every project I needed to do for the next ten years. I ran myself ragged—I painted the whole house."

In spite of being busy, she says, "The waiting was very difficult, especially watching them get on the plane." The children had to return to Kazakhstan from the United States and their parents had to rejoin them there before their adoptions could be finalized. "It was bizarre, because the children were all excited about going on a plane, but the parents were all crying."

Watching your child leave on a plane is hard, and leaving your children half a world away isn't any easier. Some countries, or provinces, require parents to make two trips in order to adopt. Jody said, "The time between our first and second trips was the worst. I remember my husband marking off every day with a red 'X,' and he's just not usually the kind of guy who does things like that. You get numb because you think it's never going to happen for you . . . but when we finally got the call, he was in Quebec. I called him, and he started yelling, he was so happy. I was so happy I started jumping up and down and knocked over a whole stack of books!"

Between marking off the days, and the numbness, and the anxiety, there's time to feel all the feelings that go with adoption. This is the time to return to the circle of emotions discussed in chapter 1. At this point in the adoption journey, parents have generally gone through most of their grief about infertility, so it has healed from a raw and gaping wound to a scar that twinges only occasionally. Our experience with this grief has given us great empathy for anyone who has experienced a loss. Any guilt related to infertility is probably fading. However, our anger about the process might still be with us, along with its evil sisters, resentment and sadness that can slide into depression.

Then there is the old demon fear, which easily shape-shifts into general anxiety. Joan said, "I was anxious about everything, every small decision—was I doing the paperwork right? Then during the waiting period, you have no control over what's happening half a world away." Adoptive parents worry about everything from birth parents' diets to visas to hidden congenital health problems in our children-to-come. So this is the time to take care of ourselves—physically, mentally, and spiritually. The top half of the circle of emotions shows us the way: we can help ourselves by developing the habit of hope and optimism, by letting others support us, by practicing faith, and by perceiving the happiness already present in our daily lives. When we're feeling very strong, we'll be ready to think about ways we can promote our child's attachment to us when she comes home.

Building a Relationship with Your Child To Come: Attachment 101

In the Harry Potter series, each book tells the story of Harry's parents at least once. Harry, a young wizard with extraordinary magical powers, survived an evil wizard's attack on his family because his mother died in his place. The adult wizards in the stories credit Harry's mother's sacrifice with protecting Harry from the worst magic that the evil ones can do. The message: intense, committed, protective parental love can save a child.

That kind of parental love is marked by a commitment to the child, and to being a parent. It develops over time, grows deeper as the months and the years pass, and changes in outward form as the child grows older. Children and parents experience it minute by minute in millions of interactions. It comes from a secure parent, who helps the child to develop a secure attachment to him or her.

That's why the discussion of attachment is in this chapter. While you wait for your child, you can begin to think about how to promote a secure attachment for your child. Even though you might not feel like a bona fide parent yet, your parenting has already started (Levy-Shiff et al., 1991).

One of the best ways to work toward a strong, secure attachment is to think about your own childhood. Your home study has probably encouraged you to think about what you learned from your own parents.

Rita said, "My most positive role model for parenting is my grandmother. When we started our home study, I was concerned because I knew my childhood with my parents was dysfunctional. I started reading books then, anything and everything. But I felt like I had enough love, and my husband did too, that we could overcome anything."

Rita's commitment to and love for her child have carried her through hard emotional work. She has mourned the loss of her "ideal" mother and father, and she has come to accept her parents as they are. She has worked to be a more responsive, nurturing, and assertive mother to her daughter Mary than her own mother was for her.

This emotional readjustment can be very important for parents, so they can help their children resolve their own grief and loss. If they are not successful, it can undermine their children's attachment and their long-term adjustment as an adoptive family. Adopted children experience the loss of their birth families, and sometimes of their native culture. An important part of adoptive parenting is helping children to take these losses in stride, to talk about them, to feel the pain that comes with them, and to proceed to heal from them. The more parents have talked about and felt and healed from their own losses, the better equipped they are to lead their children through grief.

As mentioned earlier, the terms *attachment* and *attached* are used a lot in adoption. Sometimes you'll hear these words used as synonyms for *bonding* and *bonded*. The phrases are bandied about so loosely that some people even write that "you'll know it when you see it" (*The Complete Book of International Adoption*, p. 281). On-line chat groups and lists for and by adoptive parents often feature discussions of attachment. In these contexts, the word *attachment* is used for everything from how long a baby cries to whether a toddler avoids her new adoptive dad.

Many adoptive parents are afraid that their child won't be able to attach to them, or will suffer from reactive attachment disorder (RAD). Horror stories in the media and even in publications for adoptive families have reinforced this fear, although the actual incidence of RAD is very low. Psychologists divide the disorder into two types. Children with "inhibited" RAD consistently fail to initiate social contact and to react to most social cues in a developmentally appropriate way. "Disinhibited" types, on the other hand, have what psychologists call "indiscriminate sociability." Being sociable sounds nice, but it can be dangerous. Young indiscriminately friendly children will get into cars with strangers, hug any adult, or readily leave their parents to go away with someone else. These behaviors are symptoms of the child's failure to form a healthy attachment. Children with these extreme characteristics are unusual, and they most often come from very deprived environments, where physical and emotional needs were not met and where there was frequent change in caregivers and/or grossly inadequate caregiving. Some psychologists are concerned that disinhibited RAD is over-diagnosed among adopted children, and that too many adopted children are labeled as *unattached* or *attachment disordered*. Attachment experts caution that "the conceptualization of attachment disorder within a diagnostic framework remains controversial" (Carlson et al., 2003, p. 370). In plain English, this means that we don't have reliable and valid measures for all of the proposed types of attachment disorders. Carlson calls for more research to define and classify infants' and toddlers' attachment "disturbances" before these concepts are used in psychotherapy practice.

For psychologists, *attachment* means very specifically the relationship that children have with their parents or their main caregivers.[1] It develops over time from the child's experience with his parents or with his main caregivers. Almost all children develop an attachment to their caregiver, even if that adult mistreats the child severely. Children in abusive or neglectful homes or institutions do not lack attachment, but they do lack a secure attachment.

Two aspects of the child-caregiver relationship are most important in determining the type of attachment. The first is the way that the child uses the parent as a "safe haven" when he is distressed, even only a little distressed. The secure child goes quickly and comfortably to his mom when he is upset, and it only takes him a few minutes to return to playing. The second factor is the way that the child uses the parent as a "secure base" for exploring his environment—from the playroom to the world. A secure child touches base with parents periodically as they play together, either visually, verbally, or physically. The younger the child, the more often he checks in; toddlers run back to a parent every few minutes, or call across

---

[1] Psychologists use precise methods to determine the type of attachment, and three major coding systems for placing babies' or children's behavior into an attachment category. A companion system for classifying parents' behavior was recently developed (Britner et al., 2005). Attachment research is an important subfield of developmental psychology, and thirty years of research in this area has given us over three thousand scientific papers on the subject. Training in the coding systems teaches psychologists how to observe and assess children's behavior in a lab setting. Training usually involves two full weeks of workshops and self-study with training videotapes or DVDs. Then there is a video-based test on twelve standardized mother-child pairs. Psychologists who pass the test are certified as reliable in a particular system. I am certified in the Cassidy-Marvin preschool system (Cassidy, J. & Marvin, R. S., with the MacArthur Working Group on Attachment. 1987/1990/1991/1992/2004. *A system for classifying individual differences in the attachment behavior of $2^1/_2$- to $4^1/_2$-year-old children.* Unpublished coding manual, University of Virginia, Charlottesville, VA).

the playground, "Look at me!" Adult children might touch base by e-mail only once a week.

People often wonder whether the quality of attachment is "caused" by the infant's or child's temperament or personality. This question has been studied frequently. The conclusion is that some aspects of attachment are related to temperament; for example, some babies cry more than others, or they are more likely to be distressed. But fussiness does not determine all of a baby's attachment behavior, and temperament does not cause a baby or child to be unable to be comforted by her main caregiver. The ability to be comforted in this way is the "hallmark of security" (Carlson et al., 2003, p. 367).

Why do psychologists and social workers seem fixated on attachment? Thirty years of research have linked attachment type to nearly every important aspect of child development. Early in a child's life, attachment affects the actual development of the child's brain, which creates lasting changes at the cellular level. Attachment creates the foundation for the ways in which the child learns to handle his emotions. The pattern of relationship that a child learns in attachment creates expectations, attitudes, and feelings about himself and about other people that guide new relationships with peers. Studies have confirmed this link for families in all socioeconomic groups. Many studies have also confirmed that securely attached children enjoy many positive attributes compared to their less secure peers: they are more persistent, enthusiastic, and competent in solving problems as toddlers; more flexible in preschool; more goal-oriented in early childhood; more empathetic to others at all ages; and more socially competent from preschool to adolescence. While these characteristics do not guarantee a perfect life, they do help to protect children from the negative effects of stressful events and help them to "bounce back" from problems more quickly.

Here are the very simplified basic aspects of attachment, based on thirty years of research in psychology:

- Babies are hard-wired to do things that get parents to respond to them: cry, smile, babble, and reach. This hard-wiring is there for a good reason: babies would die without a parent (or caregiver) close by. Secure babies have caregivers who come when they cry, smile back to them, talk to them, and pick them up when they reach out.

- Babies and children create a nonverbal map of relationships based on the actions of their early caregivers. Their map, called an *internal working model* of relationships, guides their behavior with their parents, and later with their peers and other adults. For adopted children, this mental map directs their behavior with the adoptive parents who come after their original caregivers.
- Babies and children have four main ways of reacting to their caregivers—or four different types of relationship road maps. Your adopted child will come with one of the four types, based on his experiences before adoption. The younger your child, the less detailed his "map" will be.
- You will rarely know ahead of time which type of attachment your child has formed, and you cannot change your child's attachment style right away. But—and this is the most important point—*while you can't force an insecurely attached child into security, you can lead him to become securely attached to you by responding in the right way.*
- If your child's attachment pattern is insecure, it can often change to secure, if you give him consistent, warm responses to his needs, and if he is young enough.
- The challenge lies in reading between the lines of an insecurely attached child's "miscues"—the challenging or difficult behaviors that make them harder to love.
- The way in which you respond to your child's emotional needs is determined to a large extent by the way your parents responded to your needs when you were little. Your own relationship road map can either show you the way to helping your child become secure, or it can lead you both to an unhappy dead end.

You started learning to be a parent on the day you were born. Your dance with your parents gave you a complicated script, as rich and complex as one of Shakespeare's plays. You will follow this script with your children. If you decide that the script is that of a happy comedy, follow it to

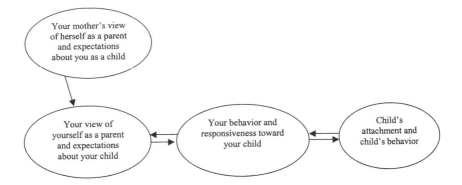

the letter and your child will have a happy ending, too. However, if you think that your script with your parents could have a tragic ending, you can rewrite it. Now is the moment to start. The figure above shows the path of influences from your parents to you to your child.

Attachment research shows us four basic types of parent-child relationships, described in the paragraphs below. Which one best describes your relationship with your parents? As you think about this, consider which parent took care of you most of the time. Also, think about how your relationship was *most of the time*. Everyone has sad days, and sick days, and "terrible, horrible, no good, very bad" days, as the delightful children's book by Judith Viorst puts it. On those days, parents might not even be basically competent, much less perfect. A few of these days, and occasional parental lapses, don't create insecure children. However, many of these days, month after month, can spell insecurity for children. As you read the following descriptions of behavior, remember that the presence or absence of one type of behavior does not indicate the type of attachment (Cassidy & Marvin, 1992). You cannot simply spot one familiar type of behavior and think, "Ah ha! My mother made me insecure!" Instead, think about general patterns of behavior, over months, years, and more years.

In the descriptions that follow, the colloquial terms are mine, and the official name for the attachment style is given in parentheses (Britner et al., 2005). These four official attachment patterns have been found across cultures in the United States, Africa, China, Israel, Japan, England, Germany, Sweden, Mexico, and Colombia (Carlson et al., 2003). I have named them *mom types* because, for most of us, our mothers were our main caregivers and our primary attachment was to them. But the types also apply to dads, aunts, grandparents, and any other important caregiver.

THE REAL MOM ("AUTONOMOUS" PARENT, SECURE CHILD)

As you can tell by the name, the Real Mom is ideal. If you had a Real Mom, you could easily come to her when you were just a little distressed. If you were upset, your first thought was to go to her because you knew that she could fix it, whatever "it" was. Contact with her soothed you quickly, or helped you to soothe yourself. You knew that you could count on her to be there when you needed her. Even if you were upset with her, she could stay with you through your anger, and tears, without becoming anxious or scared of your strong feelings. She could apologize or make amends to you when she was wrong, without feeling that she had lost "control."

You knew that she loved you because she was almost always happy to see you. She enjoyed being with you and playing with you when you invited her to, but she didn't intrude on your games if you wanted to play alone or with other children. Having her close by when you were little, and having her back you up emotionally when you were older, let you strike out on your own, to play, to try a new skill like riding a tricycle, to ride off to a friend's house, to learn a new sport. About two-thirds of middle-class biological children are securely attached.

THE TEACHER MOM ("DISMISSING" PARENT, INSECURE AND AVOIDANT CHILD)

The Teacher Mom or "dismissing" mom sometimes seems more like a teacher than a mom. If you had a Teacher Mom and you were sad or angry or upset, she would try to distract you from your distress with a toy or use a toy as a teaching tool. Eventually you learned not to show very much emotion, even when you were truly upset. A Teacher Mom was very uncomfortable with any kind of strong emotion, such as anger or sadness, either in you or in herself, so she would do everything possible to distract both of you from those scary feelings. You would learn to do the same thing, and to look very independent and unconcerned about your mom's absence or presence. As a child you paid a price, though, in not being well connected to either positive or negative feelings.

The Teacher Mom's child, like the Real Mom's child, can easily strike out on his own, play, try riding a tricycle, and go off to a friend's house. However, if you had a Teacher Mom, you could not count on her to soothe you if you got upset or to help you learn to soothe yourself. You learned early on that she wasn't comfortable with close, intimate caregiving. So you maintained your relationship with her by distracting yourself from close contact, both physically and verbally. You talked to each other about things, or people, or events, but almost never about your relationship or your feelings. The two of you kept your relationship on neutral (*safe*) ground by scarcely reacting emotionally to anything. Also, the Teacher Mom would push you to play—or to learn—and to ignore feelings. You would rarely have been close together physically; and when you were, your attention would have been directed to a toy or a game, not to each other. On the positive side, if you were the child of a Teacher Mom, you might excel in school and in your career—because you learned to use work successfully to distract yourself from your feelings.

THE SMOTHERING MOTHER ("PREOCCUPIED" PARENT, INSECURE AND AMBIVALENT CHILD)

The Smothering Mother is scared not of feelings but of the world itself. She sees the world as dangerous, and she is "preoccupied" with these fears. Like any good mother, she protects her child and is concerned about his safety in the world. However, if you had this type of mother, she overprotected you to the point that she hovered over you like the "helicopter moms" sometimes described in current media. She protected you from the very basic task of childhood, learning from playing. She needed you to need her. She appeared to be very nurturing and might have held you a lot. But all the holding didn't help to soothe you if you were distressed. You paid a price, too, in staying around her and fussing, instead of playing and exploring your environment.

The Smothering Mother's child, in stark contrast to the Teacher Mom's child, is afraid to leave his mother. At the same time, he longs to be able to play and explore on his own. If you had a Smothering Mother, both of you became very scared when you tried to explore independently and move away from her. This mom would have kept you so dependent on her that you used baby talk and acted much younger than your age. Children of

Smothering Mothers whine more than most, and cling to their moms, even though clinging doesn't help them to feel better. If left alone, they just cry. They almost never play alone.

THE BAD FRIEND MOM: ("ABDICATING" PARENT, INSECURE AND DISORGANIZED CHILD)

The Bad Friend Mom is described in psychology language as *abdicating* because she abdicates her role as a parent. If your mom was a Bad Friend, she let you take care of her, or she abandoned you to take care of yourself. Either way, her actions reversed the expected, healthy parent-child roles, and in the process deprived you of an adult parent. You would have grown up very insecure because you could never count on this mom to take care of you. She might have been abusive at times, and at other times dependent on you. This role-reversed dependency could have come out in many ways. She might have wanted you to reassure her about everything. Or she might have let you make the rules, for everything from bedtime to meal planning. She might even have let you hit her—not just once or twice in isolated tantrums, but routinely, with your fists or with objects.

If you were the child of a Bad Friend Mom, with an insecure and disorganized attachment, you were more likely than other children to "act out." Your need for comfort scared your mother so much that she abandoned you emotionally. You then became more scared, and frustrated, and angry. You didn't know what to do with this tumult of feelings, because you were a child. You might have tried to control or punish your mother, by yelling or hitting or throwing something. Or, you might have completely shut yourself down so that you were very quiet and still, and seemed to have no facial expressions.

• • •

After reading information like this, it is easy to blame parents who do not always act in their children's best interest. However, almost all parents love their children and want the best for them. Love and good will, though, are not always enough to enable parents to act in ways that help their children develop a secure attachment. This section is *not* about assigning blame to your parents. It *is* about learning what we can do as adoptive parents to heal our own childhood problems, to accept whatever behaviors our child will bring to us, and to promote secure attachment in this child to come.

QUICK QUIZ ABOUT YOUR PARENTAL REFLEXES

Think about the questions below. Write or draw your answers.	
Attachment Question	**See page 185 to interpret your answers.**
1. How will you feel when your child cries? What will you do?	
2. How will you feel when your child leaves you—crawling, walking, or riding his bike out into the neighborhood? What will you do?	
3. What will you do when you are angry with your child?	

What If You Are Not Yet a Real Mom?

Real Moms are not born but made. Your child will come to you with a unique temperament and unique pre-adoption experiences. Attachment is a process that develops over time between mothers or fathers and children—which means that you can develop the internal map of a Real Mom, even if you didn't create it during your childhood with your own parents. You can also develop the skills that you will need to help your child form a secure attachment to you.

If, after having read the previous section, you suspect that you formed an insecure attachment to your own parents, try out the quick quiz below. Then, follow the two suggestions.

If your answers to the quick quiz make you think that you need more information, try the following:

1. Read more on attachment from two very reliable sources: *Attaching in Adoption: Practical Tools for Today's Parents*, by Deborah Gray, and *Becoming Attached: Unfolding the Mystery of the Mother-Child Bond and Its Impact on Later Life*, by Robert Karen.

2. Talk about this issue with someone you trust. You might want to start with your husband or partner, or a friend. Someone who knows both you and your parents is ideal. Some, but not all, social workers and psychologists have solid training in attachment, and most can help you to talk about and think about childhood experiences and how they might affect your parenting.

The work that you do now—and it can be hard emotional work—will give you a firm foundation for being an autonomous parent to your child to come.

How to interpret your answers to the Real Mom quiz:

1. A little anxiety is normal. However, if you feel extremely anxious or scared, you might not be able to respond to your child in the way she needs. This is a signal that you should think some more about the way you were comforted when you were little.

2. A little anxiety or sadness is normal. Too much can make you overprotective and can keep your child from developing the independence and curiosity that she needs to thrive. This is a signal that you should think some more about the ways your parents helped you explore when you were little.

3. Your child needs to know when you are angry. But if you use your anger to justify punishing your child, you risk a power struggle that you will ultimately lose. Your child will lose, too, by losing the role model of a parent who models strength without bullying. This doesn't mean that you can't set limits, because of course you must. However, to pave the way for secure attachment in your child, set the limits when everyone is calm. Also, when children are old enough, they can and should help to set their own limits and consequences. Often what your child comes up with will be more strict than what you would devise! If this paragraph all seems like an alien language to you, explore the ways your parents treated you when they were angry.

As you live through the wait for your child, keep in mind the following wise words from adoptive parents.

Carol, adoptive mom of Diane: "Desperate, passive waiting is a myth. It's a ritual of tribulation that I just don't buy into. If you've got your life straight, adoption is doable. You will get your family if you've resolved to do it. It is gonna happen!"

Rita, adoptive mom of Mary: "Don't be discouraged by the paperwork. Just go with the flow and keep it going. Follow your heart and follow God."

Jody, adoptive mom of three children: "Realize that you can't control all of the process. Let it go."

Mary Landrieu, adoptive mom of two children: "You have to step out in faith; you can never be 100 percent sure about anything. Trust God to take the next step with you."

The rest of this chapter offers more ideas about ways to make the wait a positive experience and to ensure the "Harry Potter effect" for your little one.

Begin to build your relationship with your child. As we saw in this chapter, to a great extent, the way in which you think about relationships will determine what they become.

1. **Sit with your concrete object that represents your commitment to your child (from chapter 4) and your photo or video. Then, try the following visualization exercise. (If you think that it might be too overwhelming, then enlist someone to sit with you. This is a good time to enlist your spouse or partner.)**

   - ❏ Visualize your child's face.
   - ❏ Be aware of any emotions that come up inside you.
   - ❏ Talk to your child.
   - ❏ Write letters to your child about how you feel, or about what you are doing. (Here's part of a letter that I wrote when we were collecting documents.)

     > We sit in a Gypsy wagon every day when we think of you. It has every color in the universe on it: red for luck, gold for riches, blue like our mountains, purple like a queen's robe, green for May wheat to make bread, brown like your eyes, and black like your hair. Gypsies used to travel all over the world in their beautiful wagons. We don't have a horse like they did, but we want to find you badly enough that we will pull the wagon ourselves.

   - ❏ Consider the questions that your child might have about adoption.

Many of us don't want to think that our child will have questions about adoption, or we imagine that the questions won't come until our children are much older. However, the questions do come, and they come early. A psychologist and adoptive father of two said that he was surprised when his children's questions came hard and fast, beginning at age three. Your time during the wait is ideal to begin thinking about how you will answer these questions, and even to practice role-playing these conversations with your social worker, your partner, or a friend. Pay attention now to your feelings about your child's possible questions, and become comfortable with the answers.

Remember as you practice that there are at least two levels of questions and answers. One level is that of straight facts; the second is that of emotion. Adults can connect these two levels fairly easily, but children cannot, at least not consciously. A child's question might be factual and it might also have an emotional part. Start listening to both levels as soon as your child starts to talk.

2. **Here are some questions that other adoptive parents have heard:**

   - ❏ The following questions can mean, <u>Why isn't my birth mother here and why don't I live with her?</u>

- Who is my birth mother?
- How old is she?
- Where is she?
- Is she in jail?
- Is she dead?

The following questions ask for information relating to childbirth and sexuality. They can also mean, <u>How am I different from a baby to whom you would have given birth?</u>

- Did I drink milk from your breasts?
- I wish I'd been born from your tummy.
- What's my belly button for?
- [Pointing to his or her own genitalia] What's that? What's it for?

And the big one: <u>Why didn't she want me?</u> No matter how much you talk about adoption with your child when he is little, and no matter how much positive language you use when talking about adoption, almost all children will hit this emotional brick wall some time during elementary school. However, it will be much easier for your child to negotiate his complicated feelings on this issue if you have paved the way with positive, loving stories of your adoption journey. The details will be determined by your child's individual story, of course. You are already writing part of this story in your head, just by thinking through the issues in this book.

Best advice: start small. Practice by writing about and talking about what you're doing now—the waiting. Also write about and talk about the research, paperwork, and other efforts that you went through to find your child.

As a wise person once said, "God is in the details." Practice writing about and talking about all of the details, even the ones that seem tiny and boring. When you have your referral and are waiting for your child, talk about or write about your child's birth mother and birth father, his siblings, and his birth place. Talk or write about your child's birth culture, or how your friends had showers for you. If you talk about it early and often, your child will never have a Big Adoption Talk—with its echoes of a deep, dark secret. Also, you will have less anxiety about the adoption conversations that you and your child have.

You will hear this over and over, because it bears repeating: Do try to tell your child as accurately as you can why her birth mother or birth parents made an adoption plan. However, do not tell her that she was placed for adoption because her birth parents loved her so much. If you say this, she might confuse love with leaving—and that is not a message that you want to give her! One wise mother told her children that their birth mother could not have cared for any child at that point in her life. The message reinforces to a child that the birth mother did not make an adoption plan because of who the child is.

Young children in the West cannot understand poverty in developing countries, or reasons that birth parents in traditional cultures make adoption plans—such as out-of-wedlock pregnancies and social stigmas. But they do understand someone wanting the best life for them, and placing a child for adoption to guarantee that she will always have someone to provide for her. You can talk about how much you wanted children, how long you had wanted children, how you asked the agency workers to help you find your child, and how, finally, they did. You can tell your child how happy you are that he is yours to love and care for forever.

When your child gets older, he may go through some stages in which he talks about his birth family or culture a lot and have other periods when he is focused on other things. Let him direct his own interests for the most part, but also be comfortable enough that you can drop a comment about his birth family into your conversation—just to let him know that the topic is still open in your family. This is important because children sometimes cannot verbalize what they are thinking. After all, they are still young, and still learning everything, from words to feelings. Our job as parents is to help them learn to feel and identify their emotions, without being overwhelmed by them.

3. **Check in with yourself on using the four basic coping strategies from chapter 1.**

   ❑ HOPE: Are you still carrying your parent and commitment talismans? How has that felt?

   ❑ SUPPORT: Are your support people helping you through? If not, where else can you look for support or who else can you contact? Can any of them contribute to your memories about your parents, and your life with them?

   ❑ FAITH: Are you taking time to feel in contact with the universe, or God, or your higher power? How does that feel? Try writing to see what that source will reveal to you about your childhood, and what you will need to know as a parent.

   ❑ HAPPINESS: What is not wrong today? Which one thing can you do to help yourself feel happy?

4. **If you are stuck for ideas on "happiness," take a break from all your heart-stretching labor and watch a movie with an adoption-related theme. Here are some of the best picks (some because they're so bad they're good):**

   • *Raising Arizona*, 1987. This movie offers a hilarious take on infertility and baby-stealing—yes, it's possible, in the hands of the amazing Coen brothers (*The Big Lebowski, O Brother Where Art Thou*). The film is worth renting just to hear Holly Hunter say to Nicholas Cage, in a gorgeous Texas accent, "Go in there and git me a toddler!"

   • *Anne of Green Gables*. There are many versions. The first, from 1934, stars Anne Shirley. My favorite version of this adoption classic is the 1985 remake with

Megan Follows, Coleen Dewhurst, and Richard Farnsworth. Disney also brought out a television series and a film in 2000.

- *The Bad Seed,* 1956. This movie stars Nora Kelly and Patty McCormack. (See chapter 4 for discussion of the ways in which this movie reflects, and has helped to reinforce, popular myths and misconceptions about adopted children.) A sweet eight-year-old girl is a liar and a murderer. Her mother, adopted as an infant, learns that her own birth mother was probably a murderer, too, and the source of the "bad seed." This film was remade as a 1985 TV movie. The title phrase turns up even in psychology papers.

- *Secrets and Lies,* 1996. This excellent film, nominated for five Oscars, stars Marianne Jean-Baptiste as a successful British-African woman who decides to search for her birth mother. To her great surprise, her research leads her to a lower-class white woman, who denies their connection. Lies are revealed and secrets are exposed.

- *Made in China: The Story of Adopted Children from China,* 2000. Written and directed by Karin Lee, this film tells the poignant stories of adopted children from China, predominantly girls, who live in three distinct regions of Canada. Many of the children live with white families and face the challenge of making sense of their identity and their roots at a very young age. They explain how they deal with issues of race, racism, abandonment, adoption, and birth parents, and whether they will return to China to search for their roots. Their stories reflect their inner conflicts and how they have come to terms with their hybrid identities. Sometimes tough, sometimes vulnerable, the children reveal the joys and pain of living in a visibly adoptive family.

- *Marvin and Tige,* 1983. This movie stars John Cassavetes and Billy Dee Williams. A hard-drinking African-American man down on his luck is thrown together with a boy after the boy's mother dies. They discover that the boy's birth father is a wealthy white man. The film touches on issues of transracial parenting.

- *The Miracle,* 1991. This Oedipus re-make stars Beverly D'Angelo and Niall Byrne. Set in an Irish sea-coast village, it is the story of a sexual attraction between a young man and the actress who turns out to be his birth mother.

- *Mighty Aphrodite,* 1995. In this Woody Allen product (he wrote and directed the film), an adoptive father searches for his brilliant son's birth mother, assuming that she, too, will be brilliant. He is amazed to find an unintelligent prostitute and porn star.

- *Mommie Dearest,* 1981. This movie is a docudrama about the horrific family life of Hollywood diva Joan Crawford, based on the memoir by her adopted daughter Christina. The film stars Faye Dunaway and Diana Scarwid.

- *Mon Amie Max,* 1994. This movie stars Genevieve Bujold and Marthe Keller. The film tells the story of Catherine and Max, Québec's most promising young pianists in the mid-1960s. The duo breaks up when Max gets pregnant. She wants to raise the child, but her mother forces her to place him for adoption. She returns home years later, obsessed with finding her son. She locates the adoption records, and Social Services contacts her son to ask whether he wants to see her. He refuses, but she keeps trying. Is a relationship with him possible? Can she recover her musical career?
- *Orphan Train,* 1979. This well-done TV treatment stars Jill Eikenberry, Kevin Dobson, and Glenn Close in an adaptation of Dorothea Petrie's novel about the trains that transported New York City street urchins and orphans to the American West to be literally "put up" for adoption by farm families.
- *The Other Mother,* 1995. Frances Fisher stars in this film adaptation of Carol Schaefer's book about her search for the child she placed for adoption.
- *Second Best,* 1994. William Hurt stars as a lonely, middle-aged man in England who adopts an equally lonely teen from an orphanage. The son idolizes his birth father, which makes Hurt's character "second best." Critics praised Hurt's performance as the adoptive single father.
- *The Shipping News,* 2001. Directed by Lasse Hallstrom, this film version of the award-winning novel by E. Annie Proulx stars Kevin Spacey, Julianne Moore, and Judi Dench. Quoyle returns to his family's longtime home, a small fishing town in Newfoundland. He brings his young daughter, whose mother had sold her to an illegal adoption agency.
- *Soapdish,* 1991. This is another Oedipus remake, starring the excellent actors Sally Fields and Kevin Kline. This time, sexual attraction sizzles on a soap opera set between a birth father and the daughter he didn't know he had.
- *Stranger Who Looks Like Me,* 1974. Beau Bridges, Meredith Baxter Birney, and Whitney Blake star in the first made-for-TV movie about adoptees searching for their birth parents. Blake and Birney, who play the birth mother and the adopted woman, are real-life mother and daughter.
- *Superman,* 1978. This blockbuster stars Christopher Reeve, Gene Hackman, and Marlon Brando. It is considered the first story of interplanetary adoption.
- *The Ten Commandments,* 1956. This great Charlton Heston classic, often replayed on television, also stars Yul Brynner. Some describe the story as that of an adopted man (Moses) searching for his past, reconnecting to his birth people, and leading them to freedom.
- *Twins,* 1988. This movie stars Arnold Schwarzenegger and Danny DeVito as the twin results of an experiment to create the perfect child. Julius was planned and

grows to athletic proportions. The "accident," Vincent, is much smaller. He is placed in an orphanage, while Julius is taken to an island and raised by philosophers. Vincent is about to be killed by loan sharks when Julius discovers that he has a brother and begins looking for him. Together, they search for their birth mother.

References and Resources

WEBSITES

- www.aboutourkids.org. This is the website of the New York University School of Medicine's Department of Child and Adolescent Psychiatry. It includes excellent, evidence-based information on attachment, reactive attachment disorder, and other issues.
- www.aacap.org/page.ww?section=Practice+Parameters&name=Practice+ Parameters. This is the website of the American Academy of Child and Adolescent Psychiatry. The "Practice Parameters" are written by committees of experts on major issues in child psychiatry, including reactive attachment disorder, ADHD, and others. You can download the PDF files free.

ARTICLES AND BOOKS

Boris, N. W, Aoki, Y., & Zeanah, C. H. (1999). The development of infant-parent attachment: Considerations for assessment. *Infant Mental Health Journal, 11*, 1–10.

Boris, N., Fueyo, M., & Zeanah, C. H. (1997). The clinical assessment of attachment in children under five. *Journal of the American Academy of Child and Adolescent Psychiatry, 36*, 291–93.

Boris, N. W., Hinshaw-Fuselier, S., Smyke, A. T., Scheeringa, M .S., Heller, S. S., & Zeanah, C. H. (2004). Comparing criteria for attachment disorders: Establishing reliability and validity in high-risk samples. *Journal of the American Academy of Child and Adolescent Psychiatry, 43*, 568–77.

Boris, N. W., & Zeanah, C. H. (2005). Reactive attachment disorder. In H. I. Kaplan & B. J. Sadock (Eds.), *Comprehensive Textbook of Psychiatry* (8th ed.). Philadelphia: Williams and Wilkins.

Boris, N. W., Zeanah, C. H., Larrieu, J. A., Scheeringa, M. S., & Heller, S. S. (1998). Attachment disorders in infancy and early childhood: A preliminary investigation of diagnostic criteria. *American Journal of Psychiatry,* *155*, 295–97.

Bowlby, John. (1969/1973/1980). *Attachment and loss: Volumes 1–3.* New York: Basic Books. Bowlby was the first to describe attachment. His work is the basis for all later work in the field.

Britner, P. A., Marvin, R. S., & Pianta, R. C. (2005). Development and preliminary validation of the caregiving behavior system: Association with child attachment classification in the preschool Strange Situation. *Attachment & Human Development, 7*(1), 83–102.

Carlson, E. A., Sampson, M. C., & Sroufe, L. A. (2003). Implications of attachment theory and research for developmental-behavioral pediatrics. *Developmental and Behavioral Pediatrics, 24*(5), 364–79. This excellent review article from a journal for developmental psychologists and pediatricians covers the basic theory of attachment and explains its implications for foster and adoptive families.

Cassidy, J., & Marvin, R. S., with the MacArthur Working Group on Attachment. 1987/1990/1991/1992/2004. *A system for classifying individual differences in the attachment behavior of 2½- to 4½-year-old children.* Unpublished coding manual, University of Virginia, Charlottesville, VA.

Cassidy, J., & Shaver, P. (Eds). (1999). *Handbook of attachment.* New York: Guilford.

Davenport, D. (2006). *The complete book of international adoption.* New York: Broadway Books.

Gottman, J., and Declaire, J. (1997). *Raising an emotionally intelligent child.* New York: Simon and Schuster. This book for lay readers is written by the psychologist who developed the concept of emotional intelligence. Be sure to take the quiz on page 184 to assess your parenting style. I found it extremely useful in helping me to be aware of my feelings as a parent—even after a Ph.D. and plenty of therapy.

Gray, D. (2002). *Attaching in adoption: Practical tools for today's parents.* Indianapolis: Perspectives Press. This is the best book written about attachment specifically for adoptive parents.

Greenspan, S. I., & Salmon, J. (1995). *The challenging child: Understanding, raising, and enjoying the five "difficult" types of children.* Reading, Ma.: Addison-Wesley. This excellent book specifically covers parenting challenges. You might want to read through it now to get a sense of what might arise with your child or children. It is not, however, written for prospective parents.

Karen, R. (1994). *Becoming attached: Unfolding the mystery of the mother-child bond and its impact on later life.* New York: Warner Books. This book, written for lay readers, offers an excellent overview of research on attachment.

Levy-Shiff, R., Zoran, N., & Shulman, S. (1997). International and domestic adoption: Child, parents, and family adjustment. *International Journal of Behavioral Development, 20*(1), 109–29.

O'Connor, T. G. (2002). Attachment disorders in infancy and childhood. In M. Rutter and E. Tayler (Eds.), *Child and adolescent psychiatry: Modern approaches* (4th ed.), pp. 776–92. Malden, MA: Blackwell Scientific Publications.

O'Connor, T. G., Bredenkamp, D., & Rutter, M. (1999). Attachment disturbances and disorders in children exposed to early severe deprivation. *Infant Mental Health Journal 20*: 10–29.

Solomon, J., & George, C. (1999). *Attachment disorganization.* New York: Guilford Press.

Watkins, M., and Fisher, S. (1993). *Talking to young children about adoption.* New Haven: Yale University Press. This is one of the best books of its type. It includes an excellent chapter on adoption research.

Weinfield, N. S., Sroufe, L. A., Egeland, B., & Carlson, E. A. (1999). The nature of individual differences in infant-caregiver attachment. In J. Cassidy and P. R. Shaver (Eds.), *Handbook of attachment: Theory, research, and clinical applications*, pp. 68–88. New York: Guilford Press.

Zeanah, C. H. (1996). Beyond insecurity: A reconceptualization of attachment disorders of infancy. *Journal of Consulting and Clinical Psychology 64*, 42–52.

———. (2000). Disturbances of attachment in young children adopted from institutions. *Journal of Developmental and Behavioral Pediatrics 21*, 230–36.

Zeanah, C. H., & Boris, N. W. (2000). Disturbances and disorders of attachment in early childhood. In C. H. Zeanah (Ed.), *Handbook of infant mental health* (2nd ed.), pp. 353–68. New York: Guilford Press.

Zeanah, C. H., Boris, N. W., Bakshi, S., & Lieberman, A. (2000). Disorders of attachment. In J. Osofsky & H. Fitzgerald (Eds.), *WAIMH Handbook of Infant Mental Health*. Hoboken, NJ: John Wiley & Sons.

Zeanah, C. H., & Emde, R. N. (1994). Attachment disorders in infancy. In M. Rutter, L. Hersov, & E. Taylor (Eds.), *Child and adolescent psychiatry: Modern approaches*, pp. 490–504. Oxford: Blackwell.

Zeanah, C. H., Mammen, O., & Lieberman, A. (1993). Disorders of attachment. In C. H. Zeanah (Ed.), *Handbook of infant mental health*, pp. 332–49. New York: Guilford Press.

Zeanah, C. H., Scheeringa, M. S., Boris, N. W., Heller, S. S., Smyke, A. T., & Trapani, J. (2004). Reactive attachment disorder in maltreated toddlers. *Child Abuse and Neglect: The International Journal 28*, 877–88.

Zeanah, C. H., Smyke, A. T., & Dumitrescu, A. (2002). Disturbances of attachment in young children: II—Indiscriminate behavior and institutional care. *Journal of the American Academy of Child and Adolescent Psychiatry, 41*:983–89.

NOT RECOMMENDED

The American Academy of Child and Adolescent Psychiatry has issued the following statement about treatments that are not evidence-based and that have been harmful to some children:

Interventions designed to enhance attachment that involve noncontingent physical restraint or coercion (e.g., "therapeutic holding" or "compression holding"), "reworking" of trauma (e.g., "rebirthing therapy"), or promotion of regression for "reattachment" have no empirical support and have been associated with serious harm, including death. (From the Practice Parameter by N. W. Boris, C. H. Zeanah, and the Work Group on Quality Issues of the American Academy of Child and Adolescent Psychiatry. For the full text, visit www.aacap.org/galleries/PracticeParameters/rad.pdf.)

8

Family By Adoption
Spiritual Opportunities

From the womb of the morning, like dew,
Your youth will come to you.
Psalm 110:3

"This walk is nearing its end. Please attend to children and watch your step," repeated a female droid voice every few minutes from the overhead speakers near the moving sidewalk in the Pittsburgh airport. I sat beside my husband in a chilly orange plastic chair at 5 a.m., waiting for a connecting flight to Chicago, for the flight to Tokyo, for the flight to Bangkok, for the flight to Ho Chi Minh City, and to our daughter. I was half-asleep, and I was trained as a scientist, but I know an omen when I hear one, especially when it's a Voice from Above.

My walk as a childless woman was ending. My new walk as a mother, to attend to my child-to-come, was just beginning. The territory of new motherhood was as strange to me as the country of Vietnam. I had thought I was totally ready for my life to change in a day, but when that day came, it was as scary as the thought of stepping out of the plane to Tokyo while it was flying over the Pacific.

I had so many questions hanging between my dreams and the ceiling, like photos with heartless captions: *Will I love her enough? Can I really care for her?* I was almost afraid to look at my fears, as if looking would turn them into dancing trolls. If there was ever a time to turn over my fears to God, and the universe, and all higher powers, that was it—while in that orange airport chair, under blue fluorescent lights, waiting for my connection.

Many adoptive parents come to see their adoption journey as a spiritual voyage, even if they didn't begin the adoption process as religious or spiritual people. Some people move from an intense focus on paperwork, to feeling the emotions involved in becoming a parent, to deepening their emotional connection to a power greater than themselves. You don't have to have a religion to be an adoptive parent, of course. If you don't already have a religious affiliation, much less a spiritual practice, should you bother trying to develop it? You feel that you are too busy with that document collection, home study, juggling your schedules to meet with the social worker and get fingerprinted. You don't have time to go to services, much less sit and meditate (or, sit and do nothing) for even a half hour.

Here's how psychology answers the question: Yes, you should bother. Here's why: Religious faith, and prayer, help people to feel more optimistic and hopeful (Ai et al., 2004). Religious practice can help you to feel less distressed (Laubmeier et al., 2004). Personal religious beliefs and prayer can even contribute more to your health than social support from other people (Coulthard & Fitzgerald, 1999), and a higher degree of spirituality can help you to feel less depressed if you struggle with depression.

Many people find great comfort and strength in working with God or a higher power, and in feeling that they have a stronger ally than another person helping them to become parents. Rita said, "We get pulled in the direction we're supposed to go. If we pay attention, we're led, especially when you realize you have the same chance for the child's gifts whether she is biological or adopted."

Other parents, like Hanne, believe that the process was random. "I am not a believer," she said. "I have no sense of a higher power deciding that I was meant to be the mother of my daughters. It *feels* like that—once you're a parent, you feel that you couldn't possibly have been a parent to any other children than to the ones you have. But adoption is just chance. There are so many random factors that lead to exactly *that* child being referred to *that* family. . . . I've sometimes thought about the other children from our two travel groups. In both cases, we were in a pile with two other families who were matched with a pile of three children. When we were matched with Katrine, we could as easily have been matched with xxx or yyy. And when we were matched with Susan, we could as easily have been matched with zzz or xyz. We keep in touch and we see all these children and their parents on a regular basis, and it's absolutely weird to think that xyz could just as easily have been our daughter instead of Susan. Xyz is a great kid, but I mean—she's not Susan! And I'm sure that the other parents feel exactly the same way about their kids. It's one of the differences in adoption vs. giving birth—when giving birth you don't see all the potential 'could have beens'—you do when you adopt."

In this chapter, I consider *spiritual* and *religious* to describe the private practice of your relationship with whatever is greater than yourself, the god of your understanding. Spiritual or religious practice understood in this way does not necessarily involve a church, or a denomination, although some parents see their church or sangha or temple as the instrument or manifestation of a higher power. Spiritual or religious practice also does not have to involve your adoption agency, although some agencies are obviously connected with religious denominations, and some adoptive parents choose an agency from their faith. Regardless of whether you choose to work with a religiously affiliated adoption agency, you can experience the spiritual aspects of adoption and use them to deepen your preparation for parenthood.

The spiritual aspects of adoption tap into issues that many world religions address. These include:

1) honoring our families, both birth and adoptive;
2) finding meaning in suffering;
3) using conscious connection with God, Christ, a higher power, mindfulness, or all of them together to support you; and
4) enjoying the spiritual rewards of empathy and compassion.

Honoring All Parts of Our Families: Consciously Respecting All Our Relations

The opening of the Christian New Testament, the Gospel of Matthew, details the genealogy of Jesus—on Joseph's side of the family. Joseph, fiancé of Mary the mother of Jesus, in a sense adopts Jesus. According to Christian theology, Jesus's father was God the Holy Spirit. However, through adoption by Joseph, Jesus also became a descendent of David, the great historic king of Israel, and is known by Christians as the Messiah.

In another version of this idea, the apostle Paul reminds Christians that they are God's children "by adoption." He writes in his letter to the Ephesians (1:5), "[God] destined us for adoption as his children through Jesus Christ, according to the good pleasure of his will." Paul repeats this idea in his letter to the Galatians (4:3–5): "God sent his Son, born of a woman, born under the law, in order to redeem those who were under the law, so that we might receive adoption as children."

Zen master Thich Nhat Hanh (1995) reminds Buddhists that they have not only biological ancestors, but also spiritual ones. He writes, "Before I met Christianity, my only spiritual ancestor was the Buddha. But when I met beautiful men and women who are Christians, I came to know Jesus as a great teacher. Since that day, Jesus Christ has become one of my spiritual ancestors. . . . I feel stronger because I have more than one root" (pp. 99–100). Spiritual ancestors are related to us by choice and by faith, as in adoption.

Many adoptive parents describe a fuller sense of family after going through their adoption process. Their new understanding of who is close to them includes not just their nuclear family but also their extended family. Julie put it this way: "I grew up Christian and I went to a Methodist college. I'm still not definite about the nature of the thing that's greater than we are, what some call God. And as I came to adoption, I didn't feel there was a God who picked out a child for me and wrapped her up in a red ribbon." She paused, and then said, "But looking back on the certainty and peace we felt when we made the decision to go to China, and then were approved for the little girl with a heart condition—it was in tune with my feeling there's something more than me, something to rely on. I always try to do whatever I can that's within my power to do. But there was a solution I had nothing to do with, and a calm conviction with no explanations or footnotes needed."

Three months after Julie brought her daughter home, her mother-in-law was ordained as a Presbyterian minister. Julie recalled, "Her ordination sermon was on our adoption, and adoption as a metaphor for Christians' relationship to God. We were there, with our daughter Mary, and half the congregation was in tears with us."

Some parents are able to feel that their extended family includes their child's birth parents. Toni Ayers described her feelings of family connections continuing through her son. She said, "I know that I'm supposed to know my son's birth mother in the way I know her. We've impacted their family and they've impacted ours. We get to share adoption through another generation, as it was in my family. It is as it is, and it's a good thing."

Mary Landrieu said, "Openness in the modern adoption movement has helped children so much. It's important for adoptive parents to tell about the circumstances of their children's adoptions, so kids know about it and don't feel embarrassed. For mine, their dad's being adopted has made a huge impact. Recently, my son told me I was the odd one in our family because I wasn't adopted. I said, 'Well, as long as y'all love me, it's o.k.!'"

Joan never met her daughters' birth mothers because both girls were adopted in China. But she said that she feels a deep connection with them, and that she thinks of them often. She and I agreed that there should be a word for the relationship between adoptive and birth parents. It would be a word expressing a relationship similar to that of in-laws—but with only the nicest connotations; no silly in-law jokes here. Unfortunately, birth mothers and adoptive mothers are sometimes cast as enemies, or at least as competitors, by the media and our larger culture. We have probably all heard heart-rending stories of birth mothers in custody battles with adoptive mothers, or of dramatic reunions of adult children with their birth mothers. Open adoption, and adoptive parents' active desire to include the birth family in their children's lives whenever possible, go a long way toward challenging the cultural notion of competition between birth and adoptive parents (Mundy, 2007; Surrey et al., 2006).

Joan and Toni are describing what author Sara Dorow calls a conscious creation of the family (Dorow, 2006). Dorow contrasts this with the "naturalized" forms of kinship—the ones automatically produced by biology—because adoption thrusts us into a new way of seeing social relationships. This process might be more dramatic in transracial, transnational adoptions, which bring people and places from the "global political economy" into the intimacy of the home and family (Dorow, 2006, p. 5). In the best outcomes, our families become important places where new forms of racial, cultural, and social identities are constructed.

Adoptive parents can be models, as well as promoters, for new ways of seeing "family" in our culture. This process can enrich general social possibilities for families to be different from the cultural ideal. Even though this process can be rewarding, we should not minimize its challenges—especially for transracial families. As adoptive mother and psychologist Mary Watkins writes, "Most adoptive parents do not set off on the path of adoption in order to transgress societal norms regarding family, kinship, race, and ethnicity" (p. 269).

Maureen, like Carol, approached adoption firmly grounded in her family's religion. Maureen said, "We're practicing Catholics, and I felt strongly about not using birth control. We were careful when we first got married. But we wanted a big family and we thought, 'We're very spiritual people, we're married, and if a swimmer gets through, so be it!'"

After ten years Maureen finally went to an infertility specialist. Confronting infertility was, she said, "A very hard thing. *In vitro* wasn't very common, and the Catholic church was very straightforward: Nothing artificial in any way. We did what was best for us with our souls intact. That was such a hard journey. Every day a reminder that something was not right. The temperature taking, all that. The unwelcome advice—you take a bath in rainwater, wear boxer shorts. People are giving you this advice and maybe you don't even know them that well! I started isolating myself from friends, and especially from my sister, who's Fertile Myrtle."

Maureen now claims the adoptive and foster families of her daughters' siblings as dear friends in a "kind of kinship." The children have sleepovers and extended visits with these families. Maureen said, "We call each other about everything. They are our new circle of support. There aren't a lot of people who understand the kind of life choices we're making."

Committing to an Ethical Adoption

Maureen and her husband's commitment to create their family in a way that was sanctioned by their church illustrates another spiritual part of this process: doing all that we can to ensure an ethical—that is, moral—adoption. (Ethics in adoption were discussed in greater detail in chapters 2 and 3). Reaching the important goal of an ethical adoption means using an agency and facilitators who are absolutely ethical, who account for all processes and all expenditures openly and transparently. It means treating our children's birth parents as we would want to be treated ourselves. Ultimately, it means that we can assure our children that their adoptions were morally conducted. When our children are little, what matters to them is just the fact that they were adopted and that we are their forever parents. When they are adolescents confronting questions about their identity, though, the simple understanding of facts will be replaced with complex questions about *how* and *why*. How they were adopted, and under what circumstances, become important parts of their identity as adopted people. As parents, an important part of our job is to assure them that the process was ethically and morally sound.

Finding Meaning in Suffering

Most writing on adoption for the past fifty years has emphasized the theme of loss among all three members of the adoption triad: birth parents, adoptive parents, and children (Brodzinsky & Schechter, 1990). Your social worker has talked about or will talk about these losses during your home study: The birth parents lose a child, the child loses the birth family and sometimes a birth culture and language, and the adoptive parents often have lost the ability to have birth children. In the discussion of adoption losses, there is rarely a description of the meaning of those losses in universal terms, or of the potential gains in every loss. In fact, everyone has losses, not just people involved in adoption. Author Betty Jean Lifton, often regarded as an important spokeswoman for adoptees' losses, wrote: "I came to understand that all people . . . think of themselves in some sense as orphans—foundlings—who are struggling with problems around alienation. . . . Everyone is in some kind of pain" (Lifton, 1979, p. 5). Loss is such a basic human experience that many religions have a teaching that includes ways to deal with loss, through accepting it and finding meaning in it.

One of our jobs as parents is to help all our children come through their losses. They will lose their health temporarily through illnesses and boo-boos. They might lose a pet, a beloved grandparent, or other loved one. They will lose their preschool when they begin kindergarten, and their kindergarten when they begin elementary school. As years go by, they will lose contact with friends who move away or whom they leave behind. These are normal parts of life. Additionally, all adopted children will feel to some extent the loss of their birth family, and possibly that of their birth culture. Some, like Betty Jean Lifton, focus on this loss and experience it as huge. Lifton's book, published in 1979, describes the deep pain that she and other adult adoptees felt about not knowing anything about their biological roots. Lifton is widely credited with sparking the movement to open adoption records, and the broader trend toward more openness in adoption practice. Children who are adopted at older ages might come from deprived or abusive backgrounds, and have painful memories.

Other adopted people, such as Toni Ayers, acknowledge the loss, process it mentally, and integrate it into their identities. For adopted children who do not know their birth parents, and for infertile adoptive parents, the loss is *ambiguous*, as psychologists call it. It is not concrete—rather, it is a loss of a concept, an idea, and perhaps an ideal. Such losses can linger longer than concrete losses, and they might require a good deal of family discussion to allow everyone to come to grips with them.

We parents can allow children to feel as sad as they need to be—or as angry, because for some, anger is easier and less threatening than sadness. We can be strong enough and centered enough not to be blown away by their emotions. We can sit with our children while they grieve, while they feel their feelings, go through anger and resistance to acceptance and, ultimately, allow their pain to be replaced by rich spiritual gains.

We do this best when we have accumulated some experience handling our own losses, when we can consciously remember the ways we healed them. Most adults have had losses and life changes of different intensity—losses of friends, family members, jobs. We can use those experiences to help with the loss of a biological child, although for some people that is the most intense grief they have experienced. For some adoptive parents, facing the inability to have biological children was devastating and debilitating. For others, this is serious but ultimately one more loss to take in stride.

"I have mixed feelings about the importance of completely resolving infertility issues before adoption," said Rev. John Van Regenmorter, director of Stepping Stones infertility counseling for Bethany Christian Services. "I do believe that couples need to reckon with it, acknowledge it, and grieve it before they begin to have a sense of excitement about the new opportunity that adoption gives them. Some adoption workers seem to think couples need to be totally resolved to the point that infertility is not fresh in their minds. . . . If they have tears or express grief, some adoption workers might think they're not ready to be parents. But I don't think that's necessarily the case. The key is whether the couple reaches the point that they can express some sense of joy and anticipation about the adoption adventure. If they're so stuck in their grief that they cannot be excited about adoption, then I'm not sure they're ready."

Some adoption social workers might go so far as to pathologize the experience of loss, and expect that *all* parents and *all* children will be devastated by their feelings of loss. An expectation is fine, but occasionally an adoption social worker will insist that if parents and children are not incapacitated by their losses, they are "in denial," or "coping poorly." This mistaken attitude gives adoptive parents an impossible task, to heal the inevitable gaping wound in their children's psyches (Surrey et al., 2006). This task is especially impossible if the wound doesn't exist.

A social worker's naive insistence on the depth of loss can have serious consequences for both adoptive parents and children. Some workers might even explain that children's loss of birth parents, and possibly birth culture, will cause their inevitable maladjustment and even learning disabilities or delinquency. Such a claim is so obviously unscientific that it hardly needs refuting, but I'm still surprised when parents tell me about some of the "warnings" they received. If you have this experience, just give your social worker a copy of chapter 4. Then, practice empathy and forgiveness toward her.

Carol was told that her daughter Diane would "mourn her other life, the life she would have had with her birth parents," she said. "But I've never bought into the myths; she's been with me since her first day and I've always told her about her adoption. She knows her birth parents; we see them about once a year when they come to dinner with us."

Lorie reminds us that everyone has issues. She says, "All kids have issues, whether they're adopted or stepchildren or your biological children. I think sometimes adoptive parents might say when things go wrong with their children that it's because of the whole adoption issue. I just step back and think, 'He's just a normal boy. We have to work through this like a family issue.'"

For religious people, losses and suffering can present a serious problem. "Parents who have faith are able to sense that their grief can be left with God. They don't have to bear it on their own," said Rev. Van Regenmorter. "Parents in the Christian faith know a God who has his own grief in losing his own son and can identify with us in our grief and loss."

But some parents ask themselves, "If we believe in a loving God, how can that god allow us to have losses and suffering?" This is an ancient question. At one point in their history, the Hebrews unfortunately answered it like this: "The Lord's curse is on the house of the wicked, but he blesses the home of the righteous" (Proverbs 3:33). They also wrote, "I have been young, and now I am old, yet I have not seen the righteous forsaken or their children begging bread" (Psalms 37:25). In other words, this reasoning goes: good things happen to good people, and bad things happen to bad people, so if bad things happen to you, you must be bad.

Another explanation of suffering is given in the Old Testament in the story of Job. Job was a virtuous man who believed in God, but God gave him more trials than anyone. This story is widely interpreted as portraying suffering as a test of our relationship with God.

Yet another, related view of suffering derived from the Old Testament holds that God is a disciplinarian: "Endure trials for the sake of discipline. God is treating you as children; for what child is there whom a parent does not discipline? . . . Now, discipline always seems painful rather than pleasant at the time, but later it yields the peaceful fruit of righteousness to those who have been trained by it" (Hebrews 12:5–7, 11). Rabbi Harold Kushner (1981) writes about these issues eloquently and reassuringly, with a contemporary interpretation of the Old Testament stories.

In the New Testament, Jesus contradicts the psalmist's view of suffering as punishment and teaches that random suffering can be an opportunity. The Gospel of John records, "As he walked along, he saw a man blind from birth. His disciples asked him, 'Rabbi, who sinned, this man or his parents, that he was born blind?' Jesus answered, 'Neither this man nor his parents sinned; he was born blind so that God's works might be revealed in him'" (John 9:1–3). The man's blindness was a sign not that he was being punished, but rather that he was being given a chance to "see" and to show spiritual experience to the world.

Rev. Van Regenmorter said, "We totally reject the idea that [an infertile] couple must have done something wrong and God is punishing them. We believe that any grief and loss is most often a sign that we simply live in a fallen, sinful world, where loss and death and grief are part of the human experience. When someone faces a situation like infertility, it's a call to all of us that we need to be able to sense our mortality, finiteness, and a reminder that we need to trust in God. Loss and grief are part of our life."

Would the blind man have chosen blindness in order to have a spiritual opportunity? Would we embrace any loss for the free spiritual opportunity that comes with it? Being human, probably not. I don't know about you, but I wouldn't. I'd rather have my sight, all my senses, my health, a soft bed, clean hot water from the tap, an unlimited budget . . . but the world doesn't work that way.

Can we ever explain pain and loss in spiritual terms in a way that encompasses all of the causes and effects? Our understandably human attempts to explain suffering in terms of God's rewards or punishments or discipline or opportunities can be intellectual diversions from the emotional work of feeling the sadness and pain associated with any loss. Intellectual interpretations of suffering might help us for a while, but we cannot heal from the loss until we experience the pain. When my mother-in-law died, my husband said that he knew all about the stages of grief as described by Elisabeth Kubler-Ross. He had, after all, majored in psychology. However, knowing about the process did not exempt him from actually living, and hurting, through each stage.

Adoptive parents who do resolve their grief and loss are well on their way to becoming better parents, because they can help their children to resolve their own losses. This fits with the seemingly conflicting "explanations" for suffering in the Bible as many faces of the same rock. They tell us, ultimately, that suffering and loss are simply part of human life on earth.

Buddhism teaches that the existence of suffering is a holy truth, the first of the Four Noble Truths. The Four Noble Truths are the essence of the Buddha's forty-five years of teachings. For *truth*, the Chinese combine the characters for *word* and *king*, because no ordinary mortal should argue with a king's word. The Second Noble Truth is that of the origin or causes of suffering. This second truth shows that we can begin to understand suffering by looking deeply into it to identify its emotional, spiritual, or physical causes. The Third Noble Truth is that we can stop creating suffering by not doing the things that cause us to suffer. Some people have misinterpreted Buddhist teachings to mean that everything in the world is suffering and we can do nothing about it (Nhat Hanh, 1998). In fact, the Buddha taught the opposite, and the Third Noble Truth embodies the principle that we can heal pain and suffering. The Fourth Noble Truth gives Buddhists the way to heal—the Noble Eightfold Path.

Thich Nhat Hanh (1998) writes, "Without suffering, you cannot grow. Without suffering you cannot get the peace and joy you deserve. Please don't run away from your suffering. Embrace it and cherish it" (p. 5). He emphasizes that while the Buddha taught the truth of suffering, he also taught "the truth of 'dwelling happily in things as they are'" (Nhat Hanh, 1998, p. 22).

Suffering or loss might be a necessary part of life, but suffering alone is never necessary. As we've said so often in this book, social support is very important. Rev. Van Regenmorter said, "In our work at Stepping Stones, one of the most healing things emotionally and spiritually is for couples to know that they're not alone, that there's a community of people who feel lonely and abandoned. It helps some prospective parents to read the stories of infertile couples in the Bible: Jacob and Rachel, Abraham and Sara, in the Old Testament; Elizabeth and Zachariah in the book of Luke. We especially like their story, because the Bible specifically says they were righteous and without fault, so their infertility was not a punishment."

Practicing Empathy and Compassion

Rita described how her meeting with her daughter's birth mother in Guatemala helped her to overcome her own fears and reach empathy for the birth mother. She begins, "Meeting the birth mother—that was . . . how *was* that?"

This usually articulate, highly expressive woman keeps pausing, and the words that are usually her friends desert her briefly. She resumes, "When the agency told me it was a possibility, I was petrified. I thought, 'I don't want to. It's got to be so hard for this woman, it would be an emotional, horrible experience.'"

"But the more I thought about it," Rita went on, "I had so much empathy. If I were the birth mother, I'd want to see who was going to take my child to America. So we did meet her. She was forty, a very petite woman with big eyes and a gentle soul."

In addition to Rita's empathy for and connection with Mary's birth mother, the family now has a video of the birth mother with Mary. "She's telling her how much she loved her, that she was very poor and had to work in a factory and couldn't take care of her and wanted the best for her," Rita said. "That was actually really wonderful—not the huge dramatic scene I'd thought it would be. I'd recommend it for anyone who possibly can meet their child's birth mother. She was happy Mary was finally going to be with us and go to the U.S. I pray for her still."

Rita now has not only a very powerful video, but also a very powerful memory of her daughter's birth mother. When her daughter begins asking questions about her birth family, Rita will be ready with photos and her own experience of Mary's birth mother. Rita had also experienced her own suffering, in waiting for Mary, and had seen Mary's birth mother's tears and pain. If Mary feels the sadness of loss about her birth family and culture that many adopted children feel, Rita will be ready to empathize with her. She will also be in a position to answer very hard questions that Mary might eventually ask, about her birth family's poverty and her adoptive family's relative wealth.

Karen Horridge, a veteran social worker in a city's department of social services, said that some of her adoptive parent clients see birth parents as "demons, because people think, 'How can a birth parent hurt a child so much?' They don't understand poverty, or mental illness, or addiction." She describes a case in which a couple were slated to adopt a premature infant born to a young teenager in foster care. The baby was born at such a low birth weight that she was at high risk. The adoptive parents were very judgmental about the young birth mother. "But when they met her," Karen recalled, "it was almost like something came over them and they became much softer and more understanding of the birth mother. It was a good example to me of what can happen when people can put a face to their idea of a person. It also gives them a more positive picture for their child than a vague notion about an irresponsible teenager."

Using a Conscious Connection with God, Christ, a Higher Power, Mindfulness, or All of Them Together To Support You

Many parents describe a kind of peaceful, calm "knowing" that comes when they have made the decision that feels right to them, or shortly after they meet their child for the first time.

Meditation is the major Buddhist practice to help people achieve mindfulness and, ultimately, liberation from suffering (called *nirvana*). Along the way, though, the two types of meditation can bring rest (*shamatha*) and insight (*vipashyana*)—rest from the busyness of life and insight into the nature and causes of our suffering. Resting, or stopping, can seem like the very last thing an adoptive parent can afford to do during the process of adoption. I remember feeling driven to complete one more form, or check one more website, every day—if not every hour. At those times, stopping for rest would have helped me to feel much more serene and centered. And my breakneck pace didn't make my daughter arrive any more quickly.

For some, like Lorie and Julie, this blessed time of calm might be simply the end of months or years of very anxious work and waiting. For Joan, it was a sign that God or their higher power or the universe was in charge of their adoption and had somehow miraculously connected them to their child.

This is Joan's family's story. "We'd planned to adopt from Russia," Joan said. "We were saving our money and our leave time so we could travel there, working full time, doing paperwork. But then those plans fell apart. We really needed to just get out of town and take a deep breath because it was just too devastating. While we were at the beach for a week, that's when Ellen was born. I didn't realize it at first, but at some point it hit me. I find it interesting too because of having chosen her, and the other child . . . not being a child that we took with us."

She continued, "I've shared this story with people, not to say it was pre-ordained, but to say—sometimes when you're at your lowest moment in this process, when nothing has worked out, and you think this will never happen, on the other side of the world events may be taking place that you have no knowledge of, that you have no control over, that may be spinning toward you, toward your life. We were at the beach that very week and I was thinking, 'Oh, why? Why can't this come together? Are we meant to be parents? Why aren't we meant to be parents? We'd be good parents!'"

She said, "We had a lot of struggle over that, and wondered what was next. So many things had not worked out, we felt very lost and very deeply sad at the loss and also felt no sense of direction, even if we did get refocused. I thought, there has to be a way—we thought we'd reached the summit but there were more switchbacks to get us there. We did regain our energy and looked at our options. We'd eliminated Russia, so what was left? During that time was when she was born. How could that be—that somebody on the other side of the world is giving birth to a child that she cannot parent or chooses not to parent for whatever reason? When you think about that series of events, a child is making its way to a particular orphanage, and we're connecting with an agency that works in that region. We didn't have any of that information when we chose her, and found out later. This little being who's brought so much joy into our lives was being born and somebody was making a very painful decision, at the same time that we were having very deep pain. Their pain brought us joy. That feels sacred to me. It feels spiritual. It wasn't just filling out an application and sitting in a room."

Carol, who adopted her daughter through her own faith community, described a more specific connection with God. She said, "I have a spiritual approach to life and I move from the very basis that there's an all-powerful, all-good God and no other force except Him. He's prepared a very good life for me and my choices in that path are guided by Him and He has no bad ideas. He gave me the sensibility to contemplate and do good. My choices in my career put me where I was and there were too many divine coincidences to be anything but divine for me. Some people say I was lucky, but not if you believe that God is so good. There's nothing that's miraculous to God though to us humans it might look that way. I remember the absolute joy we felt when I was pregnant. It was so amazing I couldn't get my head around it. As we had Diane put in our arms, I was just as excited, the miracle of that was equal to the miracle of pregnancy to me."

Like Carol, Mary Landrieu relied on her faith. "I felt like adoption was God's will. I'd prayed about it a lot. As a strong Christian, I pray about every important aspect of my life and felt a great spiritual confidence that this was the right thing to do. We interviewed several agencies and chose the one we felt a high comfort level with. At every step, we felt we were being led. For us, we've felt that way watching them grow every year."

Rev. John Van Regenmorter has seen this sense of a divine plan among families in his work. "When they begin bonding with their child and sense their joy in their child, they have a renewed sense of the plan that God has for their life," he said. "It might not be the plan they originally had, and they need to be patient. When God fulfills his plan, they will know it and they will rejoice in it."

For other parents, there is a general sense that their families have arrived at the "right" place when their children are with them, but that sense or feeling isn't related to a religious practice, denomination, or doctrine. This feeling of "rightness" might be especially strong for people who have experienced a failed adoption or who have lost a referral. Toni Ayers said, "Now that our son is with us, I feel like he's the one that's supposed to be with us. We thought we'd be devastated by the failed adoption. But in the end, we knew she was supposed to be with her birth father. She wasn't supposed to be for us."

Adoptive parents sometimes say that the experience of parenting has helped to deepen their relationship with God. Maureen said, "My faith is deeper, my couple relationship with Henry is richer. We're not in control. It's easy sometimes when all things seem black to just let it go and know that I'm a child of God myself, and I'm being held. It may not feel like that, but it is. I've had an opportunity to not know where my children were— during what I called the runaway summer. They both ran away when they didn't like to do their chores, the younger one following the older one's role modeling. When they're away and I can't keep them safe, as I'd promised— I told the judge I'd keep them safe, all I had was my faith. My faith, my husband, and coffee! Because we were practicing our faith, it was easier for me to let go. My sense of humor couldn't get me out of the situation, all the things I used before. I was reduced to the core of who I am, a faith-filled woman who just says, 'I'm here, God. How can I serve you?' It really was an epiphany for me. And, I had never thought I would live such a rich life."

• • •

The experiences of epiphany and joy and deep peace may seem far away if you've struggled for a long time with grief after infertility. But they are there for you, and you will find them if you keep up your spiritual practice and keep looking for them. Remember that you are doing this not just for yourself, but also for your child to come. You will enjoy your child much more when you can take delight in him, and embrace him and his life with you for the treasure that it surely will be. This delight is a special strength of adoptive families, because we do indeed choose our children, and we had to continue to choose to become parents through a process we could have stopped at any time. Our joy in our children is a significant source of strength and security for them. My colleagues who spend their days studying attachment say they believe that parents' delight in their children can predict children's secure attachment. As an adoptive parent, I know that delight certainly feels good to me, and it's also fun for my daughter!

As you swing out to catch the next trapeze bar in your flight to adoptive parenthood, I wish for you all possible delight in your child to come.

1. Begin your parents' spiritual practice now. Engage in spiritual practice daily, whether that is centering prayer, meditation, contemplation, or walks in nature. Learn to feel the peace that passes all understanding, or *shalom,* and to regain it when you lose it in the bustling busy-ness of everyday adult life.

2. Write for five minutes each day about the meaning of parenthood for you, and about its connection to God and the universe in your faith.

3. Find your ability to delight in the world, so that you can find delight in your child.

4. Explore the ways in which you think about suffering in your own life. Do you see suffering as

   ❑ punishment from God?
   ❑ part of being human?
   ❑ a reason to treat yourself gently?

5. Think about what you will do when your children suffer. Will you

   ❑ have compassion?
   ❑ empathize, and validate your child's emotions?
   ❑ hold your child, and cry with him? (Be aware that anger is sometimes a mask for pain, especially for older or previously abused children.)

6. If these possibilities seem uncomfortable to you, go back and re-read chapter 7. You might want to discuss your discomfort with your spouse or partner, with a social worker, or with a spiritual advisor.

7. Make a list of people whom you need to forgive. The list might include yourself and your partner, your parents, and/or your endocrinologist.

8. Practice forgiveness and compassion every day. Start with yourself, if you are still blaming yourself for anything. Forgive your spouse or partner for his or her mistakes. Remember that the root meaning of compassion is "suffering with." If you find yourself holding on to resentments, try to make a decision each day for a week that you will not take revenge on the person whom you resent. See how you feel after a week. If you are still resentful, practice this exercise for another week. (Repeat until "done"; you will be done when you have let go of most of your

resentment.) As you become able to forgive yourself, your partner, and the world, you will find that you have many more choices in your life than you had previously imagined.

9. Become willing to apologize or otherwise make amends to everyone on your list. Imagine how good it will feel not to carry the baggage of resentment. Ask for divine guidance about when and how to make amends.

10. Collect stories from your faith tradition, even if you do not practice it any more, about parents and children, and about adoption.

11. Are you still struggling with adoption decisions? Think about ways to use your religious faith tradition to help you.

References and Resources

WEBSITES

- www.beliefnet.com. This for-profit site connects people of all major world religions, and offers on-line chat groups. The Family and Parenting area includes discussions of adoption.
- www.hannah.org. This site, run by a nonprofit corporation and volunteers, offers Christian-oriented support for infertility issues and adoption.
- www.ssministry.net. This is the site for the infertility support group run by Bethany Christian Services, an adoption agency.
- Adoption-related listservs also have threads of discussion about loss, grief, and spiritual issues from time to time.

ARTICLES AND BOOKS

Ai, A., Peterson, C., Tice, T., Bolling, S. & Koenig, H. (2004). Faith-based and secular pathways to hope and optimism: Subconstructs in middle-aged and older cardiac patients. *Journal of Health Psychology, 9*(3), 435–50.

The Bible. Quotations in this book are from the Revised Standard Version of the Old and New Testaments. New York: Nelson & Sons, 1952.

Brodzinsky, D. M., & Schechter, M. D. (1990). *The psychology of adoption.* New York: Oxford University Press.

Coulthard, P., & Fitzgerald, M. (1999). In God we trust? Organized religion and personal beliefs as resources and coping strategies, and their implications for health in parents with a child on the autistic spectrum. *Mental Health, Religion & Culture, 2*(1), 19–33.

Dorow, S. K. (2006). *Transnational adoption: A cultural economy of race, gender, and kinship.* New York: New York University Press. This is a complex book by a professor of sociology. The fascinating ideas are unfortunately wrapped in very dense and scholarly prose.

Hanh, Thich Nhat. (1995). *Living Buddha, Living Christ.* New York: Riverhead Books. This is a book of short meditations on the connections between Buddhism and Christianity, including a discussion of spiritual ancestors by adoption. The book also contains several sections on suffering as part of human life. The author is a prolific Zen teacher and a Nobel Peace Prize nominee.

————. (1998) *The heart of the Buddha's teachings: Transforming suffering into peace, joy and liberation.* Berkeley: Parallax Press. This is a longer book by the Zen master on the basics of Buddhist teachings. It is written in language accessible to Western readers. The book is translated into colloquial English from the Vietnamese.

Laubmeier, K., Zakowski, S., & Bair, J. (2004). The role of spirituality in the psychological adjustment to cancer: A test of the transactional model of stress and coping. *International Journal of Behavioral Medicine, 11*(1), 543–55.

Lifton, B. J. (1979). *Lost and found: The adoption experience.* New York: Dial Press.

Mundy, L. (2007, May 6). Open secret. *Washington Post Magazine,* pp. 18–30. This article is a feature story on a contemporary open adoption.

Surrey, J. L., Smith, B., & Watkins, M. (2006). "Real" mothers: Adoptive mothers resisting marginalization and recreating motherhood. In K. Wegar (Ed.), *Adoptive families in a diverse society,* pp. 146–61. New Brunswick, NJ: Rutgers University Press.

Watkins, Mary. (2006). Adoption and identity: Nomadic possibilities for reconceiving the self. In K. Wegar (Ed.), *Adoptive families in a diverse society,* pp. 259–74. New Brunswick, NJ: Rutgers University Press.

Index